Imperial Glass

Encyclopedia

Volume II
Cape Cod - L

by members of the
National Imperial Glass Collectors' Society

Edited by James Measell

Front Cover:
A. Free Hand vase.
B. Rubigold No. 473 Grape 10 oz. goblet.
C. Cathay 5012 Ku ribbon vase.
D. Ritz Blue Cape Cod 160/163 30 oz.
decanter and stopper.
E. Ritz Blue Cape Cod 160 wine.
F. Sample Caramel Slag No. 463 10" oval bowl.

Back Cover:
G. Lead Lustre vase.
H. Amber off-hand Swan.
I. 50/1823 Jonquil vase.
J. Free Hand vase.
K. Free Hand perfume lamp in metal holder.
L. Opaque turquoise Lace Edge bowl

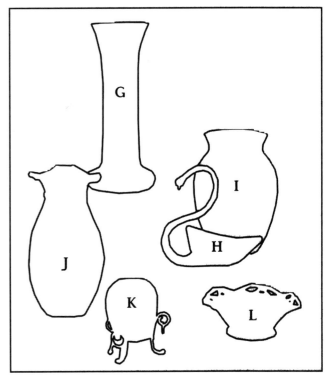

© Copyright 1997

The Glass Press, Inc.
dba Antique Publications
Post Office Box 553 • Marietta, Ohio 45750

ALL RIGHTS RESERVED

PB ISBN #1-57080-021-9   HB ISBN #1-57080-022-7

No part of this book may be reproduced, stored in a retrieval system or transmitted in
any form or by any means, electronic, mechanical, photocopying, recording,
or otherwise, without the prior permission of the publisher.

TABLE OF CONTENTS

INTRODUCTION AND ACKNOWLEDGMENTS

The book you have in your hands is part of an encyclopedic series which discusses Imperial glass from A to Z. This is the second segment, "Cape Cod-L" (the first, covering "A-Cane" in some 226 pages, was published by The Glass Press/Antique Publications in 1995). This volume contains eighty pages of color photography and numerous original black-and-white photos, many of which are from Imperial catalogs or advertisements.

Eye-catching headings appear throughout the book in the upper left or upper right corner of each page. For example, at the end of the "C" section on page 288, the heading "C/miscellaneous" can be found. The respective "miscellaneous" sections contain information about those Imperial products for which a full page could not be constructed. Captions to the eighty color pages can be found on pages 393-398 and 479-483.

Readers seeking specific articles can consult the comprehensive index (see p. 485), which embraces both this book and the previous volume. The index lists colors, item designations, pattern names and other terminology important for a thorough understanding of Imperial glass.

These books on Imperial glass would not have been possible without the determined efforts of the National Imperial Glass Collectors' Society Book Committee: Myrna Garrison (Chairperson) and members Douglas Archer; Joan Cimini; Kathy Doub; Bob Garrison; Marion George; Lucile Kennedy; Madeline Kennedy; Willard Kolb; and Betty Jane Muhleman. They secured information, located glassware to be photographed and checked (and re-checked!) facts about Imperial glass.

Photography for this book was done at the homes of Bob and Myrna Garrison in Texas and Paul and Judy Douglas in Illinois. Several days of photo work at the Bellaire Glass and Artifact Museum were made easy through the help and cooperation of Helen M. Clark, Jean Mountain and the late Clara Dankworth.

Many people loaned glass or provided information about Imperial and its products. Special thanks go to Doug and Margaret Archer; Roy Ash; Bob Burns; Joan Cimini; Helen M. Clark; Bill Crowl; Ron and Connie Doll; Kathy Doub; Paul and Judy Douglas; Laurence Evans; Frank M. Fenton; Bob and Linda Frost; Bob and Myrna Garrison; Marion George; Kirk and Jackie Glauser; Charles Hartman; Paul and Carole Hrics; Don Jennings; Lucile Kennedy; Willard Kolb; Dave and Mary Kuster; Richard Lancione; Addie Miller; Gene and Flora Ross; E. Ward Russell; John Sampson; Nathan Taves; Paul and Wilma Thurston, Ronnie Vickers; Paul and Suzanne Weimer; Monte and Kris Schroer; Tony and Kim Scialdone; and Berry Wiggins. The Gutman Advertising Agency made its files available, and some of the original black-and-white photos in this book came from those records.

James Measell, Editor
David E. Richardson, Publisher

September 8, 1997

C

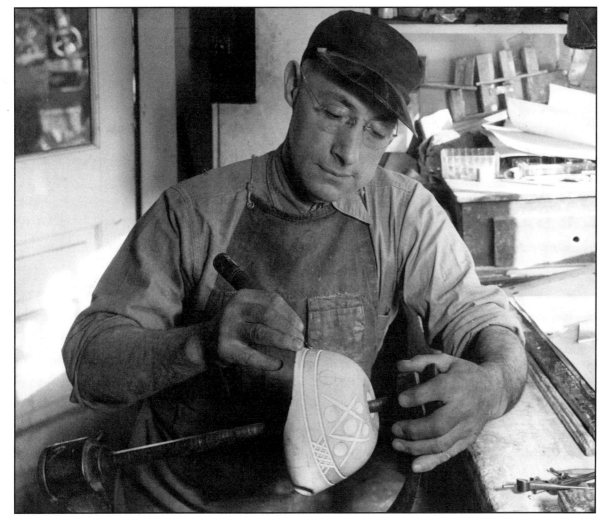

Imperial's Raymond Kraus works on the plaster model for a Cape Cod piece.

On August 17, 1931, Earl W. Newton made application at the U. S. Patent Office to register the designs for a tumbler, a bowl and a goblet (this looks more like a sherbet in the original patent drawings, however). Newton had been associated with Imperial since about 1913, and he maintained a factory representative's showroom in Chicago. By the late summer of 1931, Newton had been president of the newly-formed Imperial Glass Corporation for just a few weeks, and the organization was facing difficult economic times.

The new design was for a line to be called No. 160 Cape Cod. This pattern became Imperial's lifeblood throughout the Great Depression, and it remained important to the company's success for decades afterward. By the time the design patents were granted (March 20, 1932), No. 160 Cape Cod was well into production.

The inspiration for the Cape Cod design is somewhat difficult to pinpoint, but Imperial's immediate stimulus seems to have been the Pairpoint Glass Company of New Bedford, Massachusetts, which went out of business in 1926. A Pairpoint salesman named Axelrod traced the design back to the Sandwich Glass Co. and to a sixteenth-century Irish firm, the Waterford Glass Co. These three firms—Pairpoint, Sandwich and Waterford—were responsible for creating their respective

C

A Cape Cod tumbler is born in one of Imperial's press shops, c. 1940
(note the legend "160-6 oz. TUMB"on the mould).

motifs in cut glass, but Imperial's ware was generally made as pressed glass, a method far more economical than pressing followed by extensive hand cutting and subsequent polishing.

Imperial's large-size catalogs from the 1930s contain at least six full pages depicting No. 160 Cape Cod (two of these are in the Archers book, pp. 160-161, and the others appear in this book). Although No. 160 Cape Cod was primarily a crystal line, some pieces were made in amber, Ritz Blue (cobalt blue) and ruby in the 1930s. Some elements of Imperial's Cape Cod design resemble the firm's No. 165 Tradition pattern, and items from the two lines are sometimes shown in close proximity to one another on the catalog pages from the 1930s.

An internal Imperial memorandum summarizing sales for 1938 indicates that Cape Cod was the firm's number one seller, accounting for 818,400 pieces and about 17% of total sales (No. 699 Mount Vernon was a distant second at 5%). A Cape Cod Crystal catalogue dated January 1, 1942, depicts several dozen Cape Cod items ranging from beverage and table service to console sets and dresser sets. In the November, 1942, issue of *Better Homes and Gardens*, Imperial invited America's homemakers to "inspect the beauty of the more than 100 pieces at your favorite gift, jewelry or department store." (text continued on p. 233)

1608F. 18½ inch Torte Plate
1½ dozen in No. 1 carton, weight 65 pounds

165. Ice Pitcher
1 dozen in No. 4 carton
Weight 45 pounds

160. 36 ounce Refrigerator Jug
1½ dozen in No. 1 carton
Weight 60 pounds

1608A. 11 inch Salad Bowl
1 dozen in No. 1 carton, weight 55 pounds

160. 8-piece Wine Set
1 dozen Wine Sets in No. 1 carton, weight 65 pounds
6 dozen Wines in No. 27 carton, weight 25 pounds
One Set in No. 68 carton, weight 7 pounds

1608X. 11¼ inch Fruit Bowl
1 dozen in No. 1 carton, weight 55 pounds

160. 8-piece Whiskey Set
1 dozen Sets in No. 1 carton, weight 65 pounds
1½ dozen Decanters in No. 1 carton, weight 65 pounds
12 dozen Whiskeys in No. 32 carton, weight 40 pounds
One Set in No. 68 carton, weight 7 pounds

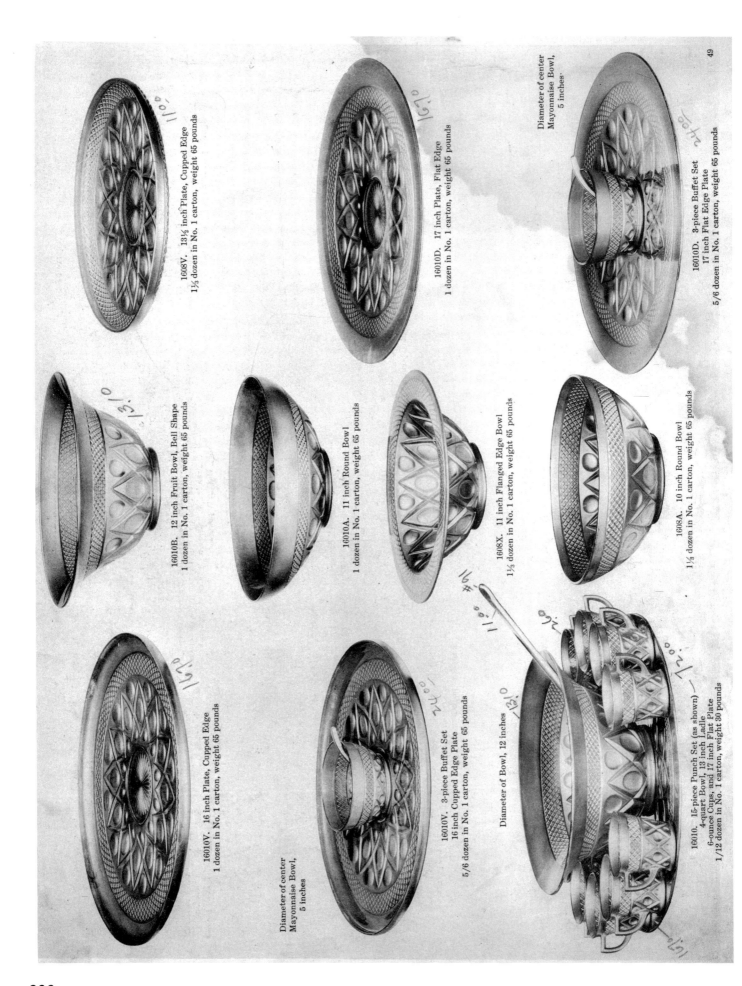

1608V. 13½ inch Plate, Cupped Edge
1⅓ dozen in No. 1 carton, weight 65 pounds

16010D. 17 inch Plate, Flat Edge
1 dozen in No. 1 carton, weight 65 pounds

Diameter of center
Mayonnaise Bowl,
5 inches.

16010D. 3-piece Buffet Set
17 inch Flat Edge Plate
5/6 dozen in No. 1 carton, weight 65 pounds

16010B. 12 inch Fruit Bowl, Bell Shape
1 dozen in No. 1 carton, weight 65 pounds

16010A. 11 inch Round Bowl
1 dozen in No. 1 carton, weight 65 pounds

1608X. 11 inch Flanged Edge Bowl
1⅓ dozen in No. 1 carton, weight 65 pounds

1608A. 10 inch Round Bowl
1⅓ dozen in No. 1 carton, weight 65 pounds

16010V. 16 inch Plate, Cupped Edge
1 dozen in No. 1 carton, weight 65 pounds

Diameter of center
Mayonnaise Bowl,
5 inches

16010V. 3-piece Buffet Set
16 inch Cupped Edge Plate
5/6 dozen in No. 1 carton, weight 65 pounds

Diameter of Bowl, 12 inches

16010. 15-piece Punch Set (as shown) —
4-quart Bowl, 13 inch Ladle
6-ounce Cups, and 17 inch Flat Plate
1/12 dozen in No. 1 carton, weight 80 pounds

230

DESIGN
PATENTED

ALL PRICES ARE PER DOZEN

EACH PIECE HAND MADE AND
HIGHLY FIRE POLISHED BY HAND

160. 6 ounce Ginger Ale or Juice
Crystal, Blue, Amber, $3.00
Ruby, 3.50
6 dozen to carton, shipping weight 40 pounds
Cartons 35¢ each net

160. 12 ounce Ice Tea or High Ball
Crystal, Blue, Amber, $3.00
Ruby, 3.50
6 dozen to carton, shipping weight 60 pounds
Cartons 40¢ each net

160. 6 ounce Sherbet
Crystal, Blue, Amber, $3.00
Ruby, 3.50
6 dozen to carton, shipping weight 40 pounds
Cartons 35¢ each net

160. 8 ounce Goblet
Crystal, Blue, Amber, $3.00
Ruby, 3.50
6 dozen to carton, shipping weight 55 pounds
Cartons 40¢ each net

1605D. 8 inch Salad Plate
Crystal, Blue, Amber, $3.00
Ruby, 3.50
6 dozen to carton, shipping weight 70 pounds
Cartons 50¢ each net

1604½D. 6¾ inch Salad Plate
Crystal, Blue, Amber, $3.00
Ruby, 3.50
6 dozen to carton, shipping weight 50 pounds
Cartons 35¢ each net

C

These Cape Cod items are shown in a 1942 Imperial catalog.

CAPE COD CRYSTAL

1601
6 piece Dresser Set

1601
Cologne and Stopper

1601
Puff Box and Cover

160
Decanter and Stopper

160/1
7 piece Whiskey Set

1604½B
3 piece Mayonnaise Set

1604½B
5½" Mayonnaise Bowl

1600D
7" Mayonnaise Plate

615 Ladle

1605W
7" Flared Bowl

160/6   4 piece Jam Set

160/6   Jam Jar Only

160/6
Jam Jar Cover Only

160/6
Jam Jar Saucer Only

160/6   Jam Spoon

160
9½" Oval Relish Dish

1600D
6½" Plate

1606D
8" Plate

1602D
10" Plate

16010V
16" Plate Only, Cupped Edge

16010V
3 piece Buffet Set

615   Ladle

1600J
5" Deep Mayonnaise Bowl

This c. 1946 publicity photo for Cape Cod was created in the New York City studio of Dana B. Merrill. The recording stars pictured in the background are Frank Sinatra and Harry James.

An Imperial price sheet dated January 1, 1943, lists about two dozen pieces of Cape Cod with decoration #208, which is described as "cranberry rim decoration." This treatment is reminiscent of the somewhat darker ruby-stain which was popular in the early twentieth century, and Imperial's cranberry-rimmed crystal pieces in Cape Cod are quite attractive (see Figs. 938-952). Incidentally, decoration #208 was also available on Imperial patterns No. 165 Tradition and No. 699 Mount Vernon at this time.

During the 1940s and 1950s, Cape Cod was advertised in many national publications, such as *Better Homes and Gardens, Brides Magazine, House Beautiful, House and Garden, Ladies Home Journal* and *Sunset*. These magazines reached retail buyers, of course, but Imperial also advertised to the trade in *Crockery and Glass* or *China, Glass and Tablewares*. Some ads combined Imperial's Cape Cod with the company's other popular line, Candlewick No. 400. Like Candlewick, Cape Cod was "open stock" glassware, and Imperial was interested in expanding the number of articles in the line. Various sizes of plates were added, and, especially after World War II, many new articles were developed. (text continued on p. 236)

C

These Cape Cod console sets appear in a 1947 Imperial catalog.

IMPERIAL CAPE COD

160/81   4″
Candleholder

160/221   10 in. Fruit Bowl
160/822   3 pc. Cottage Console Set

160/81   4″
Candleholder

160/80   5″
Candleholder

160/75L   13″
Center Bowl

160/8075L
3 pc. Console Set

160/80   5″
Candleholder

160/81   4 inch
Candleholder

160/137B   10½″ Footed Bowl

160/8137   3 pc. Console Set

160/81   4 inch
Candleholder

160/80   5″
Candleholder

160/92F   14″
Shallow Center or Float Bowl

160/8092F
3 pc. Console Set

160/80   5″
Candleholder

160/150   5½"
Double Rest Ash Tray

160/200
Handled Cigarette Holder

160/134
Cigarette Box and Cover

160/134/1   4½"
Single Rest Ash Tray

1602   Footed Cigarette Holder

160/223
Partitioned Cigarette Server

160/131B   12"
Oval Center Bowl

Ornament is removable, for use as
3 lite candleholder

160/100
2 Lite Candleholder and Ornament

160/100
2 Lite Candleholder and Ornament

Cape Cod
smokers'
accessories
and other
items from
a 1947
Imperial
catalog.

235

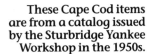

C

These Cape Cod items are from a catalog issued by the Sturbridge Yankee Workshop in the 1950s.

R-160/156

R-160/79

R-1600A   R-1600B   R-1600C

REPRODUCTION SANDWICH

In The Famous

CAPE COD *PATTERN*

The famous old house of Imperial is renowned for its fine Sandwich reproductions—especially in the Cape Cod pattern, which was one of the richest of the Sandwich designs.

#R-1600A, 10-oz. GOBLET, (shp. wt. 1/2 lb. ea.)   89c ea.
#R-1600B, 6-oz. SHERBET, (shp. wt. 1/2 lb. ea.)   89c ea.
    #R-1600C, 12-oz. FOOTED TUMBLER,
    (shp. wt. 1/2 lb. ea.)   89c ea.
        Sets of eight, any size, $6.49 set.
    #R-160/5D, 8" SALAD PLATE,
    (shp. wt. 1 lb. ea.)   89c ea.
        Set of 8 plates, $6.49 set.
    5-piece matching CONDIMENT SET, including recessed tray, salt and pepper, vinegar and oil cruets.
    #R-160/157, complete,
    (shp. wt. 2 lbs.) $5.95 set.
    4-oz. BITTERS BOTTLE and tube,
    #R-160/235, (shp. wt. 1/2 lb.)   98c ea.
    WHISKEY GLASS, 2½ oz. capacity,
    #R-160/2½, (shp. wt. 1½ lbs.) Set of four, $1.89 set.
    INDIVIDUAL SALT DIPS
    #R-160/61, set of four,
    (shp. wt. 1 lb.) $1.19 set.
    COVERED MUSTARD AND SPOON,
    #R-160/156, (shp. wt. 1 lb.) $1.49 set.
        SANDWICH HURRICANES
    An outstanding two-piece Sandwich hurricane with clear glass globe, for use singly or in pairs.
    #R-160/79, without candle, (shp. wt. 3 lbs. ea.) $4.29 ea., $7.98 pr.

R-160/157

R-160/235

R-160/61

R-160/2½

A full-page Imperial ad in the August 25, 1947, issue of *Retailing* called Cape Cod "the nation's No. 2 hit" (behind No. 1 Candlewick) and revealed that there were 196 pieces in the line at this time. Four-color ads featuring Cape Cod were scheduled for issues of *House and Garden* and *Bride's Magazine* in the fall of 1947.

Lucile Kennedy recalls that Imperial's customers requested some graceful stemware to go with their Cape Cod table service pieces. In the early 1950s, the 3600-series of blown Cape Cod stemware was created to meet this need. The intricate mitered motif on the pressed stem resembles other Cape Cod pieces, of course, and the blown crystal bowl is lightweight. The 3600 articles, including seven stemware pieces ranging from 1-1/2 oz. cordial to 12 oz. ice tea, are also shown

among the cut ware in Imperial's Catalog 53. These were available with four cut motifs—C950 Meander, C951 Celeste, C952 Today and C953 Sophisticate.

In 1953-55, a few Cape Cod items were made in Imperial's Evergreen color, and a number of other colors were made in the 1960s and 1970s. One salesman's notebook, for example, lists a special promotion of seven items (5 oz. claret, 6 oz. tall sherbet, 6 oz. footed juice, 11 oz. goblet, 12 oz. footed ice tea, 8" salad plate and finger bowl), which were available in Amber, Cranberry (also called Azalea), Heritage Blue and Verde. These were available during May-July, 1964.

Some Cape Cod articles were made in colors as special orders for a party plan called Star Exclusives, and others were produced as part of Imper-

C

IMPERIAL
Cape Cod
CRYSTAL

For the Year 'Round Brides' Market

ial's hotel/restaurant line. The Cape Cod cruet was made in Rubigold Carnival glass for the Levay Distributing Company of Edwardsville, Illinois, in the mid-1970s. Good coverage of Cape Cod production in colors can be found in Myrna and Bob Garrison's *Imperial Cape Cod: Tradition to Treasure* (see Bibliography, p. 484).

Cape Cod was marketed with a wide spectrum of consumer needs in mind. Some advertisements featured casual dining while others depicted formal, elegant settings. The "year 'round bride's market" was mentioned in some Cape Cod ads, but others emphasized a masculine theme with hunting gear, tobacco products, beer and snack food.

During Imperial's last decade of existence, Cape Cod continued in production. The 1974-1975 Imperial catalog pictured over two dozen items, and beverage items remained reasonably steady sellers for some time. Imperial's last catalog, issued for 1982-83, aptly sums up the half-century of Cape Cod's history and popularity as one of Imperial's most significant patterns: "Beautiful replicas of the much treasured Sandwich glass, these hand-pressed stems are perfect for all occasions. The splendid multifaceted pattern adds a sparkle to any beverage."

C

A. 160/200 Tom and Jerry 14-piece punch set (bowl, ladle and a dozen cups).

C

A. 1601 12 oz. ice tea tumbler.
B. 1601 9 oz. water tumbler.
C. 1601 6 oz. juice tumbler.
D. 1600 6 oz. footed juice tumbler.
E. 1600 12 oz. footed ice tea tumbler.
F. 1602 oyster/fruit cocktail with concave stem.
G. 1602 12 oz. footed ice tea tumbler with concave stem.
H. 160/225 egg cup.
I. 3600 1¹/₂ oz. cordial.
J. 3600 6 oz. sherbet.

K. 3600 12 oz. ice tea tumbler.
L. 3600 12 oz. ice tea tumbler (with cut decoration).
M. 3600 11 oz. goblet (with cut decoration).
N. 3600 5 oz. wine (with cut decoration).
O. 3600 6 oz. juice (with cut decoration).
P. 160/53/3 three-piece icer set.
Q. 160/250 bouillon cup and 160/37 saucer.
R. 160/190 footed sugar and creamer set.
S. 160/184 handled nut dish.
T. 160/183 handled nut or mint dish.
U. 160/35 teacup and saucer.
V. 160/37 coffee cup and saucer.

C

A. 160/24 two-quart ice lipped pitcher.
B. 160/176 80 oz. blown pitcher.
C. 160/19 40 oz. ice lipped pitcher.
D. 160/239 two-quart ice lipped pitcher.

E. 165 Tradition pattern ice pitcher
F. 160 36 oz, refigerator jug
G. 160/178 40 oz. blown martini pitcher.
H. 160/240 pint milk pitcher.

C

A. 160/244 26 oz. bar bottle and stopper.
B. 160/82 16 oz. cordial bottle and stopper.
C. 160/163 30 oz. decanter and stopper.
D. 160/256 18 oz. cordial bottle and stopper.
E. 160/185 26 oz. wine carafe and stopper.
F. 160/260 decanter (note "Bourbon").
G. 160 decanter (note "Scotch").
H. 160 decanter (note "Rye").
I. 160/63 6½" ice bucket and tongs.

J. 1602 2½ oz. sherry.
K. 1602 1½ oz. cordial.
L. 1600 3 oz. wine.
M. 160 7 oz. old fashion.
N. 160 14 oz. double old fashion.
O. 701 muddler.
P. 160/188 12 oz. handled stein.

C

A. 1604 two-piece hurricane lamp.
B. 160/137B 10" footed bowl.
C. 160/79 two-piece hurricane lamp.
D. 160/80/2 Eagle candleholder.
E. 160/45N 5¹/₂" candleholder.
F. 160/81 4" candleholder.
G. 160/80 5" candleholder.
H. 160/100 twin candleholder.
I. 160/45B 5" flower candleholder.
J. 160/90 4" handled aladdin candleholder.
K. 160/170 3" single candleholder.
L. 160/100 two-light candleholder (the center ornament has been removed to create a three-lite candleholder).
M. 16880 spider candleholder.
N. 160/175 4¹/₂" saucer candleholder.
O. 160/—candleholder.

C

A. 160/87F 8" fan vase.
B. 160/196 two-piece epergne.
C. whimsey.
D. 160/110B 6½" footed vase.
E. 160/27 footed bud vase.

F. whimsey.
G. 160/22 6¼" footed flip vase.
H. 160/223 8½" handled partitioned server.
I. whimsey.
J. whimsey.

C

A. 160/237 14 oz. ketchup bottle with wood screw cap.
B. 160/210 handled peanut jar and cover.
C. 160/119 4 oz. cruet and stopper.
D. 160/70 5 oz. cruet with pointed stopper.
E. 160/224 6 oz. condiment bottle and tube.
F. 160/2941 three-piece oil and vinegar set.
G. 160/207 6 oz. salad dressing and cupped plate set.
H. 160/204 12 oz. mayonnaise bowl and
    cupped plate set.

I. 160/201 18 oz. gravy bowl and cupped plate set.
J. 160/192 8¹/₂" partitioned peanut and mint.
K. 160/1112 four-piece relish and dressing set.
L. 160/25/26 square sugar, cream and tray set.
M. 160/5629 mustard and ketchup set.
N. 160/247 salt and pepper.
O. 160/2638 salt, pepper and tray set.

C

A. 160/67F 9" footed fruit bowl.
B. 160/137B 10" footed bowl.
C. 160/103D 11" cakestand (plain top and patterned apron).
D. 160/103D 11" cakestand (patterned top).

E. 160/180 4¹/₂" handled spider.
F. 160/67D 10¹/₂" flat cakestand.
G. 160/51F 6" round handled mint.
H. 160/182 6¹/₂" handled spider.
I. 160/187 6¹/₂" partitioned handled spider.

A. 160/124D 13^1/$_2$" oval platter.
B. 160/145D 11^1/$_2$" two-handled plate.
C. 160/45 6" footed comporte.
D. 160/222 12^1/$_2$" bread plate.
E. 160F 5^1/$_2$" cupped compote (note wafer stem).
F. 160/12 8" crescent salad plate.
G. 160/93 12" one-piece multiserver.

H. 160/33 3" individual jelly dish.
I. 160/34 individual butter or coaster.
J. 160/85 3" square coaster.
K. 160/78 4" round coaster.
L. 160/219 three-piece individual set: salt dip with glass spoon and pepper shaker.

C

A. 160/10F 8³/₄" bowl.
B. 160/7F 7¹/₂" bowl.
C. 160/3F 6" fruit bowl.
D. 160/45B 9¹/₂" two-handled bowl.
E. 160/5W 6³/₄" flared bowl.
F. 160/197 4¹/₂" lug dessert.

G. 160/198 5¹/₂" lug soup.
H. 160/199 6¹/₂" lug bowl.
I. 1602 finger bowl.
J. 1604 1/2A 4¹/₂" finger bowl.
K. 160/1W 4¹/₂" fruit.

A. 160/221F 9¹/₂" float bowl.
B. 160/221C 9¹/₂" crimped bowl.
C. 1602 11¹/₄" shallow oval vegetable bowl.
D. 160/131C 12" crimped oval bowl.

E. 160/124 11" oval vegetable bowl.
F. 160/125 11" oval partitioned vegetable bowl.
G. 160/221 10" oval vegetable dish.

C

A. 160/193 covered peanut butter jar with wicker handle.
B. 160/194 covered candy jar with wicker handle.
C. 160/195 6¹/₄" d. covered cookie jar with wicker handle.

D. 160/221/0 9" basket.
E. 160/73/0 11" basket.
F. 160/40 11" basket.
G. 160/40 11" footed basket.

A. 160/21 11½" footed flip vase.
B. 160/192 10" cylinder vase.
C. 160/133 covered pokal.
D. 160/110 10" footed candy jar and cover.

E. 160/143 8½" flip vase.
F. 160/128 11" covered pokal.
G. 160/186 10½" two-handled urn vase.

A. 1601 six-piece dresser set.
B. 160/459 five-piece condiment set.
C. 160/252 covered ketchup with spoon.
D. 160/52H three-piece mayonnaise set.

E. 160/49 5" heart-shaped dessert or mint.
F. 160/51H 6" handled heart mint.
G. 160/51T 6" handled heart tray.
H. 160/40H 6" handled heart (satin-finished).

A. 160/72 Tradition pattern 13" candle plate (holds 72 candles).
B. 160/72 Cape Cod 13" candle plate (holds 72 candles).
C. 160/220 10" square four-toed cake server.

C

Caramel Slag items from an original Imperial publicity photo: No. 800 Owl covered jar, No. 611 covered jar and No. 158 Rooster covered box.

When production of Caramel Slag began in earnest in 1964, it soon became quite a hit, following the success of Imperial's Purple Slag, which had made its debut several years earlier.

Indeed, the mixture of opaque brown and milk glass had been shown in Imperial's Supplement One to Our Catalog Number 62, where the No. 1608/1 24 piece "End O'Day Ash Tray Assortment" included assorted hues of "brown, green, blue, [and] purple." One of salesman Ed Kleiner's notebooks mentions the No. 602/75 salad set, but the "Caramel Slag" name may not have been associated with this ware at first. In the early 1960s, glass collectors called the opaque brown glass made at the old Indiana Tumbler and Goblet Company of Greentown, Indiana (1894-1903), "caramel slag," although Dr. Ruth Herrick had recently published a book in which the original name "Chocolate" was used.

By mid-1964, Imperial had at least 18 pieces of Caramel Slag in the line. A POPA tag purporting to reveal "Caramel Slag Glass Lore" associated the color with Harry Northwood but said that there was no proof Northwood's glass "was ever marketed commercially."

There were a few pieces added by the time of the 66A catalogue, and catalogues 69 and 71R showed more than a dozen animal figurines, most of which were made from Heisey moulds. Production continued until the mid-1970s, and then began anew about 1981. The Imperial Price List dated April 15, 1973, mentions a dozen animal figurines, as well as 25 other items (these were available in either glossy or satin finish). More than two dozen items are shown in the 1982-83 Imperial catalogue.

Because of keen collector interest in this color (and in Imperial's other "slags"), there has been quite an effort to document the articles made, including those which were not in the regular Imperial line. Thanks to the efforts of several collectors, this book shows over one hundred pieces of Caramel Slag (see Figs. 973-1082).

C

Originally made in iridescent glass as the No. 670 pitcher, Imperial's "Robin" was among the company's Carnival glass reissues.

Antiques." In the 1960s, Imperial's POPA tags on the re-issued ware reflected the popular story: "Iridescent Fired Colors now known as Colorful Carnival Glass."

Imperial reasoned that the demand for old Carnival glass which had pushed prices to $25-35 for many items in 1963 could be channeled into public acceptance of similar, newly-produced wares which would sell in the $2.00-7.00 range. This prediction proved accurate, and several other factories soon followed Imperial's lead, including the Fenton Art Glass Company of Williamstown, West Virginia. Ironically, Imperial had followed Fenton more than a half-century earlier when iridescent ware was first produced about 1908.

Imperial's revival of iridescent ware began quite modestly. Catalogue 62 shows the No. 473 Grape 10 oz. goblet in Rubigold and Peacock Blue, and they are labelled Carnival glass. No Carnival glass is listed in either Imperial's Supplement One to Our Catalog Number 62 or its Supplemental Price List (January 1, 1963).

In January, 1965, Imperial provided its sales force with three-ring binders containing descriptions and eight pages of color illustrations showing dozens of items in Carnival glass. The two colors mentioned were Rubigold and Peacock [not Peacock Blue]. The articles being made ranged from large punch bowls, tall vases and pitchers to novelty salt/pepper shakers and covered animal dishes (see Figs. 1231-1313 for some of these original illustrations). The 15-piece punch sets listed for $20 and 7-piece water sets were $15, but the majority of the items went for $2 to $6 each.

Imperial had a big display of its Carnival glass at a gift show in Atlantic City, and Lucile Kennedy recalls writing "lots of orders" for the increasingly-popular ware. Buyers in the Chicago area were also very enthusiastic, and the Marshall Field department store had a full-color ad in a Sunday newspaper supplement.

The Imperial POPA tag alluded to a recent feature story describing Imperial's old iridescent ware as "a Cinderella among Collectibles," a reference to

Although collectors today often use the term "Carnival glass" to denote iridescent glassware first made in late 1907 and continuing until about 1930, this phrase was not employed by the glass manufacturers at the time. They called the glassware "iridescent," and the glassworkers often referred to it as "dope ware." The "Carnival glass" appellation came from stories about this low-priced ware being given away as prizes during games played at carnivals and fairs.

In this book, Imperial's "old" Carnival glass (1909 to c. 1930) is discussed under the heading "Iridescent glass," its original name (see p. 364). Thus, Imperial's "new" Carnival glass (1960-1984) is discussed here. Readers may also wish to consult the three-volume *Encore by Dorothy* series produced by Dorothy Taylor to document the new Carnival glass made by Imperial and other companies over the past 45 years. Collectors should also be aware of the Collectible Carnival Glass Association, an organization devoted to new Carnival glass collectibles.

The growing popularity of old Carnival glass among collectors in the 1960s prompted Imperial to undertake what the firm termed a "genuine re-issue of its "Imperial iridescents of 50 years ago." The books published by Marion Hartung in the early 1960s certainly figured into Imperial's decision, as did an article in the Atlanta *Journal and Constitution* newspaper (August 18, 1963) which called old Carnival glass the "Cinderella of Modern

C

This Imperial POPA tag was used with Carnival glass.

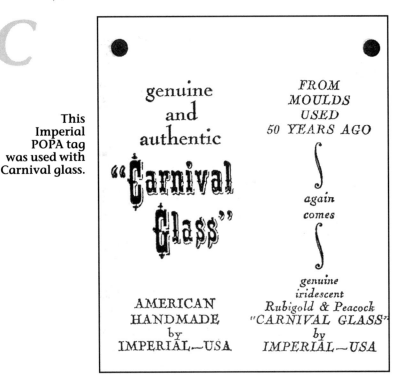

genuine
and
authentic

"Carnival
Glass"

AMERICAN
HANDMADE
by
IMPERIAL.—USA.

FROM
MOULDS
USED
50 YEARS AGO

again
comes

genuine
iridescent
Rubigold & Peacock
"CARNIVAL GLASS"
by
IMPERIAL.—USA

binders for the sales force. Noteworthy additions include the No. 524 (Mum) plate and the No. 525 (Homestead) plate, both made from original moulds. Rubigold and Peacock were the only colors mentioned, but Imperial was about to extend its repertoire of Carnival colors.

Within a short time, Imperial had introduced more re-issues of Carnival glass colors. White Carnival (see Figs. 1336-1358) imitated an old iridescent color, as did Azure Blue (see Figs. 1147-1175). Sunset Ruby (see Figs. 1314-1335) tapped into avid collector interest in the old red iridescent ware, and Imperial's revival of the name Helios (see Figs. 1176-1192), recalled the firm's green iridescent glass.

Aurora Jewels (a vivid blue iridescent) debuted in mid-1970, and Amber Carnival made its appearance in 1973. An interesting sueded version of Rubigold featured frosted panels on the Windmill pitcher and tumblers. Even when the other Rubigold items had been discontinued, this water set remained in the line (see p. 147 of the previous volume in this series).

Imperial produced several color brochures (four to six pages) to market its Carnival glass. Typically, these showed Rubigold and Peacock plus one or two other re-issue Carnival colors, such as Azure Blue, Helios or Sunset Ruby. Only Azure Blue and Sunset Ruby were mentioned in Imperial's catalogue No. 69, and no Carnival glass of any kind appears in either catalogue 71R or the 1972 catalogue. Amber Carnival was featured extensively in the catalogue for 1974-75, and White Carnival also merited a full page there, followed by a two-page spread in the 1975-76 catalogue. White Carnival was discontinued at the end of 1975.

Pink Carnival, which was in the line for about five years, was first shown in the Imperial Glass by Lenox 1978 Catalog. A limited edition compote, No. 666-1/2, was available through Imperial dealers. Horizon Blue Carnival joined the line a year later, and Meadow Green Carnival was added in 1980. Pink Carnival and Meadow Green Carnival are shown in this book (see Figs. 1193-1211).

In Horizon Blue Carnival, Imperial made a Grape punch set which was used as an incentive for dealers (see Fig. 574 in the previous volume of this series). Amethyst Carnival glass is shown in Imperial's 1981 Supplement (see pp. 38 and 157 of the previous volume in this series). A pale yellow hue called Sunburst Carnival appears in the 1982-83 Imperial catalogue.

In addition to the Carnival glass re-issues in the line, Imperial also made some Carnival glass as special orders for various customers, ranging from individuals to Carnival glass collector's clubs. Many of the articles were made in small quantities, and some were sold as limited editions (see Figs. 1359-1379 for illustrations of some of these).

the Atlanta *Journal and Constitution* newspaper article cited above. The POPA tag mentioned "genuine and authentic Carnival Glass," said that it was made "from moulds used 50 years ago" and concluded with this bit of history: "This type of Glassware was supposedly first popularized by Mr. Harry Northwood (of Wheeling Area fame) ... but it was Imperial who made and marketed the Greatest Volume, the Widest Variety of articles and in the Greatest Choice of colors."

Many old moulds were indeed utilized for Imperial's re-issue venture, including the No. 473 Grape line. The water sets included No. 289 American Beauty Rose and No. 514 Windmill. Several swung vases harkened back to the old No. 481 and No. 492 vases. The No. 356 vase, which had been called "black berry" in 1913, was re-issued under the name "Loganberry," which was, then as now, the popular nomenclature among Carnival glass collectors.

The punch sets were pattern No. 500, an imitation cut glass line which had been first introduced in a c. 1913 catalog supplement. Quite a few other imitation cut motifs from Imperial's old NUCUT lines were re-issued in Carnival glass, too. Some new moulds were used as well, and these tumblers were available in Rubigold or Peacock in January, 1965: Aloha, Bambu, Colonial Cabin and Hobnail (see Figs. 1306-1313).

Imperial's 66A catalogue (issued in early 1967) devoted four full pages to the firm's Carnival glass re-issues, although just one page was in color and only a few items had been added beyond the 1965

C

Top row, left to right (colors as indicated in parentheses):

No. 004 Grape vase (Bead Green/Milk Glass); No. 005 Hobnail vase (Amber/Milk Glass); and No. 001 Reeded vase (Aquamarine/ Milk Glass).

Bottom row, left to right (colors as indicated in parentheses):

No. 002 Fiddle vase (Madeira/Milk Glass); No. 003 Masque vase (Chartreuse/Milk Glass); and No. 006 Loganberry vase (Heather/Milk Glass). Notice the various crimped effects on some of the vases.

These six vases were being made about 1951, and other articles in cased glass were made later. Each of these began as an initial gathering of milk glass and was then covered with one of Imperial's colors before being blown to its final shape. Imperial's literature called this technique an "overlay."

Although these were made from moulds used for well-established items (No. 185 Fiddle) or pattern lines (No. 701 Reeded), each was given a new number for this offering. These were relatively expensive, ranging from $3.00 to $5.00 each when purchased in dozen lots.

CASUAL CRYSTAL

C

IMPERIAL GLASS CORPORATION, BELLAIRE, OHIO

IMPERIAL CASUAL CRYSTAL

TRAYS AND BOWLS

#81   6" Handled Bon Bon

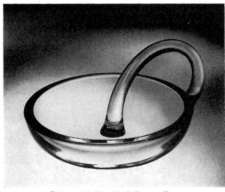

#84   6" Handled Pecan Tray

#82   6" Ash Tray, Single Rest

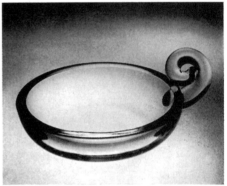

#80   6" Handled Olive Server

#85   6" 2-Handled Smokers Bowl

#83   6" Handled Mint Tray

These six articles were produced in the mid-1950s, about the same time as the Gaffer bowls and vases (see p. 336). They are shown in Imperial's 1953 catalogue and were advertised in *House Beautiful* as late as May, 1955. All were made by adding "bits" of hot glass to rather thick, plain 6" shallow bowls which were pressed ware pieces. A skilled glassworker called a finisher then shaped the bits into their final forms, which range from ashtray rests to handles in unusual shapes. Lucile Kennedy recalls that Imperial sought to make Casual Crystal items which reflected the influence of Steuben creations. Finding all six of these would be an interesting challenge for today's collector of Imperial glass.

This is a popular line today among Imperial glass collectors, and there is a wealth of information available about its history and production. In June, 1981, longtime NIGCS member Richard Lancione talked with Cathay designer Virginia B. Evans. This interview appeared in the souvenir booklet prepared for the 1981 Bellaire Glass Festival, and it was reprinted in the NIGCS *Glasszette* for October, 1995.

The development of Cathay started in 1943, when Imperial president Carl Gustkey telephoned Virginia B. Evans at her home in Moundsville. Evans was an accomplished teacher and artist who had worked in many media (particularly in oils and gouache). While teaching art at West Liberty College , she lectured frequently to various groups, maintained a studio in the Chapman Building in Wheeling, and promoted the arts through the Art Colony at Oglebay Institute and the Wheeling Women's Club in the 1930s. She agreed to come to the Imperial plant in Bellaire for a meeting.

Without mentioning the Chinese motif at first, Gustkey outlined Imperial's procedures for designing and marketing glassware. Finally, he asked about Evans' interest and training in Chinese art. As it happened, she had been intrigued by Chinese forms when studying and working at the Tiffany Foundation on Long Island in the 1920s. She related these aspects of her background and also told Gutskey that she had yet to see a careful following of the Chinese style in glassware. That was

just what Imperial needed to hear, for Gutskey and Carl Urhmann had decided to develop a Chinese-inspired line and were searching for an artist-designer. Virginia B. Evans was the perfect choice, and Cathay Crystal was the result in 1949.

She was enthusiastic about doing the necessary research—visiting department stores and art galleries in Boston, New York and Chicago—and she compiled a notebook of design ideas based on Chinese art. As her work continued, Imperial's original prospects for a line of Chinese-style tableware changed to a quest for unique decorative pieces.

Once the concept for each Cathay piece was established, Evans made a full-sized clay model of the article. The models enabled Imperial's mould shop to procure the necessary castings and to make the mould. Except for three items (5016 Fu wedding vase, base of 5019 Ming jar and chimney of 5027 wedding lamp), the Cathay line was made as pressed ware. By the time the line was complete, Imperial had invested a great deal of money in the moulds.

Although Evans was not experienced in the mechanics of glassmaking, she liked the look of "camphorated" glass, and this led Imperial to develop the distinctive frosted finish used for most Cathay pieces. Imperial took out several design patents (#156,715, #156,716, #156,717 and #159,792) to protect the Cathay line from imitations.

Cathay Crystal was introduced to the public on April 25, 1949, just as the first full-color advertisements appeared in the May issue of *House Beautiful*. An article in *Retailing Dailey* (April 22, 1949) revealed that Imperial retailers in 61 different

Imperial
Cathay
Crystal

DESIGNED BY

Virginia B. Evans

中 水 玻
國 晶 璃

C

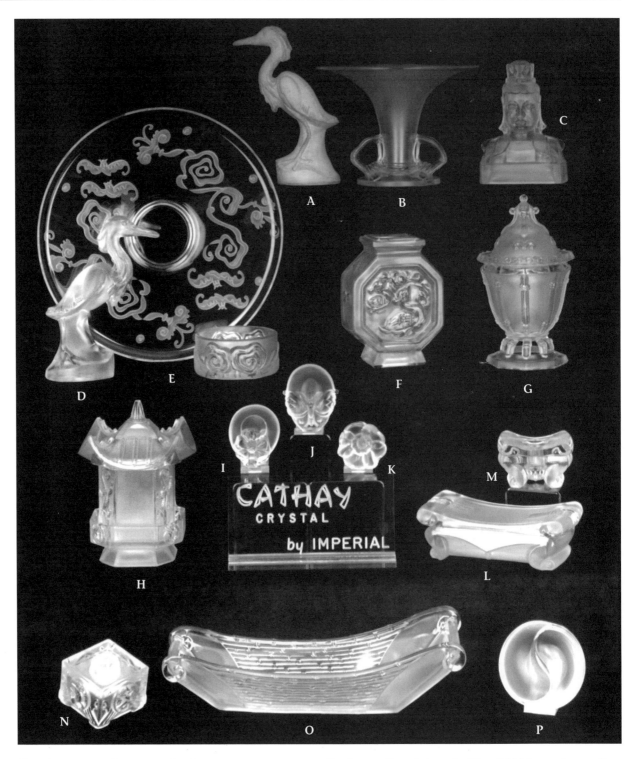

A. 5017 Egrette (wax test piece).
B. 5012 Ku ribbon vase.
C. 5029 Empress book stop.
D. 5017 Egrette.
E. 5038 Celestial center piece (carved by Franz Hess) and base.
F. 5016 Fu wedding vase.
G. 5014 Bamboo urn.
H. 5001 Pagoda.
I. Plum Blossom ash tray (sold as 5007 four-piece set).

J. Butterfly ash tray (sold as 5006 four-piece set).
K. Peach Blossom mint or nut dish (sold as 5008 four-piece set).
L. 5018/1 Pillow cigarette box (sold as 5018/3 set with two 5018/2 Pillow ash trays).
M. 5013 Pillow candle base.
N. 5020 candlebase from Shen console set.
O. 5010 Junk flower bowl.
P. 5004 Yang and Yin ash tray.

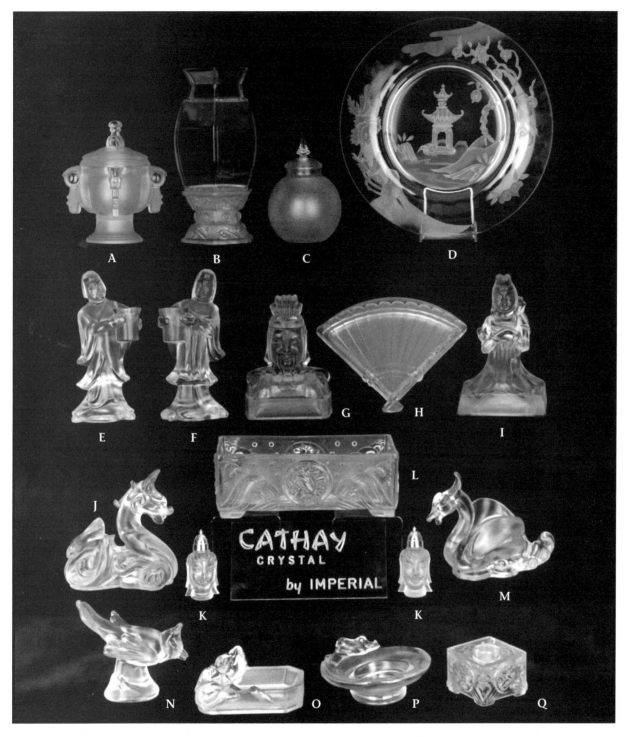

A. 5002 Shang candy jar.
B. 5027 Wedding lamp (two pieces).
C. 5019 Ming jar.
D. 5085 Pavilion tray (carved by Franz Hess).
E. 5033 Candle Servant (man).
F. 5034 Candle Servant (woman).
G. 5030 Lu-Tung book holder.
H. 5022 Fan sweetmeat box.
I. 5000 Concubine book-end.
J. 5009 Dragon candleholder.

K. These experimental shakers were difficult to make and did not become part of the Cathay line.
L. 5020/1 Shen flower box-bowl (combined with two 5020/2 Shen candlebases in the 5020/3 Shen console set.
M. 5026 Phoenix bowl.
N. 5024 Scolding Bird.
O. 5011 Wu Ling ash tray.
P. 5005 Lung ash tray.
Q. 5020/2 Shen candlebase (a pair was included in the 5020/3 Shen console set).

C

cities would display the Cathay articles, which ranged in price from $3.98 to $25.

Each Cathay item was packaged in a luxurious jade velour gift box, complete with Virginia B. Evans' signature in gold lettering on the lid and a 32-page booklet describing the entire line inside. "Cathay Crystal Sales Story" brochures were prepared for the retailers' sales staffs, and pick-up folders with the store name were available for distribution to interested customers. Virginia B. Evans was present at the Stone and Thomas department store in Wheeling for several hours on April 25, and she answered questions about the Cathay line and told customers about the development of the various designs.

The promotions for Cathay Crystal continued with full-page color advertising in *House and Garden* for June, 1949, but Imperial soon found itself beset by production problems. Some Cathay articles (such as the 5009 Dragon candleholder and the 5012 Ku ribbon vase) were difficult to make, and the company could not be timely in filling orders from its wholesale customers. Nonetheless, Cathay Crystal remained in the Imperial line for several years, and four pages in full color were at the center of Catalog 53. A few Cathay items were made in Black (and Black Suede) or Midwest Custard during the early and mid-1950s, and seven items were part of an opaque jade green grouping in 1960 (see **Dynasty Jade**).

In 1964-65, Imperial re-issued some of the Cathay pieces in a frosted hue called Cranberry and in frosted Verde; the Cranberry was actually the color Azalea, which had been acid-treated to obtain the frosted finish (see Figs. 1399-1416). In 1980-81, Imperial produced some Cathay pieces as part of an oriental-style assortment in opaque jade green.

Imperial mouldmaker Frank Moore works on the mould for the first Christmas plate.

From 1970 to 1981, Imperial issued a one-per-year series of Christmas plates based on the popular "Twelve Days of Christmas" carol. Marketed as a limited edition plate series (production was limited to orders placed during the year of issue), these were advertised in various trade publications (including the inside front cover of *China, Glass and Tablewares*), but were not mentioned in Imperial's regular catalogues until 1978.

All twelve plates were made in satin-finished clear glass, which Imperial called sueded crystal, but the Carnival glass versions (see Figs. 1417-1428) became quite collectible.

Each was made in a different iridescent color, as follows: Partridge in a Pear Tree (blue, 1970); Two Turtle Doves (dark green, 1971); Three French Hens (amber, 1972); Four Colly Birds (white, 1973); Five Golden Rings (Verde, 1974); Six Geese-a-Laying (yellow, 1975); Seven Swans-a-Swimming (Ultra Blue, 1976); Eight Maids-a-Milking (Nut Brown, 1977); Nine Drummers Drumming (pink, 1978); Ten Pipers Piping (Horizon Blue, 1979);

Eleven Ladies Dancing (light green, 1980); and Twelve Lords-a-Leaping (ruby amberina, 1981).

In an obvious mistake, some of the Six Geese-a-Laying plates were also made in the Ultra Blue with iridescent finish in 1976 (these say "Plate No. 7" on the back).

An article in the Martins Ferry *Times-Leader* (December 24, 1981) noted that Lucile Kennedy conceived the idea for these Christmas plates. A local art teacher, Robert P. Robinson of the Shadyside City School District, worked out the various designs, and Imperial's mould shop crafted the moulds. The wife of movie star George Kennedy purchased some of the plates to use as Christmas gifts, and comedienne Carol Burnett was among the recipients.

CHROMA, NO. 123

Chroma No. 123 juice, ice tea, goblet, sherbet and 8" plate, c. 1957. These retailed for $1.00 each at the time.

This short line began when Earl Newton registered the design in March, 1937 (#103,826). It was originally known as the Coronet pattern in 1938, but the name had been changed to Victorian by early 1941 (Victorian was "discontinued until further notice" in an Imperial memo dated November 13, 1945). In the early 1950s, the name was changed once more—this time to Chroma, the appellation best known to collectors today. The original 1937 design patent shows the stem with one textured ball and one smooth ball; this was altered later to add texture to the smooth ball (look closely at Figs. 1437-1443 and 1447-1449).

All three names (Coronet, Victorian and Chroma) were designated No. 123 in Imperial's records. Coronet or Victorian were made in crystal and ruby, but Chroma was offered in crystal as well as four colors—Burgundy, Evergreen, Indigo and Madiera in the early 1950s, according to an ad placed in *Crockery and Glass Journal*. A c. 1957 list in Imperial's archives, titled "Re-introducing Chroma," mentions only Burgundy, Evergreen and Madiera. Some individual items were made in other colors, such as Midwest Custard. See **Coronet** later in this book.

BELLES OF 1890

Coiffures · Sports Femmes · Fashions · Millinery

GAY NINETIES

Bicycle Courtin' · Skating in Central Park · Bowery Cop Bar Jar · Bein' Photographed

PENNSYLVANIA DUTCH DESIGNS

Spinning Wheel · Courtin' Couple · Market Day · Newlyweds' Farmhouse

These assortments of decorated milk glass jars from the late 1950s were inspired by old issues of the *Ladies Home Journal*. The name "coach lamp" is derived from the shape, which resembles lighting fixtures on horse-drawn coaches. Art student Lynne Gustkey Pepperdine created the Belles of 1890 items, and designer Jane Snead developed both the Pennsylvania Dutch series and the Gay Nineties series. These were sold in groups of four jars. Each individual jar was silk screen decorated with four different scenes, making a total of 16 different scenes.

COLLECTORS CRYSTAL

A Time for Beauty . . .

COLLECTORS CRYSTAL

Although Imperial did not begin to use the phrase "collector's crystal" until the late 1940s or early 1950s, these pieces reflect many years of Imperial's history. Quite a few articles were first made as imitation cut glass around 1910 or as part of the extensive and popular NUCUT lines several years later.

An undated Imperial brochure contains photos of Collectors Crystal Assortment No. 1 and Collectors Crystal Assortment No. 2, and most of these pieces appear in the firm's General Catalog 53. Catalogue 62 contains two pages of Collectors Crystal, and some of the articles were also offered in crystal "with fired cranberry decoration" elsewhere. Articles were added gradually, and more than fifty pieces are depicted in Imperial's Catalog No. 66A and about sixty-five in Catalog 71R. These included punch sets, cakestands and many functional items as well as vases.

Collectors Crystal was featured on the cover of Imperial's catalogues for 1974-1975 and for 1976-1977, and about seventy pieces are recorded in the April 1, 1975 Price List (this listing is particularly valuable because it preserves the "old" numbers for all items and gives the "new" five-digit numbers needed for Imperial's computer system). The catalogue for 1975-1976 called Collectors Crystal "one of the broadest ranges of popular priced gift glass available" and noted further that the items "are prized by collectors for their authentic capture of our past." More than fifty Collectors Crystal items appear in the 1982-83 catalogue, and many of them were pieces that had been in the line for more than 20 years.

IMPERIAL GLASS CORP.   BELLAIRE, OHIO

COLLECTORS CRYSTAL ASSORTMENT No. 2

No. 2   12 Unit Assortment............$38.00 Per Assortment

IMPERIAL GLASS CORP.   BELLAIRE, OHIO

COLLECTORS CRYSTAL ASSORTMENT No. 1

No. 1   14 Unit Assortment...........$20.00 Per Assortment

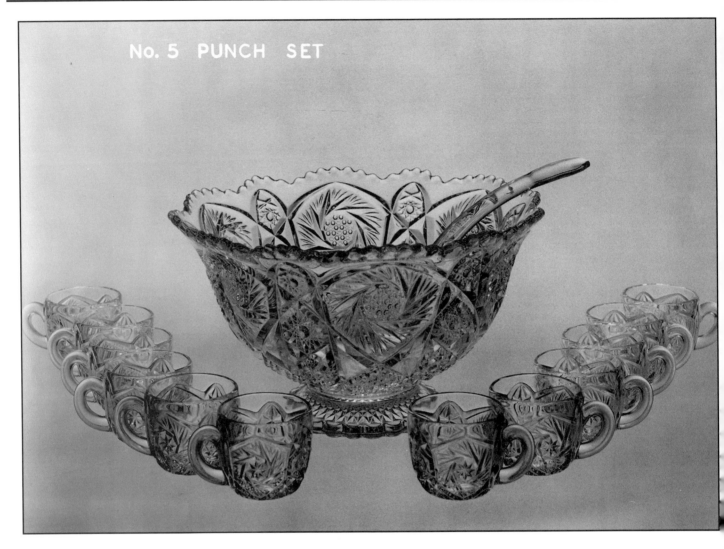

No. 5 PUNCH SET

Some items from the Collectors Crystal grouping were also marketed under other, short-lived names. A "Punch Set Special" in the summer of 1962 featured the No. 5 punch bowl with 12 cups and a ladle for a retail price of $10.00. About the same time, items from the old No. 474 and No. 612 lines were available under the aegis of "Turn O'The Century." This promotion was extended to include a half-dozen goblets and small crimped compotes made from these same goblets.

Although its may seem strange as well as contradictory, Imperial also marketed Collectors Crystal in colors! A c. 1955 brochure for Casual Crystal and Gaffer bowls and vases also lists four Collectors Crystal pieces (No. 503 oval nappy, No. 536 6" vase, No. 555 footed compote and No. 568 handled nappy) in pink and blue.

Closely related to Collectors Crystal is a small group of pieces called "Fired Gold on Crystal" (see p. 332 in this book). This was done with a specially-shaped paint roller, and many of the items were from Collectors Crystal. A firm called Crystal Clear Imports bought large quantities of this ware from Imperial. In a related development, a few of the Collectors Crystal articles were also made in dark green and decorated with gold, as were some other items then in the line which lent themselves to this treatment.

Reproductions of Genuine Antiques from *Collectors Cupboard*

PAUL REVERE
Concord 1775

LOVES REQUEST
IS PICKLES

Each
Available in
4 Colors

Wistar Purple
Honey Amber
Stiegel Green
Midwest Rose

Each item in this *Collectors Cupboard* is a replica of the 'real thing.' These designs and colors have enjoyed more than a century's popularity. To show them is to sell them . . . write today for details on this *Special* promotion assortment.

IMPERIAL GLASS CORPORATION
House of Americana Glassware
BELLAIRE, OHIO

To Retail
$2.98*

each

**Slightly higher 'way
out West!*

Imperial HOUSE of AMERICANA GLASSWARE

Imperial coined this fanciful name in 1957 for an assortment of "Authentic Reproductions of Genuine Antiques." A dozen items were available in four colors (Honey Amber, Midwest Rose, Stiegel Green and Wistar Purple), and each was to retail at $2.98. These items were offered: No. 40 Daisy basket; No. 52C Windmill crimped bowl; No. 54 8" Concord Server; No. 181 Rose vase; No. 192 Tricorn vase; No. 213 9" tray ("Loves Request Is Pickles"); No. 240 Windmill pitcher; No. 260 Watch candy box and cover; No. 270 Hobnail jar and cover; No. 474C comporte; No. 749 Lace Edge comporte; and No. 785 open edge covered candy box. A full page ad for this assortment appeared in the March, 1957, issue of *Giftwares*, and a special color brochure was printed.

COLLECTOR'S FRUIT

C

These pieces date from about 1956-57, and they can be found in at least four different colors—Bead Green, Flask Brown, Mustard and Pink.

Top row, left to right:
No. 88/1 Apple jar and cover; No. 185 two-piece Pear with brass stem; No. 186 two-piece Apple with brass stem; and No. 306 pitcher.

Middle row, left to right:
No. 217 Pineapple tray; No. 140 covered Pineapple; and No. 311 covered Pear (see Beaded Block/ Frosted Block in Volume I, pp. 49-51).

Bottom row, left to right:
No. 56, No. 72, No. 32 and No. 55 serving pieces.

This assortment of six blown bottles was marketed in 1956-57, when Imperial was involved with the Jamestown project (see pp. xx-xxi of the previous volume in this series). Imperial also referred to these as "Olde Jamestown" in some advertising promotions. These retailed for $2.00-3.00 each. Several of the colors made, particularly Blue Mist and Flask Brown, are reminiscent of hues used in glassmaking during the eighteenth century.

Top row, left to right:
No. 12 For Our Country (Bead Green);
No. 13 Washington and Taylor (Turquoise); and
No. 17 Poison Bottle (Mustard).

Bottom row, left to right:
No. 16 Colonial Jersey Scroll (Pink);
No. 14 Union (Blue Mist); and
No. 15 Handled Flask (Flask Brown).

COLONIAL CRYSTAL, No. 600

C

Open stock table glass = No. 600 COLONIAL CRYSTAL

600—pressed water bottle
3 dozen in barrel
per dozen $14.00

600—blown wine bottle
5 dozen in barrel
per dozen $14.00

Introduced in the early 1920s through Imperial's catalog 104D, this was an extensive line of open stock table glass. The catalog described Colonial Crystal as "a pure, plain colonial design without any attempt at ornamentation beyond the flutes and, here and there, the stars in the bottoms."

Catalog 104D illustrates dozens of Colonial Crystal articles, ranging from tankard pitchers and many sizes of tumblers to stemware and tableware items and a large punch bowl. In her book on Depression era glass, Weatherman labelled the tankard pitcher from this line "Chesterfield," and later writers have mistakenly concluded that this was Imperial's original name.

In the mid-1920s, the No. 600 moulds were also used to make glass in a variety of colors, ranging from Golden Green (see p. 342) to the iridescent Ice colors and hues such as Nuruby, Peacock and Sapphire. When the popularity of these colors waned, No. 600 continued to be a staple in crystal glass. In Imperial's 1938 sales summary, No. 600

was credited with about 34,000 pieces sold. Some moulds were still in use many years later, such as the No. 600 toothpick, which was marketed in several colors as "toothpick/cigarette sets" in Imperial's 66A catalog.

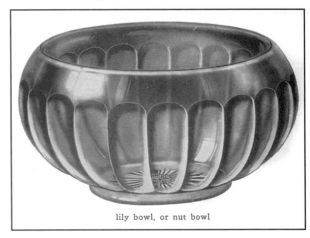

lily bowl, or nut bowl

272

COLONIAL AND GRAPES, No. 700

Imperial's catalog 100B uses the phrases "Colonial and grapes" or "colonial grapes" to refer to iridescent pressed glassware bearing a grape pattern imparted by the plunger (i. e., on the interior of the article). For some time, this pattern has been called "Heavy Grape" by Carnival glass collectors, and it was often misattributed to the Fenton Art Glass Company. Plates and bowls are known in various sizes, along with a punch bowl and cups.

8½ inch flared berry.—Colonial grapes.

Footed punch bowl—Colonial and grapes.
The inside bottom of this bowl shows a gorgeous grape design, diameter 11½ inches.

CONCORD, NO. 995

At first glance, this motif is somewhat similar to Imperial's old No. 473 Grape pattern and to the articles shown as Imperial's Vintage Ruby in Catalog 53.

The Concord line made its debut in mid-1960. There were four blown pieces (a 5" nappy and tumblers in 12 oz., 10 oz. and 5 oz sizes) and two pressed plates (6½" and 7½"). All were available in amber, crystal, Heather and Verde (Imperial salesman Ed Kleiner's notebook mentions opaque Turquoise, too). A footed sherbet and 13 oz, footed ice tea were soon added. Except for the 6½" plate, all are shown in amber, Heather and Verde in Imperial's Catalogue No. 62.

Two decoration treatments were employed on Concord, too. Selective acid etching of some areas was called "Concord Two-Tone," and these were available in amber, crystal, Heather and Verde (these were designated 995/S). The decoration called "Crowned Concord" features vivid cranberry red stain on the rims of all items and on the bases of the tumblers and footed ice tea (these were designated 995/Dec).

This name was used for these decal-decorated beverage ware articles in the 1960s. These range from a decanter with stopper and a "hospitality bowl" for snacks to a 12 oz. tumbler, a 15 oz. double old fashion, and a 14 oz. handled mug. Except for the decanter, which was No. 625, the other articles were blanks from the Federal Glass Company. All were produced for Imperial by Conrad Crafters, a decorating firm in nearby Wheeling. There was also a 7" oblong ashtray available. Another assortment, called Conrad Golden Eagles, was available in several sizes in early 1965. These were described as "burnished gold and black enamel."

CONSOLE SETS

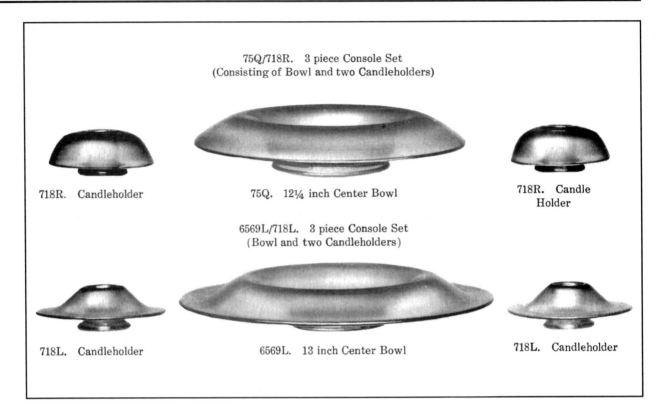

75Q/718R.   3 piece Console Set
(Consisting of Bowl and two Candleholders)

718R.   Candleholder

75Q.   12¼ inch Center Bowl

718R.   Candle Holder

6569L/718L.   3 piece Console Set
(Bowl and two Candleholders)

718L.   Candleholder

6569L.   13 inch Center Bowl

718L.   Candleholder

During the 1920s, these were quite popular, and many different glass factories created their own distinctive console sets. The most basic set consisted of two candleholders or candlesticks which flanked a large bowl; other sets came with four candleholders. In some sets, the console bowl was accompanied by a black glass "flower frog" (Imperial's No. 75 4-inch Flower Block), which went inside, and the bowl may have rested upon a separate base of contrasting color (usually black).

Imperial's console sets began in the early 1920s when bowls from the Art Glass line were combined with Free Hand candlesticks or vases (see p. 451). Two console sets were part of the Lead Lustre line (see Archer, p. 88), and these featured a dramatic 9-inch candlestick (see Fig. 1716). By the mid-1920s, Imperial was offering a wide variety of console sets (see the Archers' book, pp. 107-108, 159, 191, 198 and 204), and this emphasis continued throughout the 1930s, including such lines as No. 400 Candlewick, No. 160 Cape Cod and No. 779 Empire.

Several Imperial console sets or individual candlesticks have been named by collectors, although Imperial used only numbers in its catalogs and other records. The "Newbound" set was Imperial's No. 153, and a pair of No. 153 twin candlesticks could be combined with either a round bowl or an oval bowl (see Figs. 1450-1467). "Double Scroll" was Imperial's No. 320, and the 10½" oval bowl could be combined with either two tall candlesticks or two low candleholders (see Figs. 1468-1478). "Premium" was Imperial's No. 635, and a pair of candlesticks was combined with the No. 656 bowl (on black base).

Various bowls from Imperial's No. 749 Laced Edge line were used to form console sets by combining them with a pair of No. 749 twin candlesticks. In like manner, the No. 169 twin candlestick was combined with either the No. 648B 11" bowl or the No. 656 bowl. The Art Deco look of the 1920s is readily apparent when Imperial's No. 718 candleholders were combined with either the No. 75Q or the No. 656 center bowl as seen in the illustration at the top of this page.

C

7499B. 3-piece Console Set, 12 inch Bowl
⅝ dozen in No. 1 carton, shipping weight 65 pounds

7499F. 3-piece Console Set, 13 inch Bowl
⅝ dozen in No. 1 carton, shipping weight 65 pounds

7498B. 3-piece Console Set, 10 inch Bowl
1 dozen in No. 1 carton, shipping weight 65 pounds

7498F. 3-piece Console Set, 11 inch Bowl
1 dozen in No. 1 carton, shipping weight 65 pounds

7497B. 3-piece Console Set, 9 inch Bowl
1¼ dozen in No. 1 carton, weight 65 pounds

C

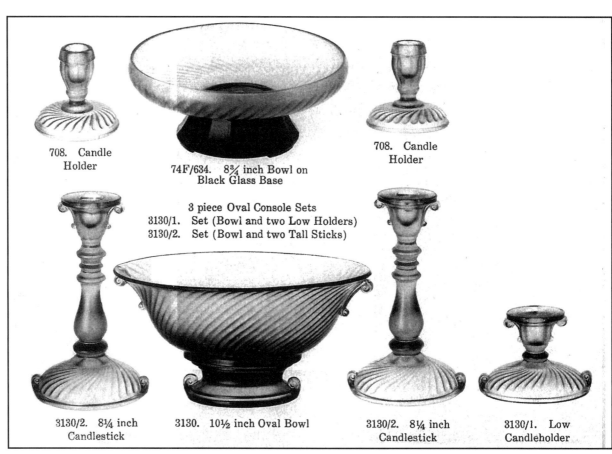

708. Candle
Holder

74F/634.   8¾ inch Bowl on
Black Glass Base

708. Candle
Holder

3 piece Oval Console Sets
3130/1.   Set (Bowl and two Low Holders)
3130/2.   Set (Bowl and two Tall Sticks)

3130/2.   8¼ inch
Candlestick

3130.   10½ inch Oval Bowl

3130/2.   8¼ inch
Candlestick

3130/1.   Low
Candleholder

808/3Q/73.   3 piece Console Set
Consisting of Bowl and two Low Candleholders.

73. Low Candle
Holder

808/3Q.   10½ inch Center Bowl

73. Low Candle
Holder

3139R/637/3.   3 piece Console Set
Consisting of Bowl and two Candleholders.

637/3. Low
Candleholder

3139R.   11 inch Bowl, Deep

637/3. Low
Candleholder

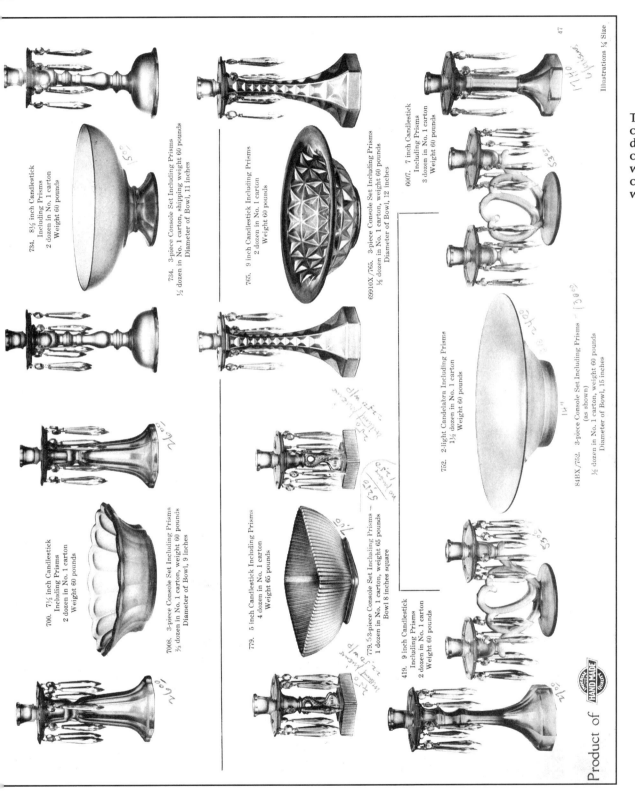

Illustrations ¼ Size

47

734. 8½ inch Candlestick
Including Prisms
2 dozen in No. 1 carton
Weight 60 pounds

734. 3-piece Console Set Including Prisms
½ dozen in No. 1 carton, shipping weight 60 pounds
Diameter of Bowl, 11 inches

765. 9 inch Candlestick Including Prisms
2 dozen in No. 1 carton
Weight 60 pounds

69910X/765. 3-piece Console Set Including Prisms
½ dozen in No. 1 carton, weight 60 pounds
Diameter of Bowl, 12 inches

6007. 7 inch Candlestick
Including Prisms
3 dozen in No. 1 carton
Weight 60 pounds

700. 7½ inch Candlestick
Including Prisms
2 dozen in No. 1 carton
Weight 60 pounds

7008. 3-piece Console Set Including Prisms
¾ dozen in No. 1 carton, weight 60 pounds
Diameter of Bowl, 9 inches

779. 5 inch Candlestick Including Prisms
4 dozen in No. 1 carton
Weight 65 pounds

779.53-piece Console Set Including Prisms –
1 dozen in No. 1 carton, weight 65 pounds
Bowl 8 inches square

419. 9 inch Candlestick
Including Prisms
2 dozen in No. 1 carton
Weight 60 pounds

762. 2-light Candelabra Including Prisms
1½ dozen in No. 1 carton
Weight 60 pounds

84BX/762. 3-piece Console Set Including Prisms
(as shown)
½ dozen in No. 1 carton, weight 60 pounds
Diameter of Bowl, 15 inches

Product of

HAND MADE

This Imperial
catalogue sheet
depicts seven
console sets
which feature
candlesticks
with prisms.

279

C

This Imperial catalogue sheet shows three bowls (No. 75X, No. 75B and No. 320), each of which could be ordered in combination with No. 75 candelabrum to form 3-piece console sets.

These were available in crystal, Stiegel Green and Ritz Blue for the same price, but Ruby was about 35% higher.

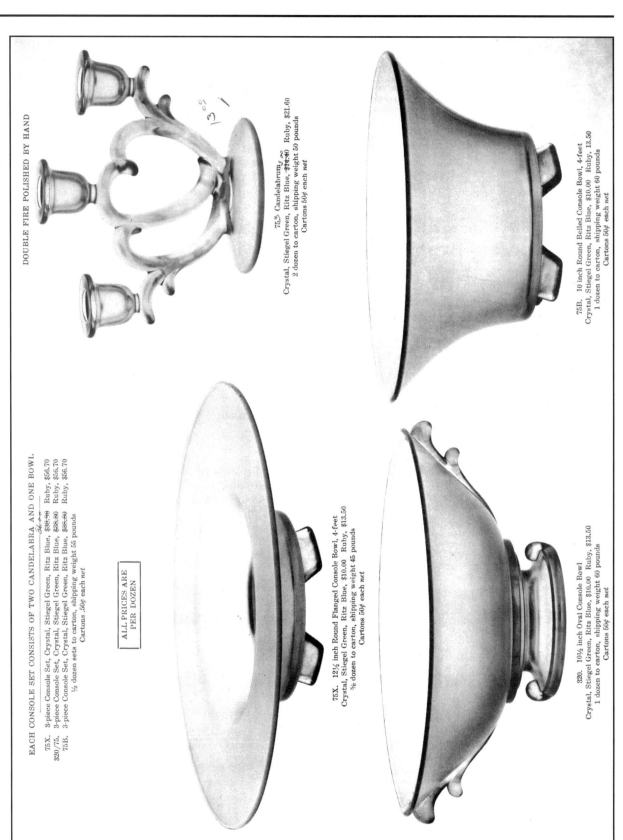

DOUBLE FIRE POLISHED BY HAND

75. Candelabrum, Crystal, Stiegel Green, Ritz Blue, $14.40 Ruby, $21.60
2 dozen to carton, shipping weight 50 pounds
Cartons 50¢ each *net*

75B. 10 inch Round Belled Console Bowl, 4-feet
Crystal, Stiegel Green, Ritz Blue, $10.00 Ruby, 13.50
1 dozen to carton, shipping weight 60 pounds
Cartons 50¢ each *net*

EACH CONSOLE SET CONSISTS OF TWO CANDELABRA AND ONE BOWL.

75X. 3-piece Console Set, Crystal, Stiegel Green, Ritz Blue, $38.90 Ruby, $56.70
320/75. 3-piece Console Set, Crystal, Stiegel Green, Ritz Blue, $38.80 Ruby, $56.70
75B. 3-piece Console Set, Crystal, Stiegel Green, Ritz Blue, $38.80 Ruby, $56.70
½ dozen sets to carton, shipping weight 55 pounds
Cartons .50¢ each *net*

ALL PRICES ARE
PER DOZEN

75X. 12½ inch Round Flanged Console Bowl, 4-feet
Crystal, Stiegel Green, Ritz Blue, $10.00 Ruby, $13.50
⅚ dozen to carton, shipping weight 45 pounds
Cartons 50¢ each *net*

320. 10½ inch Oval Console Bowl
Crystal, Stiegel Green, Ritz Blue, $10.00 Ruby, $13.50
1 dozen to carton, shipping weight 60 pounds
Cartons 50¢ each *net*

IMPERIAL CONTINENTAL

176
12 oz. Goblet

1761
11 oz. Goblet

176
7 oz. Sherbet

176
6 oz. Wine

176
12 oz. Footed Ice Tea

176
4½ oz. Cocktail

176
4 oz. Oyster Cocktail

176
Footed Finger Bowl

176
2 oz. Cordial

176
40 oz. Pitcher

176
14 oz. Tumbler

176
10 oz. Tumbler

176
7 oz. Old Fashion

176
5½ oz. Juice Tumbler

176
3½ oz. Tumbler

176
80 oz. Pitcher

This long-lived crystal line from the 1940s was featured in the April, 1948, *House & Garden*. Intended as an "open stock" pattern for beverages, Continental can be found in Imperial catalogues throughout the 1950s and much of the 1960s. Imperial's Catalog 53 shows two pitchers, five tumblers and nine footed/stemmed articles, all in crystal. Four pieces (12 oz. goblet; 7 oz. sherbet; 6 oz. footed juice or wine; and 12 oz. footed ice tea) in Sueded Verde are in Imperial's Supplement One to Our Catalog Number 62 and in Catalog 66A.

C

Imperial obtained patents in 1940-41 on this design, which was called Crystal Shell. The designer was Onnie Mankki of Cleveland. When Imperial stopped using the name Crystal Shell in September, 1940, the term Corinthian was employed. This line consisted of bowls, plates and serving pieces, but several vases (numbered 280/129-132) were made, including some with hanging prisms. As Corinthian was phased out in the 1940s, many of these vases found new life in such colors as Black Suede (see p. 63 of the previous volume of this series). In the early 1950s, Corinthian was re-named Tiara, and this line occupied the first two pages of Imperial's Catalog 53 (see **Crystal Shell** below and **Tiara** in the next volume of this series).

CORINTHIAN

280/132R   8 in. Urn Vase,
Plain

280/129R   4½ in. Urn Candleholder
Plain

280/131R   6 in. Urn Vase,
Plain

280/129RP   4½ in. Urn Candleholder,
6 Prisms

280/132RP   8 in. Urn Vase,
12 Prisms

280/129RP   4½ in. Urn Candleholder,
6 Prisms

280/100   Twin Candleholder

280/131RP   6 in. Urn Vase,
9 Prisms

280   7 in. Candy Box and Cover

280/132B   10 in. Urn Vase, plain

280/131B   8 in. Urn Vase, plain

280/130B   6 in. Urn Vase, plain

CRACKLED, NO. 841

No. 841 tumblers in various sizes. Bottom row: 80 oz. pitcher; 40 oz. pitcher; martini mixer
(the stirring rod actually belongs with this article); and 10" vase.

This interesting treatment was used in conjunction with several Imperial lines and articles in the 1950s and 1960s. The crackled effect is achieved by plunging a hot glass item into water momentarily and then reheating it in a glory hole.

More than 20 items appear in Imperial's Catalog 53, and all are designated with the line number 841. These crystal articles range from tumblers of various sizes to large vases in various shapes and pitchers with bucket-like metal "bales." Two sizes of No. 841 tumblers (14 oz. and 10 oz.) are shown in Bead Green, Flask Brown and Heather in Imperial's Catalogue No. 62.

Three stemware items (goblet, wine and cocktail) and several tumblers were made in crystal and Pink. These carried Imperial's No. 843 in 1955-57. The No. 871 tumblers and No. 83 pitcher were marketed as "Olde Jamestowne Inspired Crackled Ware" in the late 1950s. Crystal was dubbed Olde Flint, and Bead Green and Flask Brown were also available.

The crackled treatment was occasionally used for other Imperial articles. In Catalog 53 for example, three pieces from the No. 330 line (6 oz. sherbet, 5 oz. juice and 13 oz. tumbler) are shown with the crackled finish, and the catalog notes that these are "available in crystal and colors" (see the entry for **Crinkled** below).

These items, which were intended to be vases, feature a spiral of crystal glass wound from top to bottom on their exterior surfaces. The overall effect is quite striking.

CUT GLASSWARE

C

One could write an entire book just about Imperial's cut ware production. Simple gray cuttings were a part of Imperial's offerings early in its history, and quite a few motifs are shown in catalogues 101D (c. 1915-17) and 103G (c. 1918). Some of these were pictured in the previous volume of this series (see **Anemone**, **Aster**, **Butterfly** and **Buzz Star**) and quite a few are shown in the Archer's book (pp. 54-69).

In the late 1920s and during the 1930s, Imperial created various cutting designs, including "rock crystal" cut and polished pieces, many of

No. 85 tumblers with C530, C535 and C 536.

Imperial cut decanters.

286

212/C842
"ELIZABETH II"

212/C843
"BRIDAL WREATH"

212/C845
"KIMBERLEY"

212/C844
"CELESTIAL"

These four cuttings are from the mid-1950s.

No. 176 pitcher with "Denise" cut.

which were done at its subsidiary, the Crown Glass Manufacturing Company. Most of these were executed on crystal glass (see the Archer's book, pp. 94-102), but some cuttings may also be found on Imperial's green, Rose Pink, ruby and topaz colors.

In 1940, Imperial acquired moulds and equipment from the bankrupt Central Glass Company in nearby Wheeling. Many of the moulds were for stemware articles; when made plain, these sold well to hotels and restaurants, and, over a period of time, Imperial also found good markets in the upscale department stores which had bridal registry services.

These developments, coupled with work on the Etiquette No. 554 line and the steady popularity of some cuttings on Candlewick, kept Imperial involved with cut ware. Imperial's catalog 53 devoted six pages to cut stemware, and allocated four pages to other cut products, including several full pages of tumblers and bar ware. At this time. Imperial was purchasing large quantities of "blanks" (particularly tumblers such as 71) for cutting and decorating from the Federal Glass Company.

Some cut stemware and tumblers appeared in Imperial's catalog 62, but the overall quantity diminishes by the time of catalog 66A. By the 1970s, Imperial's cut glass production was confined almost entirely to bar ware such as decanters and tumblers of various sizes.

CAPRICE

(see **Cambridge Caprice** in the previous volume of this series, pp. 90-91)

CASA TILE TUMBLERS

(see **Tile Tumblers** in the next volume of this series)

CASED BOWLS

These are mentioned in an Imperial price list from early 1957, and they were in the line for several years. They were available as the No. 55 7" oval

Caveman Carvings

14 OZ   14 OZ

bowl in milk glass cased with any of the following: Stiegel Green, Heather, Verde, Flask Brown, Bead Green, Turquoise, Blue Mist, Pink or Mustard. Imperial's cased Bambu pieces were made in some of these colors (see Figs. 13 and 17 in the previous volume of this series).

CASINO

One can easily imagine a group of avid card players using these drinking glasses for various beverages with the large ashtray nearby for their cigarettes, cigars or pipes. The Clubs, Diamonds, Hearts, and Spades were a sandblasted decoration. Imperial experienced problems with the masks used in sandblasting, however, and these items were made for only a brief period.

CAVEMAN CARVINGS TUMBLERS

Designated Imperial's No. 997, these 14 oz. tumblers (a tall tumbler and a double old fashion) were from the early to the mid-1960s. One of salesman Ed Kleiner's notebooks indicates that they may also have been known as "Stone Age." Either name is a good one, as the primitive drawings depicted certainly have a prehistoric look to them.

The Caveman Carvings tumblers appear in Imperial's Supplement One to Our Catalog Number 62, where they are shown in Honey Amber

Casino

(caution: the Hobo Signs and Caveman Carvings tumblers are labeled incorrectly in this catalogue supplement). In mid-1964, both sizes were available in crystal.

CELERY VASES

Imperial billed its No. 194 vase as a "Circa 1860 Celery Vase" in January, 1964. An accompanying POPA tag explained that this was Imperial's "authentic reproduction" of the Cambridge or Sandwich "sawtooth" motif, a popular cut glass pattern that was replicated in pressed glass later by several factories. Imperial's No. 194 celery vase stands about 9" tall, and it was available in Amber (see Fig. 33 in the previous volume of this series), Antique Blue and Verde as well as crystal.

CEMETERY VASES

In the late nineteenth and early twentieth centuries, glass vases were fixtures at gravesites for floral offerings. Imperial made several of these over its early years, and some are illustrated in a c. 1913 catalog.

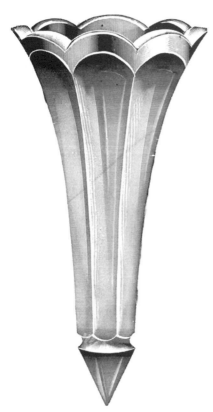

No. 700—7 in. cemetery vase.

CENTENNIAL KEEPSAKES

(see **West Virginia Centennial** in the next volume of this series)

CHAMPAGNE COLOR

(see **Svelte** in the next volume of this series)

No. 12. 6 oz.
champagne.
height 5 inches.
15 dozen in barrel.

No. 240. 6 oz. champagne.
height 4½ inches.
15 dozen in barrel.

CHAMPAGNES

Saloons and other establishments required these sorts of glassware in great quantities when Imperial first began production. These champagnes are from the firm's 1904 catalogue.

CHANGE TRAY

Long thought to be a paperweight by Carnival glass collectors, this article is mentioned in documents from Imperial's archives (see Fig. 367 in the first volume of this series).

CHARCOAL COLOR

(see **Elysian** later in this book)

CHARCOAL BROWN COLOR

This color dates from the mid- to late 1950s and was used for such lines as Dawn, Pinch and Svelte (see **Svelte** in the next volume of this series).

CHATELAINE

This is the Carnival glass collector's name for Imperial's No. 407 1/2 pattern, which was being made in crystal in 1909-10. The water pitcher and tumblers were made in Azur iridescent glass about 1910-11.

CHESTERFIELD

This is good example of the confusion that can result when names are attached to patterns. In her book on depression glass, Weatherman named Imperial's pattern No. 600 "Chesterfield" (although she also labeled the No. 600 wine set "Zak").

In his book on Imperial Carnival glass, Burns mistakenly assumed that Chesterfield was Imperial's original name. He goes to some length to show how these articles relate to Flute, Colonial and Wide Panel (other names used by Carnival glass collectors), and he does a good job of calling attention to the shapes of the handles. Unfortunately, however, Chesterfield is <u>not</u> the original name for Imperial's No. 600. The line is shown in several Imperial catalogues, and, in catalog 104D, it is called Colonial Crystal. Perhaps the discovery of this original name will now end the confusion. See **Colonial Crystal** earlier in this book.

CHINA ROSE CUTTING

This graceful cutting motif, designated C903, was developed in the early 1950s and is shown in Imperial's Catalog 53.

CHRISTMAS ORNAMENTS

Four Carnival glass Christmas ornaments are shown in Imperial's 1980 catalogue. These individually gift-boxed 3" ornaments were based on the "Twelve Days of Christmas" song. Like the similar Christmas plates, the idea for the ornaments came from Lucile Kennedy. Only the first four orna-

China Rose cutting

Chatelaine

No. 407½ pitcher.

ments (Partridge in a Pear Tree; Two Turtle Doves; Three French Hens; and Four Colly Birds) were marketed by Imperial, but, as this photo shows, at least one other ornament (Ten Pipers Piping) was made.

CHRISTMAS SEASON TUMBLERS

These 14 oz. tumblers were made in decorated crystal during the mid-1960s and were available with three finishes—bright gold, matt green or matt red. The red and green versions were available in

Above: Christmas ornaments
Below: Christmas Season tumblers

No. 525 cake plate, or wall decoration, diameter 10 inches

boxed sets of six (three of each color) for $9.00 retail. As their name suggests, these tumblers reflect the holiday season with designs of bells, fir branches, hanging bells and ornaments, holly leaves, poinsettias, and pine cones.

CHRYSANTHEMUM

This is the popular name among Carnival glass collectors for a large plate whose border is similar to the "Homestead" plate. Both of these appear in Imperial's catalog 101B, where they are described as "cake or wall" plates (see **Homestead** later in this book). The Chrysanthemum plate was Imperial's No. 525, and some carry Imperial's Nuart trade-mark at the five o'clock position on the front. These were re-issued when Imperial made Carnival glass during its last two decades of operation, and the Chrysanthemum plate can also be found in Ruby Slag.

No. 9 claret.
capacity 4 oz.
4¾ inches high.
15 dozen in barrel.

No. 203. 4 oz. claret.
height 4⅞ inches.
20 dozen in barrel.

CLARETS

Saloons and other establishments required these sorts of glassware in great quantities when Imperial first began production. These clarets are from the firm's 1904 catalogue.

CLOVER PINK

(see **Svelte** in the next volume of this series)

COARSE RIB, NO. 407

(see **Heisey moulds** later in this book)

Cobblestones

COBBLESTONES

Also known as Cobblestone to Carnival glass collectors, this was an Imperial novelty whose original number designation has yet to be discovered. The 9" crimped dish appears in Imperial's 100B catalog.

COCKTAILS

Saloons and other establishments required these sorts of glassware in great quantities when Imperial first began production. These cocktails are from the firm's 1904 catalogue.

COFFIN NAIL CIGARETTE SET

This was Imperial's No. 803/dec 4 ashtray along with a cigarette holder with the phrase "Coffin Nail" on a colonial-style sign.

COLLECTOR'S COIN PLATE

(see **Bicentennial Coin Plate** in the previous volume of this series and **Crystal Coins** later in this book)

No. 20 cocktail.
capacity 3 oz.
height 4¼ inches.
18 dozen in barrel.

No. 21 cocktail.
capacity 3 oz.
height 4⅝ inches.
18 dozen in barrel.

No. 22 cocktail.
capacity 3 oz.
height 4¾ inches.
18 dozen in barrel.

No. 23 cocktail.
capacity 3 oz.
height 4⅝ inches.
18 dozen in barrel.

Colonial
Lady

No. 746C blown vase.

No. 246—8 inch crushed fruit and cover
cover without notch
2 dozen in barrel

COLONIAL

A Carnival glass mug in this pattern is shown in Edwards' book. This was Imperial's No. 593 1/2 line about 1912. Imperial also called its No. 341 individual sugar and cream "Colonial" in Catalog 66A.

COLONIAL BELLS

(see **Bells** in the previous volume of this series)

COLONIAL CABIN TUMBLERS

Designated No. 106 in mid-1964, this 13 oz. tumbler was then available in "doeskinned crystal with buffed highlights." One side shows a large pot over a wood fire in a brickwork fireplace, while the other shows a chair, a broom and a flintlock rifle with powder horn. Designed by Bruce Hehn, these were later made in Imperial's Carnival glass colors, Rubigold and Peacock (see Figs. 1306-1307).

COLONIAL EAGLES

This decal decoration appears on several decanters, some beverage items (No. 800 and No. 801 tumblers and No. 820 mug) as well as the No. 464 covered pokal. These are pictured in Imperial's Catalog 66A.

COLONIAL LADY

This name is used by Carnival glass collectors for Imperial's No. 746 vase, which was made in a variety of shapes, including this crimped version.

COLONIAL TILE TUMBLERS

(see **Tile tumblers** in the next volume of this series)

COLUMBIA

Carnival glass collectors use this name for a few iridescent pieces from Imperial's No. 246 line. This was a good-sized, colonial style line about 1914-16. Several interesting shapes are shown in the Archer's book (pp. 26-27 and 36).

CONE AND TIE

Some Carnival glass collectors have attributed this tumbler to Imperial, and their conclusion based upon color is quite correct. Imperial had no name for it, however, simply designating the tumbler No. 382 1/2. There are no other pieces bearing this number in Imperial's catalog 100A.

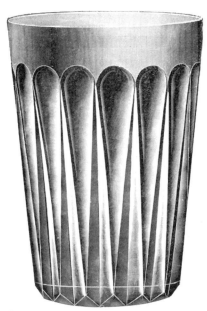

No. 382½ tumbler, 10½ oz.

No. 11. 1 oz. cordial.
height 3 inches.
40 dozen in barrel.

No. 93 cordial.
capacity 1½ oz.
height 3¼ inches.
40 dozen in barrel.

CONTINUOUS TANK GLASSWARE

This ware was made from glass batches melted in a large capacity furnace that enabled Imperial to offer articles at relatively low prices. Imperial issued a twelve-page "special catalog" showing the glassware made by this process in 1905. Imperial pattern numbers which are followed by the fraction 1/2 typically designate glassware made from the continuous tank process.

CONVIVIAL, No. 1680

This photo from one of Imperial salesman Ed Kleiner's notebooks shows four sizes of drinking glasses (14 oz. ice tea; 12 oz. hiball; 8 oz. juice; and 6 oz. old fashion). The flutes near the base of each piece were cut and polished, a technique used with the Etiquette No. 554 line.

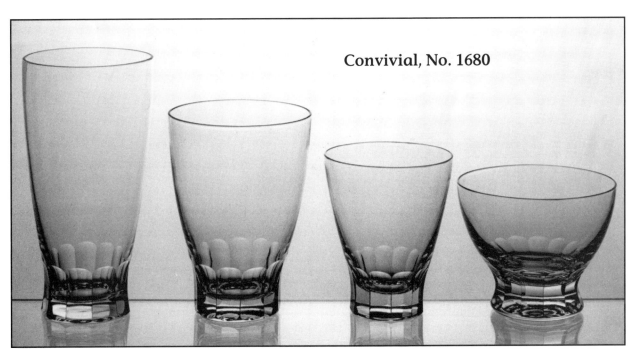

Convivial, No. 1680

CORDIALS

Saloons and other establishments required these sorts of glassware in great quantities when Imperial first began production. These cordials are from the firm's 1904 catalogue (see previous page).

CORN BOTTLE

Attributed to Imperial by Carnival glass collectors on the basis of color, this item has yet to be confirmed as an Imperial product. It does not appear in any of the numerous original catalogs consulted in the preparation of this book, and it is not to be found among any records of special orders or private mould work.

CORONET, No. 123

This pattern name appears on a list in Imperial's archives which records the lines in the 1938 factory inventory, but its name was changed to Victorian, for a January, 1941 price list which shows Victorian has this handwritten note: "was Coronet."

The design for Coronet was registered by Earl Newton and assigned to Imperial on March 30, 1937 (#103,826). There were just eight pieces in the line, and, in the early 1950s, the name was changed from Victorian to Chroma, the appellation best known to collectors today. All three names—Coronet, Victorian and Chroma—were designated No. 123 in Imperial's records. The eight articles in the line under the names Coronet or Victorian were made in ruby as well as the crystal shown in a small Imperial brochure (see **Chroma** earlier in this book).

COW BRAND TUMBLER, No. 777

This interesting 16 oz. tumbler is shown in Imperial's 1953 catalog and was discontinued at the end of 1954. The outer surface is completely covered with symbols "illustrating authentic brands of over 100 U. S. ranches." The mouldmakers also tossed in a few spurious brands, such as CJU and LJK (for Imperial's Carl J. Uhrmann and Lucile J. Kennedy). Retailing at $9.00 per dozen, the No. 777 Cow Brand tumbler was made in crystal as well as Saddle Brown, a creative name for Imperial's Flask Brown, which is an amber hue.

Cow Brand Tumbler

Two other Western-motif tumblers, Longhorn (see p. 391) and Ranch Life, were being marketed at the same time.

CRABCLAW

This name (or Crab Claw) is used by Carnival glass collectors for Imperial's No. 409 pattern which dates from about 1912 (see next page).

CRACKLE

Although some Carnival glass collectors believe this pattern to have been Imperial, others express reservations at this attribution. The pattern does not appear in any of the dozens of Imperial catalogues used in preparing this series of books, nor is there any other record from Imperial which bears on this motif.

No. 409 pitcher, large 3 pint.

Crabclaw

CRANBERRY STAINED AND CUT

Catalog 66A (p. 68) shows seven articles, mostly vases, which feature a "cut-to-clear" effect. These were purchased from the West Virginia Glass Specialty Company and sold by Imperial.

CRINKLED, No. 851

Like Imperial's various "crackled" items, these Crinkled pieces are subjected to a dip in water while still hot to create the distinctive treatment.

The moulds used for Crinkled, however, impart a twist or swirl optic to each item. Imperial's Catalog 53 shows Crinkled tumblers in six sizes (5 oz. to 18 oz.) and an 80 oz. pitcher which has an applied, reeded handle. According to Imperial's Catalog No. 62, two tumblers (10 oz. and 14 oz.) were available in Bead Green, Flask Brown and a pale blue called Turquoise.

Crinkled, No. 851

CROWN GLASS MANUFACTURING CO.

This was an Imperial subsidiary, formed about 1931, shortly after the Imperial Glass Company had been reorganized into the Imperial Glass Corporation. Many Crown products are pictured by the Archer's (pp. 179-200) and in Weatherman's books; readers should remember, however, that the names coined by Weatherman are <u>not</u> the original names for the glassware.

The Crown firm was a decorating concern, purchasing its blanks from the nearby Imperial plant. The Crown plant, operating with non-union labor, specialized in cutting work, including "Rock Crystal" polished cuttings, although some handpainting and sandblasting was also done. Crown produced assortments for the Carson Pirie Scott department store chain as well as the Butler Brothers wholesale house. Some cuttings were probably continued at Imperial after the Crown operation closed down.

Unless otherwise indicated, these cuttings occur on crystal glass only: Allard (C261); Anniversary (C259); Chardon (C257, also on rose pink, green and topaz); Chatham Rock Crystal (C257); Corona (C269); Danube (C280); Laurel (C256, also on rose pink, green and topaz); Lucerne (C251, also on rose pink, green and topaz); Manhattan (C252, also on rose pink, green and topaz); Monticello Ringing Rock Crystal (C451); Mt. Vernon (C450); Navarro Rock Crystal (C458); Noel (C253, also on rose pink, green and topaz); C600 Hand-Cut on Ruby; Primrose (C270); and Priscilla (C260). These are all Crown Rock Crystal Cuttings: Canadian Wreath (C453); Flora (C455); Oak Leaf (C459); Regina (C460); and Viking (C465).

Crown made Rock Crystal Ice Tea or Beverage Sets (with cuts 451, 453, 454, or 455) in amber, crystal, green. Ritz Blue, and Stiegel Green. These were also decorated with platinum bands, gold bands, vari-colored bands, vari-colored polka dots, cobalt blue polka dots or carmine red polka dots.

A Crown production book dating from 1933-34 lists more cutting/decorating motifs, as follows: bands (53); Cattail; Century (464); Daisy (462); dots (100); Federal (103); Festoon (101); Jupiter; Lady Addington (456); Laurel Wreath; Mallard; Mandalay; New Wreath (462); Picket Fence (452); Regina (460); Silva and Cosma (104); Rock Crystal Gray Flower (461); Rock Crystal Gray Rose (461); Twisted Gray (33); and Vintage (102). Some of these are cuttings and some are decorations, but there are no illustrations, so these have yet to be fully sorted out.

Crown jelly mould and cap

CROWN JELLY MOULD

Two sizes of this article, complete with metal caps, were available from Imperial in barrel lots at rock-bottom prices, even for 1913!

CRYSTAL COINS

Although it was made in 1971, this crystal plate featured likenesses of 1964 coinage, the last year in which silver was used in dimes, quarters and half dollars. The plate depicts (somewhat larger than life size) both the obverse and the reverse of a Lincoln penny, a Jefferson nickle, a Roosevelt dime, and a Washington quarter. The obverse of a Kennedy half dollar is at the center of the plate. These may be marked on the back: "American Numismatic Association 81st Anniversary 1972 New Orleans, LA, EWR [for E. Ward Russell]. See also **Bicentennial Coin Plate** in the previous volume of this series (see next page).

CRYSTAL, FIRED ON GOLD

(see **Collectors Crystal** earlier in this book)

CRYSTAL INTAGLIO

(see **Intaglio** later in this book)

CRYSTAL SATIN

Imperial's 1979 catalogue marked the initial appearance of some 22 items. A year later, the ranks had diminished to 19 and the line was called Satin Crystal. Collectors sometimes call this frosted glassware "camphor glass."

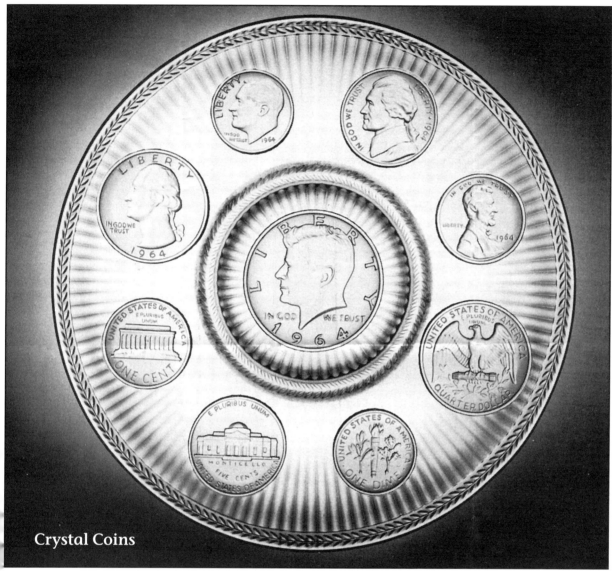

Crystal Coins

CRYSTAL SHELL

This was Imperial's original name for a late 1930s-era line that was re-named No. 280 Corinthian in the early 1940s. An ad in *Crockery and Glass Journal* mentioned these pieces—cup and saucer; 8" plate; 3-pc. mayonnaise; 4-pc. marmalade; 12" and 14" bowls; two-socket candleholder; and 3-pc. console—and noted also that "other pieces [are] in production."

Imperial held four design patents on this line: #119,864 (April 9, 1940); #120,128 (April 23, 1940); #120,408 (May 7, 1940); and #130,333 (November 11, 1941). These were assigned to Imperial, but the designer was Onnie Mankki of Cleveland, Ohio (see **Corinthian No. 280** in this book and **Tiara** in the next volume of this series).

Crystal Shell

CRYSTAL WITH FIRED CRANBERRY DECORATION

This attractive combination is reminiscent of the "ruby-stained" glassware that was quite popular during the first decade of the twentieth century. A full-page of this ware appears in Imperial's Catalogue No. 62 (see Figs. 1495-1511), and similar assortments, sometimes called "Decorated Cranberry," are present in Imperial catalogues over the next decade. Much of this ware was produced from moulds used for Collectors Crystal, and all was decorated at Imperial.

CRYSTAL VASE COLLECTION

Nine vases were listed in Imperial's 1981 Supplement. Five of the shapes (Honan, LiPo, LuChin, Mei and Meng) were also being made in Jade at the time. The other four were Ambrosia, Flora, Iris and Thalia. In the 1982-83 Imperial catalogue, nineteen different vases are listed. Most of the new shapes were also being used for an assortment called Yellow and Blue Optics (see the next volume of this series).

CROWNED CONCORD
(see **Concord No. 995** earlier in this book)

CRUCIFIX, No. 119

This item, which has an octagonal base, bears No. 119 in Imperial's 1904 catalogue. At the time, it was being made in crystal only, but production not long thereafter included both milk glass (then color number 11) and purple (color number 30). During the time iridescent ware was in production, the No. 119 Crucifix was made in Rubigold (see Fig. 1086).

Cup plates

Curved Star

No. 452½B—7 inch footed bowl.

CUP PLATES

Called "Americana Cup Plates" these four Early American-style cup plates originated in the early 1960s, when Imperial liked to use the phrase "House of Americana Glassware" to describe itself. When the winners of a contest for Wheeling-area newspaper carriers visited Spain and Portugal in 1968, sets of these cup plates were presented to the mayors of various cities (Wheeling *Intelligencer*, April 6, 1968).

They were packed in shallow gift boxes with the Imperial logo and the phrase "Collectors' Treasures" on the lid or in deep boxes with separate slots to hold the plates upright. Designated the No. 1975 4-pc. Cup Plate Set, these were shown in Amber, Bead Green, crystal and Heather in Imperial's Catalogue 62. In Catalog 66A, they appear in Amber, Antique Blue, Azalea and Verde. The four-piece set was in Catalogs No. 69 and 71R (Amberglo replaced Amber) as well as the 1972 and 1974-75 catalogues (Blue Haze replaced Azalea). In the final version of the set, the colors were Amber, crystal, Ultra Blue and Verde (1975-76 catalogue).

CURLIQUE CRYSTAL

This was Imperial's name for its re-introduction of articles in the Cambridge Glass Company's Caprice No. 3550 line. Imperial purchased these moulds in 1960, and Curlique Crystal was made in 1962-1963. See **Cambridge Caprice** in the previous volume of this series, p. 90-91.

CURVED STAR

This is a name coined by Carnival glass collectors. The comport or footed bowl, bearing No. 452 1/2 in early company catalogs, is also shown in Imperial's catalog 101B, which was devoted to "iridescent glass novelties."

CUSTARD, MIDWEST

This opaque color (see Figs. 1480-1486 and 1488-1490), produced in just a few shapes, made its debut in the mid-1950s, along with several other opaque hues: the short-lived Lichen Green, Turquoise, and Forget-Me-Not Blue (also called Opaque Blue). A few items in Chroma No. 123 were made in 1957, and Midwest Custard was also used when some Cathay pieces were reissued. Some, but not all, of Imperial's Midwest Custard production was available in either glossy or doeskin finish.

CUT GLASS, IMITATION

(see **imitation cut glass** later in this book and NUCUT in the next volume of this series)

DEWDROP OPALESCENT

To a large extent, this was a revival of an older Imperial line, Early American Hobnail (No. 741 and No. 742), which was introduced in crystal, ruby and Ritz Blue during the 1930s (see p. 312 in this book). Dewdrop Opalescent debuted in early 1965, and quite a few pieces are pictured in Imperial's catalogue 66A.

Many of the moulds from the No. 741 or No. 742 pieces were used for this line. The Dewdrop name harkened back to Hobbs-Brockunier's glassware of the 1880s, and Imperial also called this glassware "1818 Stamm House." Imperial's presi-

dent, Carl Gustkey, lived on Stamm Lane in nearby Wheeling, and both the glassware and his address derived their names from the old Stamm House, a lodging and dining tavern east of Wheeling on the old Cumberland Road which dated from 1818.

In addition to the articles shown in the color pages in this book (see Figs. 1512-1551), these were made: 1886/350 lamp; 1886 wine; 1886/163 36 oz. Leighton bottle with stopper (a large decanter); 1886/201 footed lamp; and 1886/2850 hurricane lamp.

Mm! Mm! **Look!**

Imperial
U.S.A.

Sets the scene for gay hospitality!

"Ladies and Gentlemen" . . . .
presenting "DIXIE DANDIES"

a really new tumbler decoration

GOOD TIMES . . . HILARITY . . . and
ENTERTAINMENT "in person"

8 different men
8 different names
for easy party identification!

"DIXIE DANDIES" *will sell because . . .*

they are priced for volume—
$3.98 is the suggested retail
price for the 8-piece set,

they are decorated in the
popular trend—BLACK AND WHITE,

the subjects just naturally
suggest FUN . . . FRIVOLITY . . .
and FOOLISHNESS!

This set of eight tumblers was designed by Lynn Gustkey Pepperdine and appeared in Imperial's line about 1953-56. Only one tumbler is illustrated in General Catalog No. 53, but all eight are shown in this advertisement placed by Imperial sales reps Fred and Tommie Carroll, who were based in Dallas.

Each tumbler featured the silk-screened likenesses of various minstrel show characters—Bones, Sambo, Sugar, Bayou, etc. The blanks used were No. 71, a tumbler manufactured by the Federal Glass Company and purchased in large quantities by Imperial so that they could be decorated with many different motifs.

DOG-GONE TUMBLERS

This interesting set consisted of eight silk-screen decorated 12 oz. tumblers. Each tumbler depicted eight different dogs, and the entire set was packaged in a doghouse-style carrying case, complete with peaked roof and a handle for carrying.

D

7426. 6-piece Dresser Set
1½ dozen in No. 1 carton, weight 65 pounds
742. Cologne and Stopper
6 dozen in No. 29 carton, weight 65 pounds
742. Puff Box and Cover
2½ dozen in No. 1 carton, weight 65 pounds

153. 6-piece Dresser Set
3 dozen in No. 1 carton, weight 55 pounds
153. Cologne and Stopper
6 dozen in No. 2 carton, weight 50 pounds
153. Puff Box and Cover
6 dozen in No. 1 carton, weight 65 pounds

130. 6-piece Dresser Set
With Intaglio ground stopper
3 dozen in No. 1 carton, weight 55 pounds
130. Cologne and Stopper
6 dozen in No. 2 carton, weight 50 pounds
130. Puff Box and Cover
6 dozen in No. 1 carton, weight 65 pounds

Sometimes called vanity sets by today's collectors, these articles were an important part of Imperial's production, especially during the 1930s and early 1940s. The sets typically consist of two cologne bottles with stoppers and a covered puff box for face powder.

Some sets were extensions of a pattern line. For example, Imperial's No. 7426 set was related to the No. 742 Early American Hobnail line. Two other sets No. 153 and No. 130, were independent of pattern lines. Other sets were decorated in various ways to increase the variety for wholesale purchasers. Imperial's No. 169 set, for instance, was available with two different cuttings (261 gray cutting and 465 rock crystal cutting) or the "Lalique" (acid etched) finish, with enameled flowers in white, green or yellow.

Some dresser sets came complete with trays. Imperial's No. 63 and No. 64 sets were pictured in the firm's Catalog No. 400 (c. mid-1930s). An Imperial price sheet (dated January 1, 1943) carries this interesting note: "Dresser sets and cologne and perfume bottles are to be sold *only* to perfume manufacturers and decorators. Must not be sold to dealers other than these."

During World War II, Imperial did private mould work for American-based wholesalers (such as I. W. Rice) who were unable to get bottles and puff boxes from Europe. Many Rice sets featured elaborate stoppers that resembled Czechoslovakian products. Demand was strong, and the Rice firm rented a warehouse in Bellaire to ship glassware quickly (more information about Rice products will appear in the next volume of this series)

Research continues in this intriguing area of Imperial's private mould work. Interested readers should consult Myrna and Bob Garrison's book, *Imperial's Boudoir Etcetera…A Comprehensive Look at Dresser Accessories for Irice and Others* (1996).

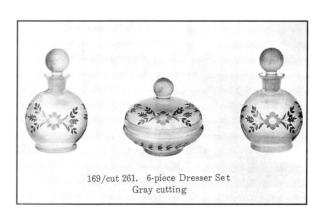

169/cut 261. 6-piece Dresser Set
Gray cutting

DAD'S COOKIE JAR

According to one of salesman Ed Kleiner's notebooks, this item was made in three sizes (1, 2 and 3 gallon) for a cookie manufacturer between 1931 and 1942. The jars, obviously intended for in-store use, were made plain and with large letters on the outside ("Property of Dad's Cookie Co."). Kleiner also records that salesman Harry Cushwa secured this item for Imperial to produce and that it was one of the largest blown items ever made at the Bellaire plant.

DAISY

Now referred to as "Field Flower" or "Field-flower" by Carnival glass collectors, this was originally called Daisy in Imperial's catalogue 101B, which was devoted to iridescent glass novelties.

DAISY BASKET

This is the Carnival glass collector's name for Imperial's No. 363 basket, which first appears in the company's Catalog No. 200 from the late 1920s. These were listed in three iridescent colors—Rubigold, Peacock and Sapphire. the basket is shown in crystal in Imperial's catalog 300, but the designation was changed to No. 303. In the 1960s, this basket (called simply No. 40 tall basket) was part of Imperial's reissues of Carnival glass.

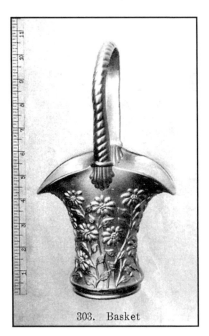

303. Basket

Large quart pitcher, Daisy design.

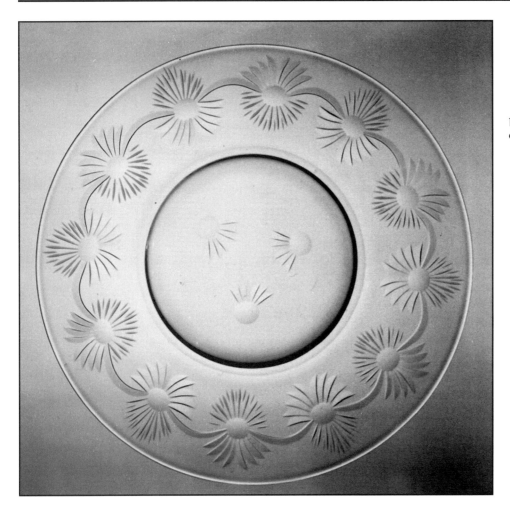

**Dandelion
cutting (C807)**

DAISY AND BUTTON BASKET

The No. 221 Daisy and Button 8" oval basket (see Fig. 966) was made from about 1959 through 1963 in the popular *House & Garden* colors (Blue Mist, Emerald Green, Mustard Yellow and Siamese Pink).

DANDELION CUTTING

Designated C807, this cutting motif is pictured on goblets and plates in materials from Imperial's archives.

D'ANGELO

This is Weatherman's name for Imperial's No. 678 "Heavy Part-Cut Glass," which was illustrated in Imperial's second Bargain Book catalog in the mid-1920s (see **Part Cut** in the next volume of this series).

DAWN, NO. 3300

This short line consisted of five pieces of stemware (footed ice tea, footed on-the-rocks, goblet, sherbet and wine/juice) accompanied by the No. 2428 plate. In the 1969 catalogue, these were shown in Blue Haze, Nut Brown and Verde; the 71R catalogue carried the same page, and the items were depicted elsewhere in crystal. By 1973, these were discontinued.

The line was first known as Svelte No. 330 when it was introduced around 1950. Articles were made in Champagne, Clover Pink, and Dresden Blue during the late 1950s (see **Svelte No. 330** in the next volume of this series).

DECORATED CRANBERRY

Also called Fired Cranberry on Crystal, this ware, like Fired Gold on Crystal, was an extension of the popular Collector's Crystal line. Like Imperial's #208 (cranberry rim) decoration, Fired Cran-

No. 434¹/₂ (Diamond Lace)

berry on Crystal recalls the ruby-stained glass which was popular early in the twentieth century. Several of the articles shown in Imperial's catalog 66A were still in the line when the company's 1969 catalog was issued (see Figs. 1495-1511).

DECORATED TUMBLERS

A black-and-white catalog sheet (probably from the mid-1920s) shows a number of realistic decorations on the No. 100 5 oz. Old Fashion, the No. 100 7 1/2 oz. Old Fashion, and the No. 8401 14 oz. plain tumbler. These range from the plain ("Polka Dots") to individual animals and even outdoor sporting scenes (see page 16 in the previous volume of this series and the Archers' book, p. 202). The Chevalier tumblers appear in a September 17, 1932, price list as do Red Rooster, Tomato, Orange and Happy Hour.

DENIM BLUE

This decoration on milk glass (along with Aspen Green and Terra Cotta) is mentioned in material from Imperial's archives dated in mid-1952 (see **Leaf** later in this book).

DEWEY

This pattern originated at the Indiana Tumbler and Goblet Company in Greentown, Indiana, in 1898. Imperial used it as the inspiration for its No. 972 box and cover (see Fig. 9 in the previous volume of this series), although the Dewey name was seldom used. This item was made in many Imperial colors, ranging from crystal with cranberry decoration to Rubigold and Peacock Carnival glass.

DIAMOND BLOCK

Two researchers have attached this name to Imperial patterns; unfortunately, they have employed it for two distinctly different lines! Weatherman uses it for Imperial's original No. 330, which is shown in both catalogue 200 and catalogue 300 (later, Imperial used No. 330 for its Svelte line). Burns uses it for Imperial's No. 699 line, which had several different name—Prism Crystal, Lincoln, Mount Vernon and Washington (see **No. 330** and **Washington No. 699** in the next volume of this series).

DIAMOND LACE

Carnival glass collectors use this name for Imperial's No. 434 1/2 pattern. About 1910, this was a regular line in crystal, but only a few items were made in Azur or Rubigold iridescent glass. The water pitcher and tumbler appear in an original Imperial ad for Azur in late 1910 (see the previous volume in this series, p. 33).

DIAMOND QUILTED

Depression glass collectors use this name for two Imperial patterns, No. 414 and No. 625, both of which will be discussed in the next volume of this series.

Diamond Ring

DIAMOND RING

This iridescent motif is depicted in Imperial's catalog 101B, but an original number, if any, has yet to be determined.

DIMPLED TUMBLERS

Designated No. 861, these Imperial tumblers were available in five sizes—6 oz., 9 oz., 11 oz., 13 oz. and 16 oz.—in the mid-1960s. The largest was called Big Cooler in some of the company's sales materials. See **Big Cooler** in the first volume of this series.

No. 349$^{1}/_{2}$
(Diamond and Sunburst)

DIAMOND AND SUNBURST

Carnival glass collectors have been unable to agree on the origins of this wine set, debating whether it was made by Imperial or by the United States Glass Co. The set is shown as No. 349-1/2 in original Imperial catalogs, however, so there can be no doubt of its origin. Incidentally, the trays supplied with the iridescent wine sets were crystal.

DOESKIN FINISH

From time to time throughout its history, Imperial marketed glassware with a satin finish. This was typically obtained by the action of hydrofluoric acid, and Imperial called this effect "suede" or "Lalique finish" in the 1940s, until the French firm objected and the latter term was dropped (see **acid etched glass** in the first volume of this series). The doeskin finish, however, was actually obtained by sandblasting the glass prior to acid dipping.

In 1949-50, Imperial began to advertise its doeskin finish in conjunction with a new line of milk glass. A memo to Imperial's sales reps described doeskin as follows: "This finish was inspired by Imperial's Cathay finish, a study of alabaster, salt-glaze, suede, frosted, blasted and acid-eaten finishes formerly applied to glass by Imperial or other glass producers of modern or olden days, and by earthenware, pottery, crockery, stoneware and china makers over hundreds of years." Imperial predicted that its "trade secret" doeskin finish would "give the milk glass picture the shot-in-the-arm it has needed for 100 years."

DOGGIES TUMBLERS

This assortment of eight decorated tumblers was usually called Working Dogs. Those depicted include American Fox Hound, Hill Collie, Cocker Spaniel, Mister Pointer, English Setter, Basset Hound, Springer Spaniel and Dalmatian Coach. These are on the No. 176 14 oz. tumbler with gold rim and were made in the 1960s.

DOODLER CUTTING

This simple cutting looks like a tic-tac-toe symbol with a few added lines. The roly-poly Doodler tumblers and an accompanying pitcher were advertised in the May, 1952, issue of *Sunset* magazine.

You'll Use **DOODLER** tumblers Everyday

Smart and new...cut designs on practical, tough-to-tip shapes...tumblers that serve you well on every occasion, for they're styled to our American way of casual ease and informality. Crafted by American artisans in five easy-to-handle, roly-poly sizes. Open stock and modestly priced—see them now!

THE IMPERIAL GLASS CORPORATION
BELLAIRE, OHIO

DOUBLE DUTCH

This was Imperial's No. 514, but it now has two names in Carnival glass circles—Double Dutch and Windmill. The various items all carry No. 514 in the older Imperial catalogues, but the company did use the Windmill name as early as 1912. In its 1960s re-issues of Carnival glass, Imperial again used the Windmill appellation.

DOUBLE SCROLL

Here is another instance where Carnival glass collectors have one name for a pattern and depression glass collectors have different names. The 8¼" tall candlesticks and 10½" oval console bowl come in two versions, plain or with a spiral optic. The plain three-piece set is known as "Double Scroll" among Carnival glass collectors and "Packard" by depression glass collectors, but Imperial simply used the designation No. 320 (see Figs. 1468-1477).

This three-piece set was offered in Amber, Green and Rose Marie in Imperial's catalogue 201, which dates from the late 1920s. The spiral optic console set, which features either the 8¼" tall candlesticks or 3½" tall candlesticks, is actually part of Imperial's extensive No. 313 line, which Weatherman calls "Twisted Optic." See **console sets** earlier in this book and **No. 313** in the next volume of this series.

Double Dutch

DRESDEN BLUE

(see **Svelte** in the next volume of this series)

DUNCE CAP DECANTERS

The No. 701—26 oz. (in Stiegel Green or Crystal) and 18 oz. (in Smoke or Black) Dunce Cap decanters—were introduced in July, 1955, along with the "Tall Boy" shaker and three sizes of No. 701 Forester vases (in crystal, Turquoise, Stiegel Green or Mustard).

DYNASTY JADE

This name was used when Imperial introduced a few items in the opaque color (designated by the prefix 12) during 1960. Most were pieces from the Cathay line, but this original photograph (used in *Crockery and Glass*, August, 1960) also shows five items in the Atterbury Scroll pattern, which had been introduced in crystal in March, 1960, although only the pitcher is numbered in this assortment. According to one of salesman Ed Kleiner's notebooks, the Dynasty Jade items did not appear in any of Imperial's regular price lists, so production was quite short-lived. The jade color was revived in 1980, and many of the Cathay pieces were produced along with several sizes of plain vases. See **Imperial Jade** later in this book.

DYNASTY TUMBLERS

Designated Imperial's No. 115, these 12 oz. and 16 oz. tumblers date from the mid-1960s. They were made in crystal and decorated with gold

newly created

DYNASTY TUMBLERS

Quality Pipe Blown raised-pattern Imperial Crystal Tumblers, delicately decorated with kiln-fired 22 carat Gold, lend Dignified Uniquity to Gracious Hospitality. Tired of mass-made sameness? Then use or give the Tall 16 oz. Ones, or the smart new Low 12 oz. Ones. Sets-of-Six, gift boxed, either size, $9 each, prepaid. We'll insert your card.

Old Hay Shed Gift Shop
P. O. Box 563
Bellaire, Ohio, U.S.A.

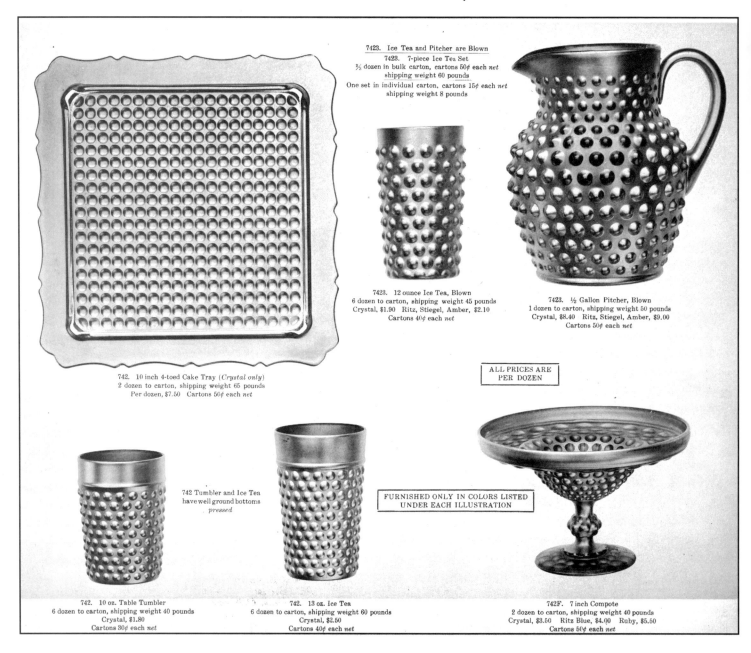

7423. Ice Tea and Pitcher are Blown

7423. 7-piece Ice Tea Set
⅗ dozen in bulk carton, cartons 50¢ each *net*
shipping weight 60 pounds
One set in individual carton, cartons 15¢ each *net*
shipping weight 8 pounds

7423. 12 ounce Ice Tea, Blown
6 dozen to carton, shipping weight 45 pounds
Crystal, $1.90   Ritz, Stiegel, Amber, $2.10
Cartons 40¢ each *net*

7423. ½ Gallon Pitcher, Blown
1 dozen to carton, shipping weight 50 pounds
Crystal, $8.40   Ritz, Stiegel, Amber, $9.00
Cartons 50¢ each *net*

742. 10 inch 4-toed Cake Tray (*Crystal only*)
2 dozen to carton, shipping weight 65 pounds
Per dozen, $7.50   Cartons 50¢ each *net*

ALL PRICES ARE
PER DOZEN

742 Tumbler and Ice Tea
have well ground bottoms
pressed

FURNISHED ONLY IN COLORS LISTED
UNDER EACH ILLUSTRATION

742. 10 oz. Table Tumbler
6 dozen to carton, shipping weight 40 pounds
Crystal, $1.80
Cartons 30¢ each *net*

742. 13 oz. Ice Tea
6 dozen to carton, shipping weight 60 pounds
Crystal, $2.50
Cartons 40¢ each *net*

742F. 7 inch Compote
2 dozen to carton, shipping weight 40 pounds
Crystal, $3.50   Ritz Blue, $4.00   Ruby, $5.50
Cartons 50¢ each *net*

This short Imperial line, numbered either No. 741 or No. 742, was made in many different colors in the late 1920s and early 1930s. Advertisements mention crystal, amber, Ritz Blue, Golden Ophir, Stiegel Green, Rose Marie, ruby, and black. Shortly thereafter, another ad lists several Sea Foam opalescent colors: Harding Blue, Moss Green, and Burnt Almond [amber opalescent].

The line included round and square plates as well as a large square cake tray which is much like the Cape Cod cake tray. The compote and footed ivy

ball were made from the same mould, which has pattern on the underside of the foot. The blown pitchers and tumblers were considerably more expensive than their pressed counterparts. Furthermore, the hobs on blown pieces have a pointed character to them, while those on the pressed articles are circular and relatively flat.

Many of the No. 741 and No. 742 moulds were given new life as the Stamm House/Dewdrop Opalescent assortment in the 1960s and again as Hobnail in 1977.

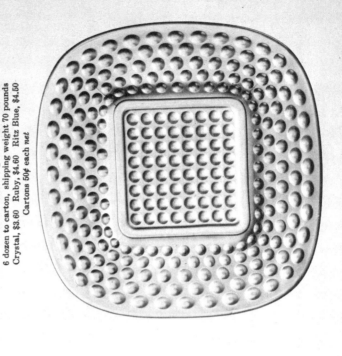

742.   8 inch Salad Plate, ground bottom, round
6 dozen to carton, shipping weight 70 pounds
Crystal, $3.60   Ruby, $4.60   Ritz Blue, $4.50
Cartons 50¢ each *net*

7415D.   8 inch Salad Plate, square
6 dozen to carton, shipping weight 70 pounds
Crystal, $1.60   Ruby, $3.50   Ritz Blue, $3.00
Cartons 50¢ each *net*

ALL PRICES ARE
PER DOZEN

741. 7-Piece Water Set
Six 9 oz. Tumblers and one Pitcher
5/6 dozen in bulk carton
Shipping weight 70 pounds, cartons 50¢ each *net*
one set in individual carton
Shipping weight 8 pounds, cartons 10¢ each *net*

741.   55 ounce Pitcher, pressed
1 dozen to carton, shipping weight 50 pounds
Crystal, $4.00   Ruby, $8.00   Ritz Blue, $6.00
Cartons 50¢ each *net*

FURNISHED ONLY IN COLORS LISTED
UNDER EACH ILLUSTRATION

742.   9 oz. Sherbet
6 doz. to carton, shipping weight 45 pounds
Crystal, $1.60   Ruby, $3.50   Ritz Blue, $3.00
Cartons 35¢ each *net*

742.   9 oz. Goblet
6 dozen to carton, shipping weight 55 pounds
Crystal, $1.60   Ruby, $3.50   Ritz Blue, $3.00
Cartons 50¢ each *net*

741.   9 oz. Table Tumbler
6 dozen to carton, weight 35 pounds
Crystal, $1.00   Ruby, $1.80   Ritz Blue, $1.40
Cartons 30¢ each *net*

7412.   12 ounce Ice Tea
6 dozen to carton, shipping weight 60 pounds
Crystal, $1.60   Ruby, $2.70   Ritz Blue, $2.00
Cartons 50¢ each *net*

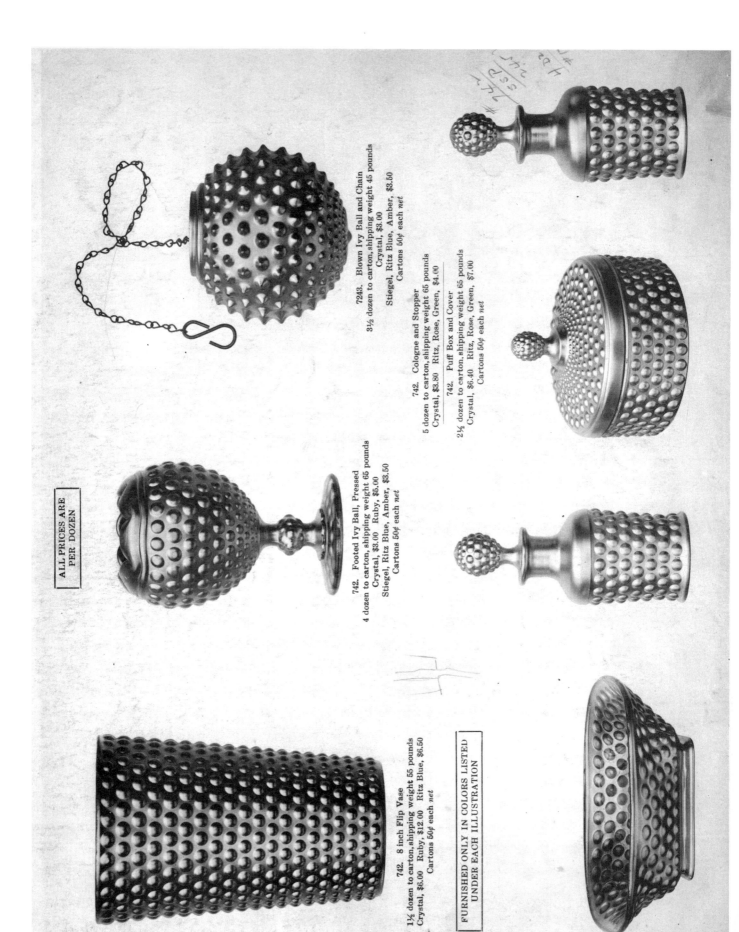

ALL PRICES ARE
PER DOZEN

7243. Blown Ivy Ball and Chain
3½ dozen to carton, shipping weight 45 pounds
Crystal, $3.00
Stiegel, Ritz Blue, Amber, $3.50
Cartons 50¢ each *net*

742. Cologne and Stopper
5 dozen to carton, shipping weight 65 pounds
Crystal, $3.80 Ritz, Rose, Green, $4.00

742. Puff Box and Cover
2½ dozen to carton, shipping weight 65 pounds
Crystal, $6.40 Ritz, Rose, Green, $7.00
Cartons 50¢ each *net*

742. Footed Ivy Ball, Pressed
4 dozen to carton, shipping weight 65 pounds
Crystal, $3.00 Ruby, $5.00
Stiegel, Ritz Blue, Amber, $3.50
Cartons 50¢ each *net*

742. 8 inch Flip Vase
1½ dozen to carton, shipping weight 55 pounds
Crystal, $6.00 Ruby, $12.00 Ritz Blue, $6.50
Cartons 50¢ each *net*

FURNISHED ONLY IN COLORS LISTED
UNDER EACH ILLUSTRATION

314

EISENHOWER PITCHER AND TUMBLERS

After the death of former President Dwight D. Eisenhower in 1969, Imperial created a silk screen likeness to honor him. A Columbus firm, Richard Conn Associates, was involved in this project. The rendering was done from an original photo (see inset) sent to Imperial with the approval of the President's widow, Mrs. Mamie Eisenhower.

The Eisenhower set used the No. 760 Continental pitcher and tumblers as blanks for the silk screen portrait. Imperial's Carl Uhrmann prepared sketches of more items (comport, vase, and hospitality bowl) using the No. 760 line.

A Novel Wedding of Crystal and Charcoal

Imperial's NEW Elysian Glass

Distinctive in design—vibrant with decorative contrast—Imperial's New Elysian was a hit at recent shows. Styled to bright, exciting artistry, all pieces easily adapt to multiple use. Just display them—these conversation pieces will interest every customer.

Stock Elysian now! It's profit-priced for all-occasion selling.

E-1	Crimped Tray	$4.00	list
E-3	Compote	4.00	"
E-4	Compote	4.00	"
E-6	Square Shallow Tray	4.00	"
E-8	Crimped Bowl	7.00	"
E-9	Cake Stand	6.00	"
E-13	Square Bowl	8.00	"
E-14	Compote	10.00	"

Not shown—Matching Candleholders
$1.25 to $1.50 each (list)

Buy the *full* Elysian Line
See it at:

225 Fifth Avenue
New York 10

320—2nd Unit, Santa Fe Bldg.
Dallas 2

Room 404, Brack Shops
Los Angeles 14

1633 N. W. 21st Avenue
Portland 9

IMPERIAL GLASS CORPORATION, Bellaire, Ohio

In 1958, this contemporary-styled glassware was advertised in both *Crockery and Glass Journal* and *China, Glass and Tableware*. The bent-glass bowls were purchased from the H J. Houze Glass Company of Point Marion, Pa., and shipped to Bellaire. Imperial's workers then glued bases made from Heisey moulds onto the bowls (charcoal glass purchased from Houze was also used for other Imperial creations; see **Grecian Key decoration** in this book

and **Symmetry** in the next volume of this series).

An Imperial advertising folder described Elysian as "a novel wedding of crystal and charcoal." The charcoal color was sometimes described as "dense Smoke glass." Imperial added various candleholders from such lines as Sculpturesque to create interesting console sets. In mid-1960, Imperial offered four Elysian items with a blue and platinum decoration called Florentine.

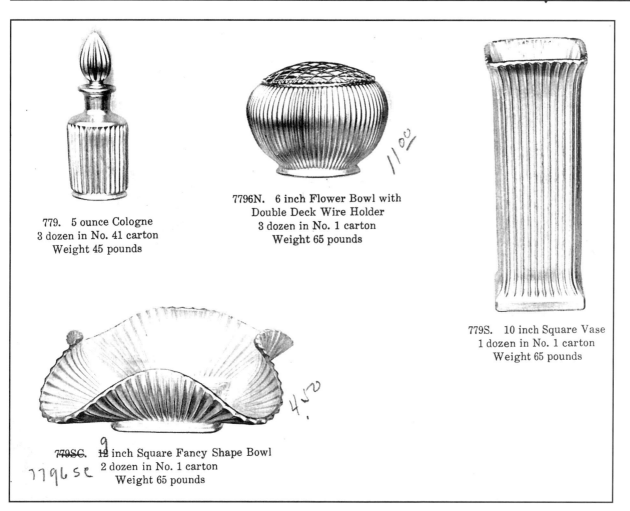

779. 5 ounce Cologne
3 dozen in No. 41 carton
Weight 45 pounds

7796N. 6 inch Flower Bowl with
Double Deck Wire Holder
3 dozen in No. 1 carton
Weight 65 pounds

779S. 10 inch Square Vase
1 dozen in No. 1 carton
Weight 65 pounds

779SC. 9 inch Square Fancy Shape Bowl
2 dozen in No. 1 carton
Weight 65 pounds

7796 se

*T*his rather plain but interesting line, which dates from the mid-1930s, consists mostly of bowls and plates of various sizes, along with occasional pieces such as ashtrays, candleholders, relish dishes, a canape set and an individual salt dip. The pattern is rather subdued on the round candleholder, and the 5-inch square candlestick is so dominated by the dolphin motif (see p. 418) that one might not notice the pattern. Imperial catalogue pages dating from the mid-1930s (see the Archers' book, pp. 167-168) show more than two dozen different items. An Imperial sales record from 1938 lists Empire as the company's third strongest seller, behind only No. 160 Cape Cod and No. 699 Mount Vernon.

ETIQUETTE, NO. 544

To Selected Jewelers We Offer

Etiquette Crystal

In mid-1941, Imperial was laying big promotional plans for the debut of this extensive line of beverage service. According to an Imperial memo dated July 23, 1941, there were to be about 20 items in the line, ranging from three different champagnes and five different sizes of wine glasses to a large pilsener glass. Later, tumblers suitable for such drinks as Tom Collins, old-fashioneds and "hi-balls" were added. Imperial's Catalog No. 53 shows more than 30 beverage items, including several decanters and a cocktail pitcher (see the next two pages).

The stemmed items were made as paste mould blown items, and then the stems were "pulled" and the bases attached by a skilled worker called a foot setter. This method is more costly than simple blowing or pressing, and it is difficult to make pieces to exact size requirements. The fluting was done by stone wheel cutting and polishing, another labor intensive and, hence, costly procedure.

The Etiquette line was designed by Louise Flather of Macy's Department Store in New York City. In exchange for the exclusive rights for initial marketing of this Imperial line, Macy's planned a preview dinner for editors, columnists and wine experts in conjunction with the California Wine Growers Association. Macy's also agreed to feature the Etiquette line in its stores and to advertise in *The New York Times* and *Life* magazine.

IMPERIAL ETIQUETTE

554
11 oz. Goblet

554
6 oz. Saucer Champagne

554
6 oz. Low Sherbet

554
6 oz. Parfait

554
4 oz. Whiskey Sour

554
7½ oz. Red Wine

554
5 oz. White Wine

554
4 oz. Dessert Wine

554
3 oz. Sherry Wine

554
5½ oz. Rhine Wine

554
5 oz. Sparkling Burgundy

554
6 oz. Double Cocktail

554
3½ oz. Cocktail

554
3½ oz. Cognac

554
1 oz. Pousse Cafe

554
1½ oz. Cordial

554
3 oz. Frappe Liquer

554
6 oz. Hollow Stem Champagne

554
21 oz. Brandy Inhaler

554
7½ oz. Tulip Champagne

554
13 oz. Pilsener

No. 19 egg cup.
3¾ inches high.
15 dozen in barrel.

No. 109 egg cup.
4 inches high.
15 dozen in barrel.

No. 117 double egg cup.
4 inches high.
15 dozen in barrel.

EAGLE

(see **No. 1776** in the next volume of this series)

EGG CUPS

These staple items in pressed glass were part of Imperial's production during its early years. Those illustrated here are from the company's first catalogue, which was issued in 1904.

EL TABIQUE DE ORO TUMBLERS

According to one of Imperial salesman Ed Kleiner's notebooks, this pattern "was designed by and for Alfred Dunhill, Inc." and Dunhill had the exclusive rights to sell El Tabique de Oro in New York City, Chicago, San Francisco and Philadelphia. These were made in several sizes and were decorated with bright gold.

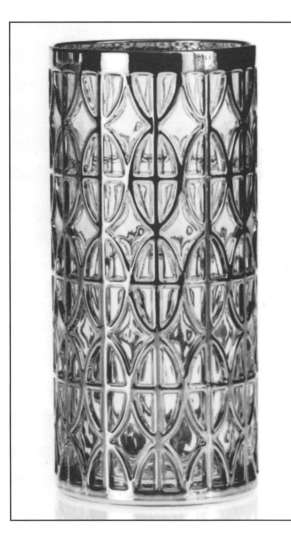

El Tabique de Oro

No. 54C pressed electric shade.   crimped.
for 2¼ inch holder.
12 dozen in barrel.

No. 48C pressed electric shade.
crimped.   for 2¼ inch holder.
packed 12 dozen in barrel.

No. 216 pressed electric shade.
for 2¼ inch holder.
packed 12 dozen in barrel.

ELECTRIC SHADES

These products were quite important to the Imperial Glass Company, especially in its early years. The 1904 general catalog illustrated several lines of shades and globes for both electric and gas use, and two specialty catalogs issued about this same time covered "Engraved gas and electric glassware" and "Plain and engraved gas and electric glassware." Several electric shades are shown in the Archer's book pp. 1-19 (see also **illuminating goods** later in this book).

ESQUIRE

This was another name for the "Roly Poly" No. 1420 pitchers (3 sizes) and tumblers which were available with various cuts, such as C969 (Doodler) and C968 (Polka Dots), in the early 1950s (see **Doodler** earlier in this book).

ESSEX STEMWARE

Lenox designers were responsible for the Essex, Flower Fair, Linear and Reflections lines The small Essex grouping (15 oz. iced beverage, 11 oz. goblet, 8 oz. dessert and 7 oz. wine) was featured on the first page of Imperial's 1980 catalogue. The articles were available in crystal, Nut Brown, Sunshine Yellow and Ultra Blue. The 1982-83 Imperial catalogue also lists a 16 oz, footed iced tea and says that all items could be ordered in Verde, too (see next page).

ETCHED LUSTRE

This name is used erroneously by Carnival glass collectors to describe a line of transparent iridescent vases which have patterns cut on them.

EVERGREEN GLASS COLOR

This was Imperial's color 52. It was used in the mid- and late 1950s with various articles, such as the Chroma No. 123 line (see p. 434) and the Candlewick 400/2701 two-tier tid-bit (see Fig. 730 in the previous volume of this series).

E
MISCELLANEOUS

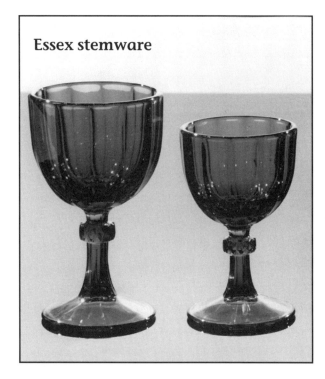

Essex stemware

EXPRESSION

These plain items were shown in Imperial's 1977 catalogue. All were produced in crystal, Nut Brown, Sunshine Yellow, Ultra Blue and Verde. Obviously intended for casual dining or snacks, these six items were available: candleholder/cigarette holder; 11" salad bowl; 8" salad plate; 7" salad bowl; 9 oz. tumbler; and 16 oz. tumbler. The tumblers had been made earlier as the No. 861 Big Cooler, and the other articles were part of the Jamestown assortments during the late 1950s. The Expression pieces were used for table service at Manuche's, an Italian restaurant in New York City.

Expression

Thoroughly contemporary in design, Imperial's Expression is suitable for many uses. Parties, buffets, or just plain snacking are just several of this line's versatile functions. Available in Crystal, Fern Green, Ultra Blue, Sunshine Yellow and Nut Brown.

OPEN STOCK **IMPERIAL** TABLE GLASS

DESIGN AND TRADE MARK ARE PATENTED

IMPERIAL

The Salesman
ART DEPT.

This advertisement for Imperial's new No. 582 line appeared in the August 20, 1914, issue of *Pottery, Glass and Brass Salesman*.

The design for this pattern was registered by mould room foreman Charles Oldham and assigned to Imperial on July 7, 1914 (#46,060). A special eight-page catalog was issued about mid-1914 to launch this pattern, which was a staple for many years as part of Imperial's lines of "open stock table glass" (see the Archers' book, pp. 72-77).

An early order blank lists more than 80 different pieces in No. 582, making it easily one of the largest and most diverse arrays of articles in one pattern then being offered by an American glassmaker. A few months earlier, *Crockery and Glass Journal* (November 20, 1913) alluded to this line, noting that the new moulds "will cost about $15,000." Another trade publication, *Pottery, Glass and Brass Salesman* (December 18, 1913), said the ware was "remarkable for its high quality of glass and finish, and it gives every evidence of being a real winner."

The 1914 catalog promised a line "of over 150 different pieces, so that you will be able to furnish your customers practically any article of table glass they may ask for in the same pattern." Many pieces prominently display the Imperial "iron cross" mark, and production continued well into the 1920s. Imperial's catalog 201 contains eight full pages devoted to "No. 582 Fancy Colonial open stock table glass," and the seventy-four different items shown were available in either crystal or Rose Marie, a new color which debuted in late 1926 (the name was later changed to Rose Pink).

Fancy Colonial articles are known in crystal as well as iridescent glass and in several colors, such as blue and green (see Figs. 1576-1596) as well as Rose Marie/Rose Pink (see Figs. 1552-1575). Carnival glass collectors usually call this pattern "Optic and Buttons."

F

CRYSTAL as well as ROSE MARIE glass

In open stock

5822 — 6¼ oz. Oil Bottle
14 dozen in barrel

5821 — 5½ oz. Oil Bottle
13 dozen in barrel

582 — 8 inch Vase
6½ dozen in barrel

5822/3 — 10 inch Rose Vase
varies from 9 in. to 11 in. in height
about 3¾ dozen in barrel

5822 — Pressed Water Bottle
3 dozen in barrel

0582 — Table Tumbler
16 dozen in barrel

5821 — 3-pint Jug, large size
2¼ dozen in barrel

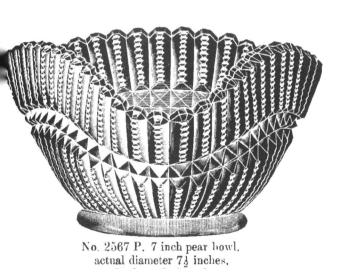

No. 2567 P. 7 inch pear bowl,
actual diameter 7½ inches,
3½ dozen in barrel.

Once misattributed to a Findlay, Ohio, glass factory, this motif, called File by pattern glass collectors, was Imperial's No. 256 line of "low priced tableware." It was an early crystal pattern, and about three dozen pieces were illustrated in the firm's 1907 catalog. These range from the usual four-piece table set and various bowls (banana, berry, cracker and nut) to several sizes of plates and triangular-shaped bowls intended for pears! Some items were made in iridescent glass, too.

FLAME, NO. 680 AND FLARE, NO. 670

These Imperial pieces were created by Russel Wright, whose designs influenced much of American household china in the 1940s. Flame was described as "a twisted, handblown design with a fairly heavy sham." There were three sizes of tumblers (6 oz., 11 oz. and 14 oz.) as well as an 8 oz. sherbet (see next page).

In later Imperial advertising, the Flame tumblers were often combined with Imperial's No. 110 Twist, a stemware line created by Carl Uhrmann. Wright also designed Imperial's No. 670 (see **Flare** below) and No. 675 (see **Pinch** in the the next volume of this series).

These three Imperial tumblers (see next page), which were advertised as 14 oz., 11 oz. and 6 oz.,were also created by Russel Wright. In addition to crystal, the No. 670 Flare tumblers were made in these colors: amber; blue; Charcoal Brown (also called Ripe Olive); Hemlock (deep forest green); Turquoise (also called Seaspray and described as "the palest aqua"); and the distinctive yellow-green, later called Verde, which was developed for Wright by Imperial.

There is a noticeable texture to the outside of the Flare tumblers, caused by minute flecks of mica or vermiculite (Imperial called this "seed glass"). Wright also designed Imperial's No. 680 (see **Flame** above) and No. 675 (see **Pinch** in the next volume of this series).

IMPERIAL...

Flare

Made expressly for color harmony with currently popular colored pottery and linens . . . . . Colors on tables are no longer seasonal . . . . . Smart tumblers are fast replacing colored stemware in the minds of most hostesses everywhere! . . . . . **PINCH** design is #675 . . . . . **FLARE** design is #670 . . . . . **FLAME** is #680 . . . . . Color descriptions: "Seaspray" is the palest aqua . . . . . "Hemlock" is a deep forest green . . . . . "Ripe Olive" is a deep brown . . . . "Verde" is a green gold.

Pinch

Flame

IMPERIAL GLASS CORPORATION
BELLAIRE, OHIO

Member Glass Crafts of America

FREE HAND

F

This advertisement for Imperial's "New Free Hand Glass" appeared in the September 12, 1923, issue of *The Jewelers' Circular* (a similar ad was carried in the July 5, 1923, issue of *Crockery and Glass Journal*).

NEW
Free Hand Glass

as the name says, this exquisite glass is entirely made by the hands of skillful artists, no moulds being used.

The illustrations cannot do justice to the exquisite colorings and decorations, which are not done with a brush, but by hand with different colors of flowing glass.

To become acquainted with this truly artistic ware, let us send you by express an assortment of 12 different, specially selected pieces for $50.00—f.o.b. Bellaire.

Barrel $1.25 Extra.

Be the first in your vicinity to put it on sale.

Imperial glass company
Bellaire
Ohio

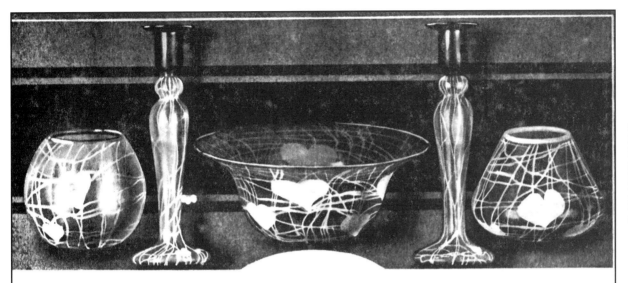

This advertisement for Imperial's Free Hand appeared in the December 18, 1924, issue of *Crockery and Glass Journal.*

Why Go To Europe?

Why do you want to go to Europe, to buy vases and fancy glass, tying up your money, so that you are handicapped for a year in your department, and then can not buy what you need in the regular way at home.

When you can secure dandy lines for small investment, in Bellaire, get prompt shipment, which means quick turnover, on which you make more money and have no worry.

Think It Over

We will not exhibit in Pittsburgh, but will be glad to welcome you at the factory in Bellaire or you can see our complete line on display in New York.

Imperial Glass Company
Bellaire
Ohio

Cox & Company
120 Fifth Avenue
New York

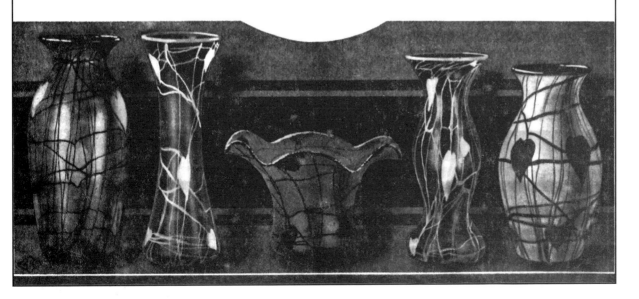

F

Left: Label on base of
Imperial Free Hand vase.

Right: This paper label
with handwriting ("F. H. 231")
is on the base of an Imperial
Free Hand vase.

These colorful, dramatic products represent some of the very best glassmaking efforts in Imperial's history. They were made in the early 1920s when Imperial's Victor Wicke realized a "long cherished ideal ... [the] consummation of a vision spanning some two decades." According to a lengthy account in *Crockery and Glass Journal* (June 7, 1923) headlined "New Imperial Line Rivals World's finest Glassware," Wicke wanted Imperial to make off hand wares for some time, but he was unable to procure the skilled workers needed and was also deterred by the costs involved. Finally, Wicke got a "a little group of artisans together" and "because these skilled workers are primarily interested in their art for art's sake, ... this dream has come true."

Free Hand ware must be differentiated from Imperial's earlier Art Glass and from the later Lead Lustre line, which is quite similar to some Free Hand pieces. Called "stretch" glass today, Imperial's Art Glass was made in five colors (Pearl Amethyst, Pearl Green, Pearl Ruby, Pearl Silver and Pearl White), mostly between 1916 and about 1926 (see the discussion of **Art Glass** on pp. 25-27 of the first volume in this series). Lead Lustre came after Free Hand in the mid-1920s and was developed as a lower-cost product which used some of the color and/or decorative treatments available in Free Hand ware (see **Lead Lustre** later in this book).

The *Jewelers' Circular* (September 23, 1923) shows a dozen different Free Hand shapes and actually provides wholesale price information: $50.00 for a dozen Free Hand pieces, plus $1.25 for the barrel! These articles were likely intended to retail at about twenty-five dollars, a considerable sum even in the economic boom times of the roaring '20s.

An original Imperial catalog of about two dozen pages shows a great array of Free Hand ware (see pp. 451-462 in this book). Free Hand pieces range from bowls and candlesticks to baskets and vases. The dominant colors are blue, green or orange, and many articles have applied handles, an applied foot or applied edging, the color of which contrasts with the body of the piece.

As shown in the catalog, Free Hand articles in a particular treatment generally have original numbers in close proximity to one another. The treatments include vivid iridescent effects, various "hanging hearts" or "King Tut" motifs, and colored threading. Some pieces made with crystal bodies exhibit elaborate hand-cutting.

On the first page of the catalog, Free Hand vases (F. H. 150 and F. H. 160) or candleholders (F. H. 164 and F. H. 165) are grouped with Art Glass bowls to form console sets. This was "Special Lot No. 1906" and is labelled "Free Hand and Art Glass" (see p. 451). Three of the Art Glass bowls are designated "P. A." (Pearl Amethyst) and one is designated "P. G." (Pearl Green). There were three other colors in the Art Glass line: Pearl Ruby, Pearl Silver, and Pearl White). This is the only page in the catalogue which shows items from the Art Glass line. The other 23 pages, all consisting of Special Lots, are headed "Free Hand Glass" and show the "iron cross" trade-mark.

Imperial obtained a design patent on December 4, 1923, for a high-quality paper label which resembles sealing wax with a signet impression. The labels have the Imperial iron cross mark in the center and bear the words "Free Hand" and "Made in U. S. A." Some Free Hand pieces also have an oval paper label with the handwritten initials "F. H." and the shape number of the item as given in the color catalog reprinted in this book.

The group of workers who made Free Hand at Imperial also worked at the Durand plant in Vineland, New Jersey, and the Fenton Art Glass Company in Williamstown, West Virginia. The men were immigrants, and Richard and Wilma Ross identified one of them, Oscar Eckstead, as the head of the shop of "five Swedish glassmakers" (*Imperial Glass*, p. 1). In his research on the history of Fenton, Dr. Eugene Murdock identified three more workers—Fritz Alberg and two men named Peterson and Brandt. Their creations at Fenton in 1925 were sometimes similar to Imperial's Free Hand ware, often employing the "hanging hearts" motif, but colors such as Karnak Red were developed (see William Heacock's *Fenton Glass: The First Twenty-five Years*, pp. 26-27, 96, 106-107 and 136).

Fashion

FACE AND FANNY TUMBLERS

As the name implies, these decorated tumblers from the mid-1950s have a "face" on one side and a "fanny" on the other. The animals so depicted include dog, cat, horse, cow, mouse, pig, goat and mule. The decoration was a silk-screen process, and the tumblers also have black or gold enamel.

FANCY FLOWERS

This is the name used by Carnival glass collectors for Imperial's No. 737. It was available as a footed salad bowl (No. 737A) and a crimped fruit bowl (No. 737C).

FASHION

This is the Carnival glass collectors' name for Imperial's No. 402½ pattern. This was a very extensive line in crystal glass, and it also enjoyed considerable production in iridescent ware.

Fancy Flowers

No. 737A—8½ inch footed salad.

FEDERAL EAGLE
(see **No. 1776** in the next volume of this series)

FERN GREEN

First introduced in 1975-76, Fern Green was featured with two full pages in Imperial's 1976-77 catalogue. Quite a few articles were shown, but this was the last appearance of this color. Fern Green was later produced with an iridescent treatment and called Meadow Green Carnival.

FIDDLE VASE

This was Imperial's No. 1850 Smoky Mountain Fiddle vase in 1956, when it was marketed in milk glass along with the No. 1860 Blue Ridge Mountain Banjo vase. It was also made in cased glass; see **cased glass vases** in this book and **Americana Folk Vases** in the previous volume of this series.

FIELD FLOWER

This (or Fieldflower) is the Carnival glass collectors' name for Imperial's No. 494 pattern, which was also originally called Daisy (see **Daisy** earlier in this book)

FIGHTING COCK
TUMBLER

This silk-screen decorated beverage tumbler was in Imperial's line during the early 1960s. Like many other decorated tumblers, this 12 oz. tumbler was designated No. 71; the blanks were purchased from the Federal Glass Company.

FIRED GOLD
ON CRYSTAL

This phrase was first used about mid-1964 in conjunction with offerings of Collectors Crystal pieces (see **Collectors Crystal** earlier in this book). These were decorated with bright gold that was fired in a decorating lehr for permanence (see Figs. 1597-1622). The gold was applied using a specially-shaped paint roller, a technique which was speedy and resulted in uniform quality. A company called

Fighting Cock

Crystal Clear bought a good deal of this glassware from Imperial.

FIRED GOLD ON GREEN

In mid-1964, some of the articles being made in Collectors Crystal were also produced in green glass (see **Collectors Crystal** earlier in this book). The effect was heightened when these were decorated with bright gold and fired in a decorating lehr for permanence. The gold was applied using a specially-shaped paint roller.

FISH ORNAMENTS

These were available in mid-1964. Imperial's sales literature described them as "off-hand" and "crackled," and a POPA (Point of Purchase Aid) tag called them "An Imperial Off Hand (no mould) Item." Four colors were mentioned—opalescent crystal, opalescent green, opalescent pink and iridescent Rubigold. These are pictured in the first volume of this series (p. 167) as are some others in unusual colors (p. 168).

FLAG DECORATIONS

These appear on crystal tumblers from the No. 451 Georgian line and are listed in an April, 1932,

Floral and Optic

price list. The decorations, which depict semaphore signal flags, are as follows: In Distress; Dispatches; No; Yes; and Man Overboard, A plain Sail Boat silhouette was listed, too; it is not a flag, but does continue the nautical theme. The Sail Boat was also available on Ritz Blue and Ruby glass, but the flags were not "because colors in flags will not harmonize with Ritz Blue or Ruby."

FLASK BROWN

This term was used to designate Imperial's amber glass, particularly during the 1950s-60s when Imperial used the "House of Americana Glass" phrase to describe itself (see Figs. 1623-1627). One would be hard pressed to differentiate among Imperial's synonyms for amber: Amberglo, Autumn Amber, Flask Brown, Honey Amber and Madeira.

FLAT DIAMOND

(see **Diamond Quilted** earlier in this book)

FLAT IRON

This name was often used for an Imperial novelty item, the No. 971 box and cover (see Fig. 42 in the previous volume of this series). These were shown in amber, Heather and Verde in Catalogue No. 62.

FLORAL AND OPTIC

This is the Carnival glass collectors' name for several Imperial bowls which were produced in the mid-1920s. The interior may be plain or it may be the No. 514 Windmill pattern, which is also known as Double Dutch. In either case, the bowls carry No. 514 in Imperial catalogs.

FLEUR DE LIS
TUMBLERS

This sandblasted decoration was available about 1958. The 12 oz. tumblers, designated No.

F

MISCELLANEOUS

71, were blanks purchased by Imperial from the Federal Glass Company.

FLOWER FAIR

This short line of highly patterned stemware made its first appearance in Imperial's 1975-76 catalogue, and it was created by Lenox designer Chet Molzen. The catalog described Flower Fair as "casual stemware with a delicate feminine touch. Spritely bouquets of flowers decorate the bowl of each hand-pressed piece." The four items (9 oz. wine, 10 oz. dessert, 12 oz. goblet and 13 oz. iced beverage) were available in Fern Green, Nut Brown, Sunshine Yellow and Ultra Blue. These were in the line about two years (see Figs. 1628-1635).

FLOWER HOLDERS

Several of these are shown in Imperial's very first catalogue, which was issued in 1904. Later, the term "vase" was used to describe these.

FLUTE

This plain pattern, Imperial's No. 700 Colonial, was a large and important early line in crystal, so it is not surprising that quite a few items can also be found in iridescent glass. Much confusion over this pattern has existed among Carnival glass collectors regarding this and other Imperial colonial lines, such as No. 393 and No. 600 Colonial Crystal (mistakenly called Chesterfield), but Burns attempts to sort these out in his *Imperial Carnival Glass*. Moulds for the No. 700 line were used with plungers bearing a grape motif to create articles called "Heavy Grape" by Carnival glass collectors (see **Colonial and Grapes** earlier in this book).

FLUTE AND CANE

(See **Cane** in the previous volume of this series)

FORESTER VASES

These were introduced in July, 1955, along with the Dunce Cap decanters, the Tall Boy shaker and three sizes of No. 701 Forester vases (in crystal, Turquoise, Stiegel Green or Mustard).

No. 700 Colonial pitcher, ½ gal. size

No. 9 size 1 flower holder. 4½ inches high. 8 dozen in barrel.

No. 9 flower holder. Size 2 height 5⅝ inches. packed 5 dozen in barrel. Size 3 height 6 inches. packed 4 dozen in barrel. Size 4 height 7¼ inches. packed 3 dozen in barrel. Size 5 height 8¼ inches. packed 2 dozen in barrel.

FOUR-SEVENTY-FOUR

As its popular name among Carnival glass collectors indicates, this was Imperial's No. 474 line. It was not among Imperial's earliest iridescent wares, but it was in production by about 1913.

FREEFOLD

Not part of any Imperial line, this vase, named Freefold by Carnival glass collectors, originally carried Imperial's No. 188. It was made as a "swung" vase, and this operation was quite important to Imperial's production of both crystal and iridescent ware from about 1911 to 1916. First pressed in moulds about the size of a typical spooner, these pieces were snapped up and warmed-in before the glassworker would "swing" the snap like a pendulum, causing centrifugal force to extend the length of the vase. Imper-

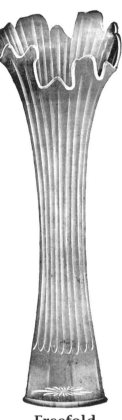

Freefold

ial's catalogs suggest that some swung vases could reach as much as 21 inches tall.

FRIEZE TUMBLERS

Made in two sizes—8 oz. and 14 oz.—these tumblers were produced in the early and mid-1960s. In Imperial's Catalog 66A, the larger size appears in Amber, Azalea, Antique Blue and Verde. According to one of salesman Ed Kleiner's notebooks, they were also available in crystal or crystal decorated with a fired-on cranberry band, a plain gold band or a cutting (C560)

FROSTED BLOCK

(see **Beaded Block and Frosted Block** in the previous volume of this series, pp. 49-51)

Four-Seventy-Four

GAFFER BOWLS AND VASES

G

This original Imperial publicity photo shows the Footed Gaffer items.

Top row: 150/74 footed bowl.

Insert: 150/75 6" bowl

Middle row: 150/70 footed vase and 150/73 footed vase.

Bottom row: 150/72 footed vase, 150/75 footed bowl, and 150/71 footed vase.

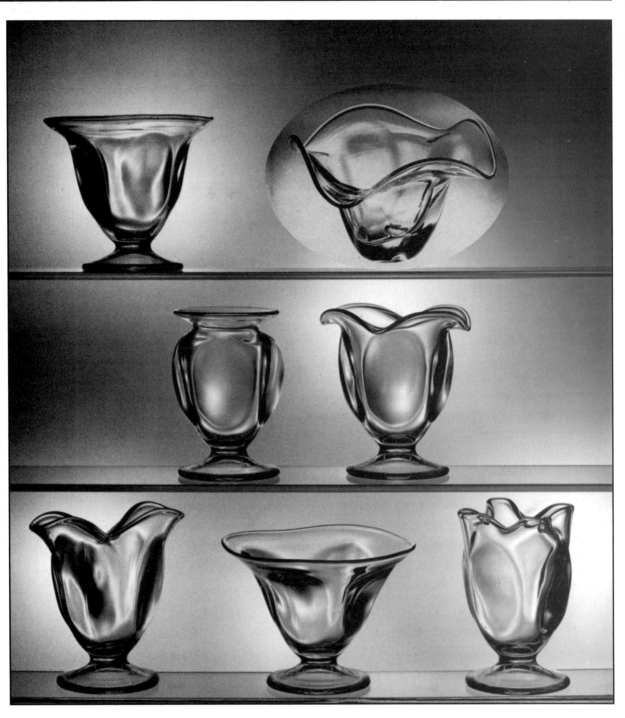

These pieces began as pressed ware items and were flared, crimped or otherwise finished to create pieces with an "off hand" look. There were six flat-bottomed Gaffer items in Imperial's 1953 catalog (see inset), and these were advertised along with Casual Crystal (see p. 258).

About 1957, six footed pieces, called "Footed Gaffer" vases and bowls, were available in either crystal or Imperial's Mustard color. The prefix 150/ was used for the Footed Gaffer articles, whose shapes are similar to the earlier Gaffer items.

G

These items, officially known as Imperial's No. 37 10¹/₂" vase and No. 83 9¹/₂" vase in satin-finished Antique Blue cased with opal glass, take their informal name after Edith Gaines, a glass enthusiast from New York who visited Imperial several times in 1964-65. Gaines was associate editor of *The Magazine ANTIQUES*, and she also published a well-illustrated series of articles on American glass for the popular *Woman's Day* magazine in the early 1960s.

During her visits to Imperial, Gaines spent many hours in the plant observing various aspects of the glassmaking process and asking many questions of both workers and management. Workers in Hot Metal took quite a liking to her, calling her "Gaffer Gaines" and making her an honorary member of AFGWU Local Union No. 13. Although Gaines was reportedly (Martins Ferry *Times-Leader*, June 10, 1965) working on a book about American collectible glass, no publication was forthcoming (see also **Peachblow** in the next volume of this series).

GARDEN ARBOR

This deep plate etching was a prominent part of Imperial's line in the early 1940s. Shown here are the 1488D 10½ cake plate, 1470 goblet and 1470 wine. These etching plates were acquired when Imperial bought many of the assets of the defunct Central Glass Company of nearby Wheeling. The Garden Arbor etching was designated DE 436, and it can be found on stemware from the No. 147 line and serving pieces from the No. 148 line as well as a few pieces of Candlewick (see p. 144 of the previous volume in this series).

G

Like their counterparts for use with electric light, these products were quite important to the Imperial Glass Company, especially in its early years. The 1904 general catalog illustrated several lines of shades and globes for both electric and gas use, and two specialty catalogs issued about this same time covered "Engraved gas and electric glassware" and "Plain and engraved gas and electric glassware."

In January, 1911, Imperial advertised its gas and electric shades as "Five and Ten Cent Wonders" in *Pottery, Glass and Brass Salesman*. These sold for 34 to 80 cents per dozen (wholesale) and included some with iridescent treatments. Quite a few other shades are shown in the Archers' book, pp. 1-19 (see also **illuminating goods** later in this book).

No. 44 pressed gas shade.
for 4 inch holder.
packed 5 dozen in barrel, or 15 dozen in cask.

No. 95 pressed gas shade.
for 4 inch holder.
packed 5 dozen in barrel, or 12 dozen in cask.

No. 97 pressed gas shade.
for 4 inch holder.
packed 5 dozen in barrel, or 15 dozen in cask.

GAS LIGHT ERA TUMBLERS

This boxed set of eight decorated tumblers features silk-screened, rather comic scenes reflecting the early twentieth century. Among them are Keystone cops, a barbershop quartet, a couple on a bicycle built for two, and a woman struggling with a tight-fitting corset. The tumblers were purchased as blanks from the Federal Glass Company and decorated at Imperial. A free lance designer, Jane Snead, developed the various designs for Imperial. The tumblers were packaged for sale in a specially printed box.

G

Sets illustrated consist of one 80 ounce pitcher and 12½ ounce tumblers, both HAND BLOWN

One-half dozen sets in bulk carton,
Seven or nine piece
Shipping weight 40 pounds

One set in individual carton,
Seven or nine piece
Shipping weight 10 pounds

451/cut 451.   7 piece Ice Tea Set,   Per set, $4.50
451/cut 451.   9 piece Ice Tea Set,   Per set, $5.60

This extensive line of beverage service items dates from the 1930s, and some pieces were still being made in the late 1940s. In addition to crystal, Georgian No. 451 was also made in amber, green, Ritz Blue, Rose Pink and Stiegel Green. Crystal beverage sets were available with colored bands and polka dots, and colored beverage sets were made with gold or platinum bands. Many Georgian pieces are also known with cuttings, two of which are illustrated here.

GOLDEN GREEN

70/1 GOLDEN GREEN DRINKING SETS

contain 4 each of 3 sets shown, or 1 dozen assorted sets.
Price per dozen $15.00 (barrel extra)

70/84/3 — 7-piece water set, pitcher 9" high

70/599/3 — 7-piece ice tea set, pitcher 9¼" high

70/06003 pressed 8-piece ice tea set, pitcher 11 inches over all

70/3 GOLDEN GREEN VASES

contain ½ dozen each of 7 vases shown, or

3½ dozen assorted vases.

Price per assortment
$9.38
(barrel extra)

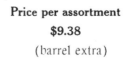

70/768/3
9" high

70/771/3
6" rose bowl

70/223/3
9½" high

70/119/3
7½" high

70/731/3
7½" high

70/729/3
7½" high

70/313-B
8" high

Introduced during the 1920s, Imperial's color #70 was billed as the company's "latest creation in colored glass" and was described as "what the name indicates, a light green with flashes of golden yellow" (see Figs. 1470-1471). Collectors today often call this hue "Vaseline glass."

These beverage service items were an important part of Imperial's gold-decorated offerings in the 1960s, along with Bambu, Dynasty, El Tabique de Oro, Sekai Ichi, Sortijas de Oro and Toril de Oro (all are in Catalog 66A). The Golden Shoji line, Imperial's No. 104, sold well through the B. Altman department stores in the New York City area. The Golden Shoji line ranged from 2 oz. tumblers and a 30 oz, bottle (for rice wine called saki) to various sizes (5 oz., 11 oz. and 15 oz.) of tumblers and a Hospitality Bowl for pretzels or other snacks. Catalog 66A also shows a 10" vase and a 6¹/₂" bud vase. Golden Shoji articles are usually gold-decorated crystal glass, but mat finish black was sometimes applied before the gold, making for a striking combination (see Fig. 957).

GRAPE, NO. 473

Tumbler, grape design.

Large 3 pint pitcher, grape design.

Goblet

Without doubt, this was one of Imperial's most important pattern lines when the firm began to produce iridescent glass. It should not be confused with Imperial's other distinctive grape motif (see **Colonial and Grapes, No. 700** earlier in this book).

The first appearance of No. 473 in an Imperial catalog dates to about 1914-15, when catalog 100B was published. Quite a few "Grape design" items are shown: berry bowl and sauces, both round and crimped; goblet; small crimped comport (probably made from goblet); oval plate; pitcher and tumbler; punch bowl and cup; round plate; blown vase; and wine bottle (w/stopper) and wine glasses. In the 1920s Imperial Bargain Book and its Supplement, quite a few items were still listed.

As one might expect, No. 473 figured prominently in Imperial's plans when Carnival glass was reissued in the 1960s. The No. 473 Grape 10 oz. goblet is shown in Rubigold and Peacock Blue in Catalogue 62, and they are labelled "Carnival glass." Within a few years, most of the early No. 473 Grape items had also been added to Imperial's new offerings.

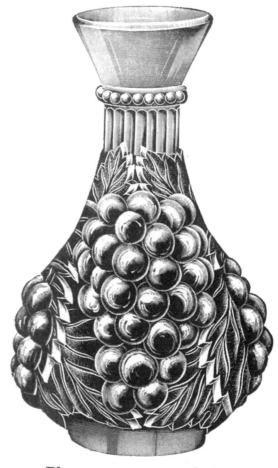

Blown vase, grape design.

Except for this publicity photo (c. late 1950s) which shows eleven different items, not much is known about this pressed ware motif, which bore the number 200. The stemware pieces have thick, square feet, but the beverage glasses have round bases. The background area around the raised Greek Key is sandblasted to create a frosted look.

G
MISCELLANEOUS

GALLOPIN' DOMINOES TUMBLER

Bearing No. 7850, this large roly-poly style 18 oz. tumbler was shown in Imperial's 1953 catalog. The silk screen decoration depicts a pair of dice, using a different color on each of the eight tumblers in the set. These were discontinued in late 1954.

GIRAFFE TUMBLER

This interesting decorated tumbler was marketed by Imperial about 1955.

GOBOONS VASES

Imperial president Carl Gustkey coined the name "goboons," and these spittoon-shaped vases were made in the late 1950s and early 1960s. In addition to Burgundy, crystal, Madeira and Stiegel Green, they were also marketed in crystal completely covered with bright gold (this decoration was called Midas; see Figs. 1737-1739).

GOLD DECORATED GLASSWARE

Imperial sometimes decorated glassware with all-over gold (see Figs. 1721-1741). After being fired, the gold finish is quite durable and very brilliant (although some pieces were burnished to diminish the effect). The 400/128 punch set was marketed as early as 1943 (see Figs. 799-800 in the first volume of this series), and other Candlewick pieces were decorated with all-over gold. In the late 1950s and early 1960s, an Imperial line called Midas featured brilliant gold on items from the No. 710 Reeded line and some other pieces.

Goboons vase

Golden Spiral Tumblers

Let Hospitality have Uniquity! Use or give Imperial Iron Mould, Pipe Blown, Patterned Crystal Tumblers, with 22 Carat Gold carefully hand-applied onto the BAS-RELIEF Spirals, then kiln-fired. EIGHT Tall 15 oz. Ones, or EIGHT of the newer, un-usually-different Squat 12 oz. Ones; either Set $12 each, Prepaid, Gift boxed.

Old Hay Shed Gift Shop
P. O. Box 563
Bellaire, Ohio, U.S.A.

GOLDEN SPIRAL TUMBLERS

Intended to retail for about $1.50 each in the mid-1960s, these crystal tumblers feature bright gold decoration on the raised spiral which wind around the body of the tumblers. Two sizes, a high-ball glass and an old fashioned, were produced (see **Space Spiral** in the next volume of this series).

GOLDEN TACKHEAD

These tumblers, Imperial's No. 1002, were made in three sizes—9 1/2 oz., 12 oz. and 14 oz. The rosette-shaped "tackheads" are decorated with bright gold. Introduced in 1961, these were sold in considerable quantities to Bechtel, Lutz and Jost, a longtime wholesale customer in Reading, Pa.

GOLDEN TILE TUMBLERS

(see **Tile Tumblers** in the next volume of this series)

Golden Tackhead

GOTHIC ARCHES

Not part of any Imperial line, this vase, named Gothic Arches by Carnival glass collectors, was originally Imperial's No. 338A. A swung vase, it was made in various sizes, ranging from a sweet pea vase (8 -11 inches) to a tall vase (17-19 inches).

GRANADA, No. 136

These unusually-shaped articles were introduced in the mid-1930s, but the line proved to be short-lived, for Imperial's 1938 sales figures show No. 136 to be one of the company's slowest sellers, accounting for less than one-half of one percent of sales at that time.

Some of the Granada No. 136 items, such as the 80 oz. pitcher and various sizes of tumblers, were made as blown ware, but others, such as plates, were made as pressed ware. The blown pitcher and tumblers may have a vertical rib optic, and collectors might also find No. 136 items decorated with cuttings.

Records from 1939 list the following items: 80 oz. pitcher; four sizes of tumblers (5 oz., 10 oz., 13 oz. and 16 oz.); four sizes of footed tumblers (2½ oz., 4 oz., 9 oz. and 12 oz.); three sizes of plates (6" 8" and 12"); three sizes of violet balls (2" 3" and 4"); sugar and cream set; cup and saucer; low sherbet; finger bowl and salt and pepper set. All were available in crystal, and many were made in the other Imperial colors from the late 1930s: Golden Amber, Hock Green, Ritz Blue and Ruby.

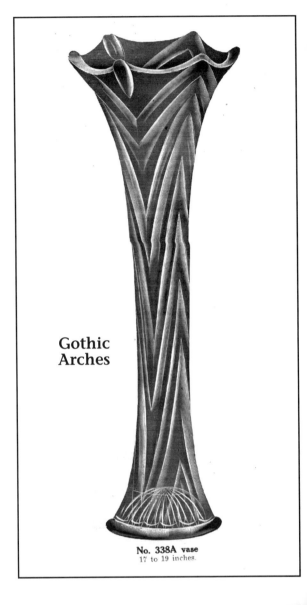

Gothic Arches

No. 338A vase
17 to 19 inches.

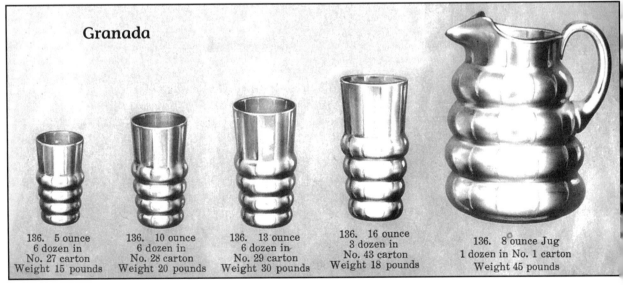

Granada

136. 5 ounce
6 dozen in
No. 27 carton
Weight 15 pounds

136. 10 ounce
6 dozen in
No. 28 carton
Weight 20 pounds

136. 13 ounce
6 dozen in
No. 29 carton
Weight 30 pounds

136. 16 ounce
3 dozen in
No. 43 carton
Weight 18 pounds

136. 8 ounce Jug
1 dozen in No. 1 carton
Weight 45 pounds

Greek Key cutting

Grecian Key decoration

GRECIAN KEY DECORATION

This white silk screen decoration contrasted nicely with the "charcoal" glass. Imperial purchased this ware—shallow bowls and plates—from Houze (see **Elysian** earlier in this book).

GREEK KEY CUTTING

Designated C904, this plain motif was done on plates and goblets. Despite its apparent simplicity, this cutting is difficult to execute, for curved lines are somewhat easier to cut than straight lines. The goblets have a facet-cut, polished stem, too. The goblet, plate and sherbet were shown in Imperial's catalog 53.

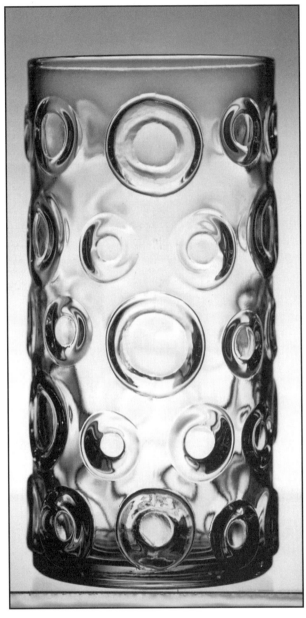

GUINEVERE CUTTING

Designated C804, this elaborate cutting on plates and stemware was intended for the bridal registry market and sold through major department stores in the 1950s.

GYPSY RINGS TUMBLER

This 15 oz. tumbler, designated No. 116, was in production for about five years, 1962-67. In addition to crystal, it was made in Amber, Antique Blue, Azalea and Verde.

Harlequin

HAPPINESS TUMBLER

This silk-screen decorated beverage tumbler was in Imperial's line during the early 1960s. Like many other decorated tumblers, this 12 oz. tumbler was designated No. 71; the blanks were purchased from the Federal Glass Company.

HARLEQUIN TUMBLER

This silk-screen decorated 12 oz. beverage tumbler was in Imperial's line during the early 1960s. It was designated No. 71, and the blanks were purchased from the Federal Glass Company.

HATTIE

Imperial's original designation for this pattern in iridescent glass was No. 496, and the company also called it Mikado. This motif was used when Imperial reissued Carnival glass.

HAWTHORNE

This handpainted decoration was probably overshadowed by several of its more popular contemporaries, Western Apple and Western Rose, but it continued in Imperial's line for some time. Mentioned on price lists from the early 1940s, it is also shown in Imperial's catalog 53 (see Fig. 798 in the previous volume of this series as well as some mentions of various decorations in the NIGCS *Glasszette* newsletter, February, 1991).

Hattie

HAZEN

This is Weatherman's name for Imperial's No. 760 line, which is called "Square" in one of the firm's price lists from 1931 (see **Square** in the next volume of this series).

HEATHER

This pale amethyst color, which is similar to Burgundy, was used with quite a few individual Imperial articles and several lines in the early 1960s, especially No. 123 Chroma and No. 995 Concord (see Figs. 963-965 and 969 and p. 404).

HEAVY DIAMOND

This is the Carnival glass collectors' name for Imperial's pattern No. 330 (unfortunately, Weatherman calls No. 330 Diamond Block, and Carnival glass collectors compound the confusion by calling Imperial's No. 699 Diamond Block!). Imperial's No. 330 dates from the late 1920s. It was offered as "low priced staples in crystal glass" in catalog 300, but items are also known in iridescent glass, typically in Rubigold (see **No. 330** and **Washington No. 699** in the next volume of this series).

HEAVY GRAPE

Although this name has been used by Carnival glass collectors for many years, it does not appear in the old Imperial records. The interior grape motif is shown in original Imperial catalogs with the designation No. 700, and it was sometimes called "Colonial Grape" or "Colonial and Grapes."

HEISEY MOULDS

As noted in the overview of Imperial's history presented in the first volume of this series, the company acquired the moulds and other assets of A. H. Heisey and Company of Newark, Ohio, in late April, 1958. Heisey was in business over sixty years, producing many successful lines. Imperial had made glass for Heisey to help fill orders, and the relationship between Imperial and Heisey executives was cordial. In November, 1960, Imperial purchased the assets of the Cambridge Glass Company. Imperial felt that it could market the most popular Heisey and Cambridge

items (see pp. 89-94 of the previous volume in this series for a discussion of Imperial items made from Cambridge moulds).

Imperial did not suppress the Heisey name. Its advertising typically made clear that the articles were from Heisey moulds, and many Heisey items continued to bear the distinctive Heisey H-in-diamond mark. This was no attempt to deceive, for Imperial needed to make popular Heisey patterns quickly to meet market demand. Removing the marks would have taken time, not to mention labor costs. Before long, however, Imperial received complaints from glass collectors, and the company made an effort to remove marks from these moulds. This can result in confusion among glass collectors, especially when a Heisey pattern turns up in an Imperial color.

Today, the phrase "Heisey by Imperial" is well known. Imperial used the Heisey moulds to continue production of such lines as Provincial and Old Williamsburg as well as novelty items such as animal figurines (see pp. 18-20 of the previous volume in this series). Imperial also replicated some Heisey colors. Fortunately, much of the history of the Heisey-Imperial relationship was carefully investigated by the Newark Heisey Collectors Club before Imperial closed. The result was a fine book, *Heisey by Imperial and Imperial Glass by Lenox*, published by the Heisey Collectors of America, Inc., in 1980. This book is valuable for detailing the various colors made by Imperial when using Heisey moulds.

Sometimes Imperial made and marketed Heisey items without changing numbers or names (see **Cabochon** on p. 86 of the first volume of this series). On other occasions, Imperial changed the name but retained the Heisey number; for instance, Imperial's No. 1425 had been Heisey's No. 1425 Victorian, but Imperial sold it under the names Early Americana Waffle and, later, Americana Waffle (see pp. 37 and 156 of the first volume of this series).

On June 1, 1958, the Imperial Glass Corporation issued a series of mimeographed sheets to its sales force under the title "Heisey Items to be Produced by Imperial Glass Corporation, Bellaire, Ohio." This document listed articles in the following Heisey lines: Old Williamsburg, Crystolite, Waverly, Lariat, Cabochon, Revere, Country Club, Coleport, Tempo, Oxford, Orchid, Rose, Moonglo, and Southwind. A few individual items were listed in Provincial, Plantation, and Puritan. The document also listed articles by type, such as candleabra and cocktail service.

HELIOS

Helios was an iridescent treatment introduced in Imperial's May, 1911, catalog, where it was described as "a beautiful light green glass with silver iridescent tints." In Imperial's 100B catalog, Helios iridescent was illustrated in color and described as "our own creation" with a surface effect "of metallic silver with shades of green gleaming through the silver" (see Fig. 1190).

When re-issues of Carnival glass became popular, Imperial revived both the color and the original name, and Helios was re-born in 1967, as pieces were introduced in both January and July (see Figs. 1176-1188 and 1190-1192). The color was very much like the original Helios, although some pieces tend to have a gold iridescence. These were accepted reasonably well by collectors in 1968-69, and Helios was discontinued at the end of 1970.

HEN ON NEST, No. 145

This little covered animal dish first appeared in Imperial's line during the 1920s, and it was made in many different colors over the years, sometimes called simply "Chicken" (see pp. 14 and 159 of the previous volume in this series).

HERITAGE TUMBLERS

(see **Tavern**, **Toasting** and **Wayside tumblers** in the next volume of this series)

HERRINGBONE AND BEADED OVAL

This name is used by Carnival glass collectors. The Imperial pattern line is an early one, and it appears in the firm's 1904 catalog (see the No. 54 bouquet holder on p. 68 of the previous volume in this series).

HEX BOX AND COVER

Two bases could be stacked upon one another to create the No. 735 "2-section hex box and cover" which was shown in crystal, sueded crystal, Antique Blue and milk glass in Imperial's Supplement One to Our Catalog No. 62 (the milk glass version is also shown on p. 20 of Imperial's 66A catalog). There is a grape pattern on each of the six sides as well as the cover.

HEXAGON AND CANE

As part of Imperial's extensive NUCUT line, this pattern was designated No. 502.

502 — 9 inch Salad Bowl, Nucut
extra heavy, very brilliant

Hexagon and Cane

Hobnail
Nut Brown

51110
12 oz. Tumbler

51150
60 oz. Blown Pitcher

51720
5" Crimped Compote

51876
Box & Cover

51700 †
10" Bowl

51696 †
8½" Bowl

51783
4" Candleholder

51680 †
4" Bowl

51762
7¼" Lamp Vase

51750
4¼" Crimped Vase

51480
Salt & Pepper Set

HOBNAIL

Imperial's 1977 catalogue shows a short line of Hobnail pieces (both pressed and blown) in Milk Glass and two colors—Nut Brown and Ultra Blue. Some had been made earlier as part of the Stamm House Dewdrop Opalescent offering in the mid-1960s, and others reached back to the days of Early American Hobnail, which was No. 741 and No. 742.

HOBNAIL, NO. 615

Imperial's Supplement One to Our Catalog No. 62 shows an interesting bowl and cover. This consisted of a milk glass foot joined to a transparent covered bowl in a sharply-pointed Hobnail motif. The cover was also made of milk glass. This item was shown in four colors—Amber (see Fig. 1493), Antique Blue, Heather and Mustard. The idea of using a milk glass foot with a bowl in some other color was also a feature of Imperial's

Parisian Provincial line, which will be covered in the next volume of this series.

HOBNAIL, EARLY AMERICAN

(see **Early American Hobnail** in this book)

HOBO TUMBLERS

There are two versions of these tumblers. The first, called Hobo Code or Hobo Signs, was designated No. 1001 and was introduced in the early 1960s. Two sizes were made, a 14 oz. tall tumbler and a 14 oz. double old fashion. These were pressed tumblers and the design is in low relief on the exterior. The Hobo Signs 1001 tumbler appears in Imperial's Supplement One to Our Catalog Number 62, where it is shown in Mustard. In mid-1964, both sizes were available in crystal.

No. 3027 N.   7 inch nut bowl.
actual diameter 7 inches.

No. 302P.   5 inch footed jelly.

Hobstar and Arches

line which was revived in part when the Americana jars were produced in the mid-1950s (see the first volume in this series, pp. 36-37).

HOBSTAR AND ARCHES

This name was coined by Carnival glass collectors, but they unfortunately use the name Hobstar Flower for the same Imperial motif! This was Imperial's No. 302 pattern, and it is shown in the 1909 catalog.

HOBSTAR AND TASSELS

This was Imperial's No. 3334 pattern, and it may also have been made as No. 333 1/2. The firm's 1909 catalog shows many different pieces, although it was not a major pattern line (see catalog reprint on the next page).

The second version, called Hobo Code, also dates from the early 1960s. These were silk-screen decorated, however, and the 12 oz. No. 71 blanks were purchased from the Federal Glass Company. To accompany these tumblers, Imperial published a booklet containing an essay by Erwin van Swol and illustrations of these crude marks. The booklet said the tumblers were "decorated with secret signs actually used by American hobos," and van Swol's article depicted the curious symbols which are supposed to direct hobos to safe places and away from dangerous places when on the road (see the October, 1996, issue of the NIGCS *Glasszette* newsletter for a lengthy article on the Hobo tumblers).

HOBSTAR

Carnival glass collectors use this name for Imperial's No. 282 pattern, an extensive early

Hobo

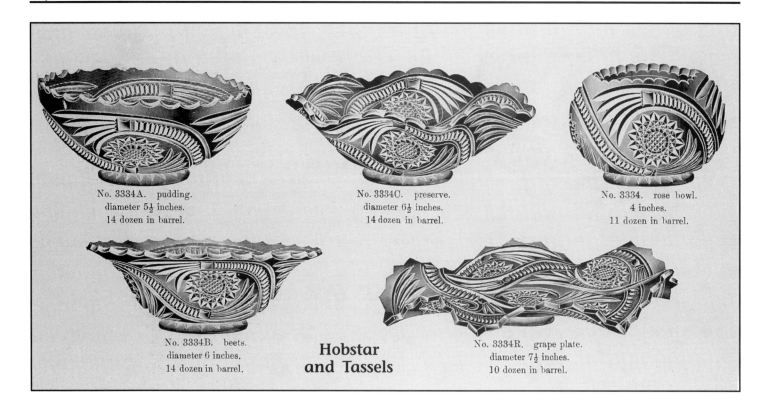

No. 3334A. pudding.
diameter 5½ inches.
14 dozen in barrel.

No. 3334C. preserve.
diameter 6½ inches.
14 dozen in barrel.

No. 3334. rose bowl.
4 inches.
11 dozen in barrel.

No. 3334B. beets.
diameter 6 inches.
14 dozen in barrel.

**Hobstar
and Tassels**

No. 3334R. grape plate.
diameter 7½ inches.
10 dozen in barrel.

HOBSTAR FLOWER

This name was coined by Carnival glass collectors, but they unfortunately use the name Hobstar and Arches for the same Imperial motif! This was Imperial's No. 302 pattern, and it is shown in the 1909 catalog.

HOFFMAN HOUSE

This was a name for a stemware shape, and it spans almost the entire length of Imperial's history. Called No. 11, some of these were illustrated in Imperial's first catalog in 1904. They are fairly thick and, hence, quite durable for either commercial or home use. In his *Imperial Carnival Glass*, Burns illustrates an iridized amber Hoffman House goblet; this is probably Imperial's "Old Gold," a relatively short-lived iridescent treatment.

By the mid-1960s, Imperial was marketing these vigorously for casual dining. The Hoffman House name was linked to "a famous hotel of that name" and the shape was said to be popular in Germany "hundreds of years ago." Imperial added a plate and small nappie to the Hoffman House listing, which was dubbed No. 46. These were available in crystal as well as several colors—Amber, Antique Blue, Heather, Ruby and Verde. Some of these colors, as well as a crystal version with cranberry (fired on) bowl, are shown in Imperial's Catalogue No. 62.

The shape continued to occupy a niche in Imperial's catalogues. In 1975-76, Hoffman House stemware was available in Amber, Nut Brown, Fern Green, Sunshine Yellow, and Ultra Blue. When Fern Green was discontinued, the Hoffman house pieces were made in Verde. These continued to be shown in Imperial catalogues as late as 1980 (see Figs. 1742-1756).

IMPERIAL'S 1962 MID-YEAR SPECIAL

ON

HANDMADE - HANDLED - HOLIDAY-HOSTESS HOSPITALITY TRAYS

IN FOUR COLORS

400/68D REGAL RUBY

160/68D BRONZE BROWN

148 PORT PURPLE

725 VERDANT VERDE

FOR SERVING FESTIVE

- Hors d'oeuvres - Cocktail or Tea Sandwiches - Petit Fours - Cookies -
- Cup Cakes - Cheeses - Crackers - Candies - Sliced Cake -
- Candied Fruits - Fruit Cake - Stuft Celery - Scones -
- Shallow-Ring Festive Moulded Salads -
- Fresh Fruits - Desserts - Buffet Service -
- 100 ET CETERAS -

- FOUR SEPARATE TRAYS - EACH IN ITS OWN COLOR -

HOLIDAY-HOSTESS HOSPITALITY TRAYS

This early 1960s ad is a good example of Imperial's ability to stimulate dealer interest by combining items from different lines. Notice the rhetorical flourishes used to describe the colors: Ruby is called Regal Ruby, and Verde is Verdant Verde; Flask Brown becomes Bronze Brown, and Heather is renamed Port Purple. The 400/68D tray is Candlewick, of course, and the 160/68D is Cape Cod. The No. 148 tray mould was acquired from the Central Glass Company in 1940 (see p. 55 of the previous book in this series). The No. 725 tray comes from the Octagon line (see p. 186 of the previous book in this series).

Home/Office Tubs Trio

No. 524 cake plate or wall decoration
diameter 10 inches

Homestead

HOME/OFFICE TUBS TRIO

This assortment consisted of three No. 801 tumblers in crystal with a black-and-white silk-screened decoration motif. An Imperial sales bulletin emphasized the styrofoam Handipak, which was an innovation at this time. This assortment was scheduled for delivery on May 1, 1965. Later, these were also offered as the Buffet Icer Trio.

HOMESTEAD

This is the popular name among Carnival glass collectors for a large iridescent plate whose border is similar to the No. 525 plate, which is called Chrysanthemum. Both of these appear in Imperial's catalog 101B, where they were called "cake or wall" plates (see **Chrysanthemum** earlier in this book). Both were reissued when Imperial

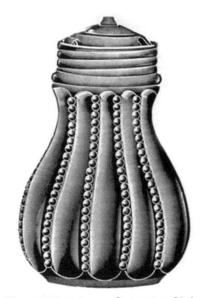

No. 65A blown horse radish.
shown with nickel top.
4¼ inches high
including top.
1 dozen in paper box.
also sold with
silver top.

made Carnival glass during its last two decades of operation.

The Homestead plate was Imperial's No. 524, and it was described in some detail in the June 13, 1912, issue of *Crockery and Glass Journal*: "This is a plaque bearing a picturesque scene of an old fashioned American homestead by the side of a stream. An artistic rustic bridge crosses the water, under which are ducks peacefully enjoying a swim. The brilliant sunset obtained through the coloring of the glass is one of the attractive features of this new creation."

HORIZON BLUE CARNIVAL
(see **Carnival glass** earlier in this book)

HORSERADISH JAR
At the turn of the century, horseradish was a common table condiment. A horseradish jar is shown in Imperial's 1904 first catalogue.

HORSESHOE BOTTOM JELLY TUMBLERS
These common tumblers were made by many American glass factories, so it is not surprising to find them in Imperial's 1913 catalogue supplement.

HUCKABEE
This is Weatherman's name for Imperial's No. 666-1/2 line (see **Cane** in the previous volume of this series).

No. X562½—8 oz jelly glass without cap
glazed edge

6567/2B. 9 inch Salad Bowl.

The Supplement to Imperial's Bargain Book offers six "Satin iridescent colors" in mid-1925. These served to extend the firm's offerings in various bright iridescent colors and in Lead Lustre. One color, Iris Ice, had been introduced in the first Bargain Book, and a selection was also shown in the second edition of the Bargain Book.

Imperial's original descriptions of these satin iridescent colors are quoted in brackets here:
color 44 Iris Ice ["white crizzled on crystal glass"];
color 56 Rose Ice ["pink crizzled on crystal glass"];
color 50 Blue Ice ["blue crizzled on crystal glass"];
color 58 Amber Ice ["crizzled on amber glass"];
color 25 Green Ice ["crizzled on green glass"]; and
color 54 Amethyst Ice ["crizzled on mulberry glass"].

These Imperial iridescent Ice colors are the epit-ome of that which collectors call "stretch" glass, often exhibiting an onionskin-like effect near the edges (see Figs. 1757-1773). The items are typically plain or colonial in style, so the color becomes the dominant feature of each.

Three of the Ice colors (Blue, Iris and Rose) were also available with decorative cuttings. Imperial's No. 664 fruit bowl/sandwich tray was illustrated with two different cuttings, and there were other Ice articles available with these motifs. Imperial's cut 30 was a simple floral motif, and cut 12 has been called "Balloons" by today's collectors. Cut 12 was also available on Imperial's lustre iridescent blown vases (in Nuruby, Sapphire and Peacock), but these should not be confused with the satin iridescent Ice colors.

No 307N. nut bowl.
massive high foot.
diameter 5½ inches.

Although a few articles in the Imperial Glass Company's 1904 catalogue resemble imitation cut ware, it was not until 1907 that the firm really began to expand into this area. A pressed ware high footed bowl novelty dubbed simply No. 307 was introduced. The 1909 and 1911 catalogs contain many imitation cut motifs, and some of these were later used in the production of iridescent glassware (see **Hobstar and Arches**, **Hobstar Flower** and **Hobstar and Tassels** elsewhere in this book).

About the middle of 1911, Imperial's management decided that its pressed ware imitation cut glass had a real foothold in the marketplace and that many more similar motifs should be developed. The result was NUCUT, a trade-mark first used in September, 1911, which was finally approved by the U. S. Patent Office in September, 1915. By that time, Imperial had issued entire catalogues devoted to its NUCUT ware, and the name continued to be used until well into the 1930s. Some of these imitation cut glass pieces were revived when Imperial hit upon the idea for its Collector's Crystal, another successful line. See **Collector's Crystal** elsewhere in this book and **NUCUT** in the next volume of this series.

INTAGLIO

I

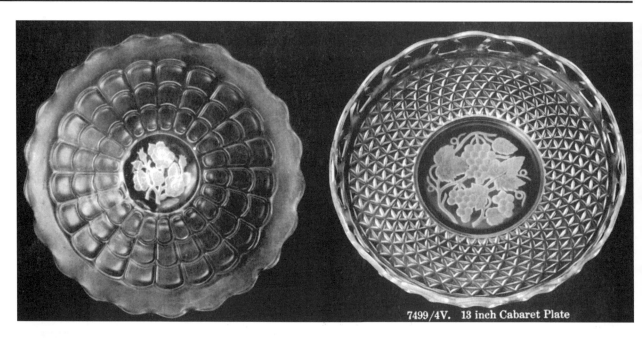

7499/4V. 13 inch Cabaret Plate

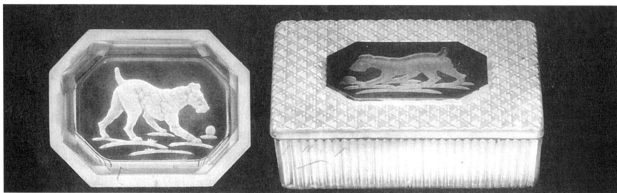

698/5. 10½ inch Square Salad Plate
2 dozen in No. 1 carton, weight 65 pounds

The term "intaglio" refers to designs "below the surface," and Imperial created several interesting motifs, especially between the early 1930s and the early 1950s. These were pressed ware pieces with a moulded design on the underside which was later acid etched to emphasize its texture and shadows.

One of the first intaglio designs consisted of fruit—a large pear or two accompanied by an apple and several large raspberries. This was given the designation 3D, but workers and salesman may have called it "Intaglio Pears." Used on the cover of an Imperial brochure (c. 1943), it is often found on articles from Imperial's No. 788 and No. 800 lines as well as Laced Edge pieces (see the Archers' book, pp. 174-175). One Imperial price list from mid-1932 refers to these lines collectively as "Intaglio Crystal." An Imperial illustrated sheet also shows the Intaglio No. 785 cigarette box and No. 785 ash tray, both of which have a dog playing with a ball.

Other early Intaglio motifs consisted of two bunches of grapes or a pair of roses. Imperial cata-

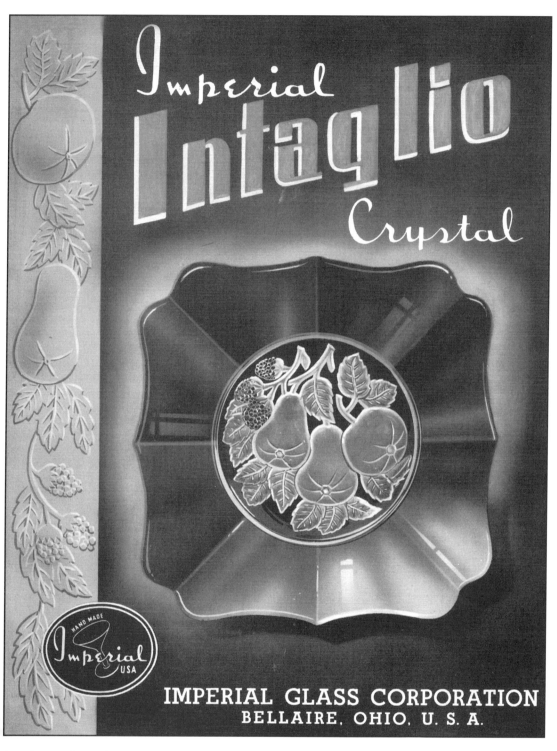

Imperial Intaglio Crystal

IMPERIAL GLASS CORPORATION
BELLAIRE, OHIO, U. S. A.

log sheets show the grape intaglio on several Lace Edge pieces, but Intaglio Rose, as it was known, is depicted on items from the No. 255 and the No. 698 lines as well as Lace Edge articles and a few other pieces.

By the early 1950s, the firm was marketing a number of otherwise plain bowls, plates, and miscellaneous pieces. These ranged from 14" plates and sectioned serving pieces to cups and saucers and individual salad dishes of various shapes. All were decorated with the fruit motif.

A series of Heisey moulds called Revere (No. 1183) were used to produce the blanks for Intaglio pieces which are illustrated in Imperial catalogues 71R and 72 (most of these bear No. 900). These consist primarily of bowls and plates, and the intaglio motif is quite similar to the groupings of fruit first used back in the 1930s.

IRIDESCENT WARE

I

The Imperial Glass Company used the phrase "iridescent glass" to describe many of the lines and novelty items it began to market in the fall of 1909. Collectors came to know these wares as "Carnival glass" years later, and Imperial itself used this popular phrase when iridescent ware was revived in the 1960s (see the discussion of Imperial's **Carnival glass** earlier in this book).

Those interested in Imperial's iridescent ware should consult the landmark books by Marion T. Hartung as well as Carl O. Burns' well-illustrated *Imperial Carnival Glass*. Burns lists the known articles in Imperial's "old" Carnival glass, but he does not detail the full history of Imperial's iridescent production and he does not detail all of the original Imperial names and/or numbers for the company's colors or patterns.

The story of Imperial's entry into the competitive arena of iridescent ware is intriguing, and there are many connections among family members and friends. Iridescent glass was made in England during the 1880s, and knowledge of the techniques for making this ware (spraying metallic salts on hot glass) was well-known to American glassmakers in the early twentieth century.

Louis Comfort Tiffany is given much credit for the development of iridescent ware in America, but he was not the only innovator. At the Steuben plant in Corning, the Englishman Frederick Carder was creating sensational but expensive iridescent articles. For over a decade, Carder had worked closely with John Northwood, Sr., at Stevens and Williams in Stourbridge, England. In the early twentieth century, another English immigrant, Joseph Webb, made an iridescent line called Muranese at the New Martinsville Glass Manufacturing Company.

In the Wheeling area, Northwood's eldest son, Harry, had established H. Northwood and Co. by refurbishing the old Hobbs-Brockunier plant (ironically, his career commenced there in 1881 after he emigrated from England). In 1904, Harry and his family were living on Front Street on Wheeling Island. Among the nearby neighbors was Capt. Edward Muhleman, who was then getting the Imperial plant completed and ready to make glass. Among Northwood's employees were two brothers—John W. Fenton and Frank L. Fenton (later to marry into the Muhleman family)—who had earlier been employed by Northwood at Indiana, Pa., in the late 1890s. Also in 1904, two of Northwood's cousins—Thomas E. A. Dugan and Alfred Dugan—were busy establishing the Dugan Glass Company in the old Northwood plant at Indiana, Pa. All of these experienced glassmakers knew about iridescent glassware, and one wonders what conversations must have been had among them about it!

Speculation aside, the rest, it can be said, "is history." The Fenton brothers built the Fenton Art Glass Company at Williamstown, West Virginia, in 1906 and entered the marketplace with their iridescent glassware in late 1907 and early 1908. Northwood and Imperial followed suit later in 1908, and the Dugan firm was not far behind.

Northwood's first iridescent line was dubbed Golden Iris, but Imperial had two colors, Rubigold and Peacock. Within a few months, labor-management agreements (dated March 22, 1909) were drawn up to govern the making of "dope ware," as it was called by the glassworkers after the liquid "dope" sprayed on the glass. The Dugan firm was apprised of these agreements in the fall of 1909, a sure indication that production was underway there as well. In the meantime, John W. Fenton left Williamstown in 1908 to start the Millersburg Glass Company, and, after some initial production of crystal glass, his firm began to market its iridescent lines, called Radium, in 1910. The rivalry among these factories was keen, and Imperial general manager Victor Wicke observed that "sharp competition on these lines has reduced the prices of iridescent ware practically to the level of those asked for crystal goods" (*Crockery and Glass Journal*, August 10, 1911).

Imperial's October, 1909, general catalog contains this note, clearly documenting that Imperial's first iridescent color was to be known as Rubigold (see next page).

Among the earliest records pertaining to Imperial's iridescent glass is a report in the November, 1909, issue of the *American Flint*, which was just commencing publication by the American Flint Glass Workers Union from its Toledo headquarters. A feature of this monthly magazine was a section devoted to regular letters from the "press secretary" of various local unions, such as L. U. No. 13 and No. 34, both of which enrolled Imperial workers. The correspondence from Bellaire (dated November 7, 1909) relates that Imperial's workers were making such articles as tumblers, gas shades and cup-foot wines and goblets. The letter also notes that "ten shops [are] working on the new iridescent colored ware, producing goblets, tumblers, vases [sic], berry sets, jugs, a general line of table ware, novelties, etc."

The "iridescent ware workers" were also listed by name: D. Roberts, T. Lynsky, E. Baird, W. Auth, H. Cook [probably Harry Cook, who later became the AFGWU's national president], T. Tracey, H. Yohn, L. Pracht, J. Kleber, J. Billgore, M. Dougherty,

Rubigold Iridescent ware

This new ware is one of the most important novelties that ever appeared in the glass market.

You may have seen some of the high priced glasswares in changeable colors which were sold for a number of years in jewelry stores and other stores where expensive goods are being featured, at necessarily high prices.

Our Rubigold Iridescent ware resembles this high priced ware closely, having the same changeable colors in all the shades of the rain bow, but our prices are very much lower, in fact are only slightly higher than the prices of the corresponding plain goods.

We have not yet been able to secure illustrations which do justice to the beauty of this ware, and have to depend therefore on actual samples to introduce it.

On the next page we give you the composition of a special assortment, arranged for this purpose.

Do not neglect to investigate for yourself by ordering one of the following assortments:

J. Murphy, T. Dobbins, J. Flaherty, J. Lappertt, J. McAfee, C. Bickerel, H. Marshall, T. Brady, F. Tiber, W. Powell, G. King, E. Duke, H. Weyrick, [and] W. Kleber. A later note in *Pottery, Glass and Brass Salesman* (January 12, 1911) says that 14 of Imperial's 48 shops were producing "iridescent or sprayed ware, such as vases, water, wine, berry or lemonade sets and a number of novelties."

The November, 1909, letter in the *American Flint* also makes this revelation about Imperial's iridescent glass: "This line of ware is under the supervision of John T. Gordon, an old ex-Flint, formerly of Williamstown, W. Va., and it is an understood fact that this is the most beautiful line of iridescent col-

ored ware that was ever placed upon the market."

Who was John T. Gordon? What had he been doing down in Williamstown, home of the Fenton Art Glass Company? The earliest surviving Fenton pay records (dated November, 1907) list a "J. Gordon." His pay rate at the time, $2.67 per turn, was the highest of some 30 skilled employees, suggesting that he was an accomplished glassworker, probably a "finisher" who could attach handles to jugs and shape many other articles (see William Heacock's *Fenton Glass: The First Twenty-Five Years*, p.129).

An interesting bit of Fenton lore concerns the arrival of a mysterious, eccentric glassworker in a

I

railroad boxcar. As the story goes, he knew how to make iridescent ware, and he worked with Fenton factory manager Jacob Rosenthal to launch the production of iridescent glass at Fenton before leaving. Could this mystery man have been John Gordon? Or did glassworker Gordon simply pick up his knowledge of iridescent ware while working at Fenton and then move on to a supervisory position at Imperial?

The answers to those questions may never be known, but there can be no doubt that John Gordon played a key role in Imperial's success with iridescent glass. In their book *Imperial Glass* (1971), Richard and Wilma Ross note that Gordon "had the formula for the lustre" used to make iridescent ware. The *American Flint* for August, 1915, mentioned that Gordon "who worked last at the Fenton Art Glass works ... now has charge of our dope department" and that he was building a home in Bellaire at 48th and Jefferson street. Gordon was still employed by Imperial when he died more than fifteen years later. Thus, he would have been responsible for the spraying operation throughout two decades, embracing the earliest iridescent ware in 1908-1909, followed by Art Glass (1916-1924), Free Hand (1923-1924) and Lead Lustre (1925-1926) as well.

Shortly after Gordon passed away, Imperial glassworker Cliff Vogt said this about him in the February, 1930, issue of the *American Flint* magazine: "By this man introducing the the iridescent spray or dope ware system at the Imperial Glass Works many men were given work, and that if it had not been for him they would have lost many a day's work. I remember as a boy when I learned my trade at the Imperial we made dope ware only, so I think if it had not been for Mr. Gordon's effort our work would not have been so good. But he has gone to his reward which we all must do some day. He shall always be in the thoughts of the writer."

The first iridescent color introduced by Imperial was Rubigold, and it was soon followed by Azur and Helios, both of which were well established in the line by 1911 (a mysterious "amethyst" is listed along with Rubigold in the 1911 catalog, but only Azur, Helios and Rubigold appear in the 1913 catalog supplement, so the term was likely dropped in favor of Azur. Old Gold, which was iridized amber glass, was added in mid-1911. All four of these iridescent hues were illustrated in color in Imperial's catalog 100B.

Imperial used a simple code for its iridescent colors; each was given a letter, as follows: Azur (L), Helios (K), Old Gold (R) and Rubigold (M). The usual pattern line numbers were abandoned, and catalog designations for iridescent glass assortments began with the iridescent color code letter. In the May, 1911, catalog, there are two full pages which cross-reference Imperial's iridescent wares to corresponding pieces in crystal. This important catalog section enables one to pinpoint the original designations for many of Imperial's iridescent products.

Later, new iridescent colors were introduced and new names were sometimes coined: the term Rainbow appears in the second edition of Imperial's Bargain Book, but not in the Supplement to the Bargain Books or in later Imperial catalogs. In the Supplement to the Bargain Book, however, no fewer than seven "bright iridescent colors" were listed; Imperial's descriptions are given in brackets:

color 22, Peacock ["This glass has a very brilliant iridescence, but the effect is not loud. Every color of the rainbow is represented; a golden yellow predominating. Many color variations"];

color M, Rubigold ["Our famous dark red iridescent glass with tints of other colors. The biggest selling line of iridescent glass in the world."];

color 52 Nuruby ["Very similar to Rubigold, but because used mainly on plain designs, a slight change in chemicals was necessary."];

color 53 Saphire ["a dark blue-gray iridescent color on crystal glass. An entirely new, expensive looking effect."];

color L Azur ["A very brilliant blue iridescent effect, on dark amethyst glass. All colors of the rainbow such as : yellow, green, rose, combine in this treatment."];

color 12, Purple Glaze ["A very brilliant blue iridescent effect, on dark amethyst glass. The effect is similar to that of the plain blue iridescent on the expensive lead lustre glass."];

color K, Helios ["A silvery iridescence on green glass, very beautiful."].

The Supplement to the Bargain Books also served to introduce six "Satin iridescent colors" as follows: color 44 Iris Ice ["white crizzled on crystal glass"]; color 56 Rose Ice ["pink crizzled on crystal glass"]; color 50 Blue Ice ["blue crizzled on crystal glass"]; color 58 Amber Ice ["crizzled on amber glass"]; color 25 Green Ice ["crizzled on green glass"]; and color 54 Amethyst Ice ["crizzled on mulberry glass"]. Some of these were also available with cutting motifs (see **Ice** earlier in this book).

I

Several assortments of "lustre iridescent on transparent blown glass" are pictured in the Supplement to the Bargain Books. There were just seven different vase shapes, but these were not part of Imperial's Lead Lustre line, despite the similarity in terminology (see **Lead Lustre** later in this book). All seven lustre iridescent vases were available in four Imperial colors—Nuruby, Sapphire, Peacock and Purple Glaze—and several decorative cutting motifs were also available.

One of the cutting motifs, Imperial's cut 12, has been labelled "Balloons" by Carnival glass collectors, and another, Imperial's cut 99, is called "Etched Lustre" (there is, however, no etching involved). In their *Imperial Glass*, Richard and Wilma Ross noted that a Belgian worker, Telesphore Naome, joined Imperial in 1925. He was in charge of the cutting department, and he might have developed these motifs.

The Supplement to the Bargain Books also mentions Blue Glow and Red Glow, describing them as "similar to Nuruby and Sapphire." Three plain colors (i. e., "without iridescence") were also described: color 20 Nugreen ["a bluish green plain glass"]; color 30 Mulberry ["a plain amethyst glass"]; and color 40 amber ["a plain amber glass"].

Imperial catalogs 200 and 201 (both issued in the late 1920s) list Rubigold, Sapphire and Peacock as well as three of the satin iridescent colors—Rose Ice, Blue Ice and Iris Ice. Sapphire, the 200 catalog explains, "takes successfully the place of the more expensive old Azur, which is made no more."

Clearly, the ranks of Imperial's iridescent colors had been greatly diminished by about 1930. Imperial's catalog 300 mentioned only Rubigold, and there is no iridescent ware in the firm's catalog 400. Imperial catalogs and price lists from the 1940s and 1950s list no iridescent wares. In the early 1960s, the iridescent hues Rubigold and Peacock were reborn as "Carnival glass" and became one of Imperial's most successful lines (see **Carnival glass** earlier in this book).

No. 1081 ice cream.

No. 2081 ice cream.

698. Basket

ICE CREAMS

During the first few years of its existence, the Imperial Glass Company produced quite a few different dishes suitable for ice cream or sherbet. These illustrations are from the firm's 1907 catalogue.

IDA

This is Weatherman's name for a series of rather plain items shown in a 1930s Imperial catalogue. In addition to a relish tray, five sizes of plates, a cream/sugar set, and cups and saucers, this grouping includes two soup bowl, a baked apple dish and a shrimp cocktail bowl with insert. Imperial's numbers on these suggest that most come from the No. 85 line, which will be discussed in the next volume of this series.

ILLUMINATING GOODS

In the American glassware industry, the phrase "illuminating goods" was used to embrace all sorts of appliances used in this area except for various sorts of pressed and/or blown lamps. Included among the Imperial's early illuminating goods were bobeches, globes, smoke shades, stalactitites, and Welsbach shades (see the Archers' book, pp. 1-20). These were available in a wide variety of styles ranging from elaborate pressed patterns similar to tableware motifs to plain articles which could be decorated by frosting, engraving or sandblasting.

IMPERIAL'S BASKET

Carnival glass collectors use this name to refer to Imperial's No. 698 basket, which was part of a large line of glassware in this pattern.

No. 9 ink stand.
diameter 5¾ inches.

244 ink stand.
2⅝ inches high.

IMPERIAL JADE

(see **Jade** later in this book)

IMPERIAL JEWELS CANDLE HOLDERS

These are mistakenly attributed to Imperial in Edwards' books on Carnival glass. They were made by the Diamond Glass-Ware Company of Indiana, Pa., about 1924 (see *Dugan/Diamond: The Story of Indiana, Pennsylvania, Glass*, p. 112) .

IMPERIAL JEWELS LINE

(see **Jewels, Imperial** in this book and **Art Glass** in the previous volume of this series)

IMPERIAL PAPERWEIGHT

Long thought to be a paperweight by Carnival glass collectors, this article is actually a "change tray" and is mentioned in documents from Imperial's archives (see **Change Tray** in the previous volume of this series).

IMPERIAL RUBY COLOR

From time to time through its history, Imperial produced some excellent quality ruby glass. Some articles from the Candlewick line, for example, were first made in ruby in 1937-38, and production of stemware items apparently continued into the early 1940s (see p. 193 of the previous volume of this series). Ruby was popular in the 1960s, and Imperial's catalog 69 contained an impressive assortment of ruby pieces called "Imperial's ruby" (see Figs. 1774-1796).

INCA TILE TUMBLERS

(see **Tile tumblers** in the next volume of this series)

INCAN TUMBLERS

The same tumbler motif, Imperial's No. 996 Toltec, had four different names, depending upon the color of the glass and the decoration. "Incan" was decorated with black and gold on crystal, while "Aztec" consisted of mat black on crystal glass and "Peruvian" was decorated with satin white on crystal. The fourth, "Pizarro," was made of amber glass and decorated with satin yellow. Each was made in three sizes (see **Aztec** on p. 43 of the previous volume in this series).

INK STANDS

Several of these utilitarian items are shown in Imperial's first catalogue, which was issued in 1904.

INTERIOR RIB

This name is used by Carnival glass collectors. The item in question is a vase, and it was shape 119 in Imperial's line of transparent Lustre Iridescent pieces.

IPSWICH No. 1405

(see **Heisey moulds** earlier in this book)

IVORY SATIN

This color made its debut in Imperial's 1978 catalogue, where 15 giftware items were shown. The color is reminiscent of Imperial's Midwest Custard glass. A few additional items of Ivory Satin were added in 1979, and the color was shown for the last time in Imperial's 1980 catalogue.

Imperial Glass
Handcrafted by Lenox

1981 Supplement

This opaque green color was made about 1960 (see **Dynasty Jade** earlier in this book) and again in 1980-83. The color varies among pressed and blown items, but the 1960 wares tend to be somewhat lighter in color.

Jade was featured on the covers of both Imperial's Mid-Year 1980 brochure and the subsequent 1981 Supplement. A two-page spread appears in Imperial's 1982-83 catalogue. Among the items made in 1980-83 were articles from the Cathay line (see Figs. 1380, 1382, 1385-1386, and 1388) as well as the Hun (or Lovebirds) vase, two plain bowls, called Dynasty and Kwangsi, which were made from the same mould, another plain bowl (Hai) and several plain vases: Honan, Mei, Li Po, Lu Chin, Meng, and Tian.

$5.00 RETAILER

3-TIER JAR TOWERS SELL!

In Crystal, Verde or Charcoal

Yes, Imperial's lovely new JAR TOWERS
literally sell on sight!
Because they are so versatile,
clever homemakers will adapt them
to many uses, singly or in double
or triple tier . . . as planters,
in the bath or for handy snack service.
Most homes will use several.
And how wonderful for giving!
Ask for No. 400/655.

NEW ACCOUNTS:
We'll gladly tell you
how to become an
Imperial dealer. Please
write us.

For storage of cotton puffs, bubble
tablets, dusting powder or other
bath accessories.

Sell a JAR TOWER
for quick
snack service.
It takes so little
space but offers
three kinds of
goodies.

Part of Imperial's extensive Candlewick line and designated 400/655, the Jar Tower was also featured on its own with full-page ads in *Giftwares and Home Fashions* and *Gift and Art Buyer* during 1960. These were touted for a variety of uses, ranging from planters or bathroom storage to containers for snacks. In addition to crystal, these were produced in Charcoal and Verde (see Fig. 729 in the first volume of this series).

JEFFERSON, No. 1401

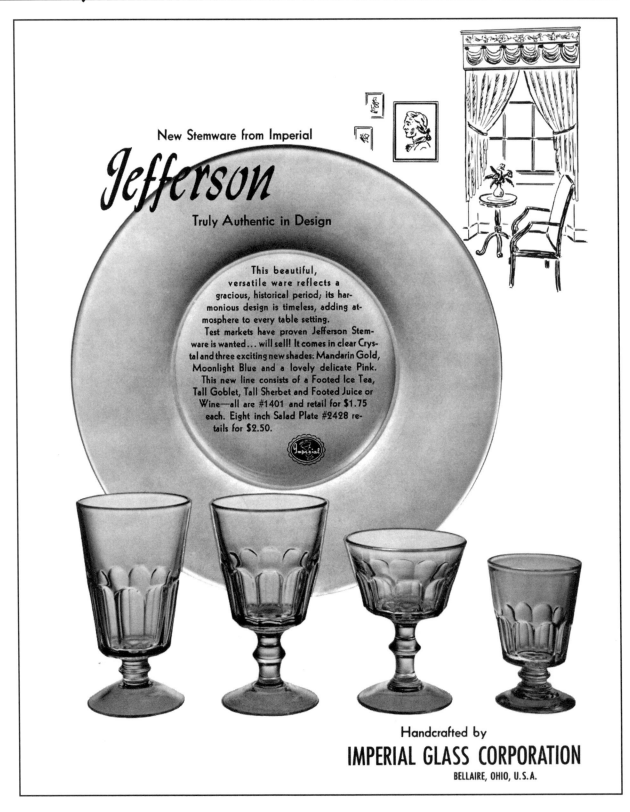

New Stemware from Imperial

Jefferson

Truly Authentic in Design

This beautiful, versatile ware reflects a gracious, historical period; its harmonious design is timeless, adding atmosphere to every table setting.

Test markets have proven Jefferson Stemware is wanted... will sell! It comes in clear Crystal and three exciting new shades: Mandarin Gold, Moonlight Blue and a lovely delicate Pink. This new line consists of a Footed Ice Tea, Tall Goblet, Tall Sherbet and Footed Juice or Wine—all are #1401 and retail for $1.75 each. Eight inch Salad Plate #2428 retails for $2.50.

Handcrafted by

IMPERIAL GLASS CORPORATION

BELLAIRE, OHIO, U.S.A.

This four-piece line of stemware (iced tea, goblet, sherbet and footed juice) was in Imperial's 1962 catalogue and was advertised on color postcards about the same time. These items were made with moulds purchased from the Cambridge Glass Co. in the late 1950s. The No. 2428 salad plate plate accompanies the stemware, and all were made in crystal, Mandarin Gold, Moonlight Blue and Pink.

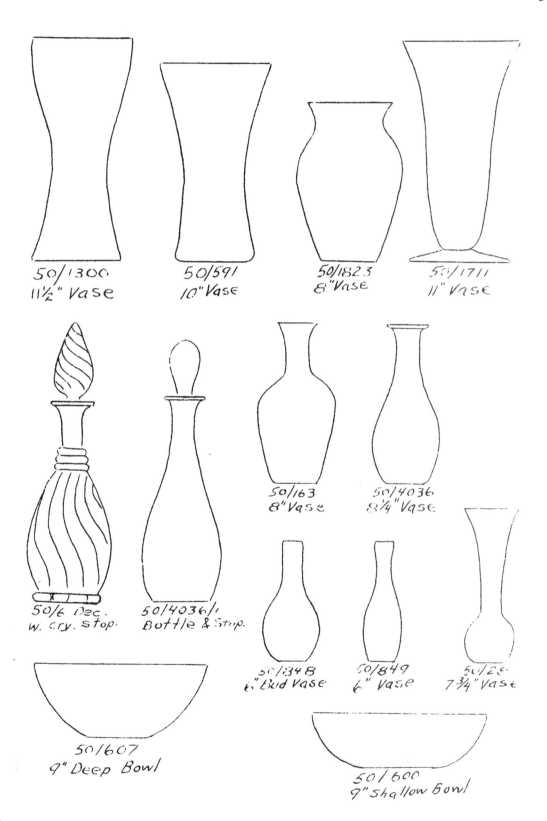

50/1300
11½" Vase

50/591
10" Vase

50/182.3
8" Vase

50/1711
11" Vase

50/6 Dec.
w. cry. stop.

50/4036/1
Bottle & Stop.

50/163
8" Vase

50/4036
8¼" Vase

50/348
6" Bud Vase

50/849
6" Vase

50/25
7¾" Vase

50/607
9" Deep Bowl

50/600
9" Shallow Bowl

This vivid yellow opaque glass (Imperial's color 50) was a feature of the plant's line in 1959, along with Burnt Orange, Murrhina and Spangled Bittersweet. There were 13 different pieces made in both Jonquil and Burnt Orange, a transparent color. The various shapes are shown here in Imperial's original line drawings.

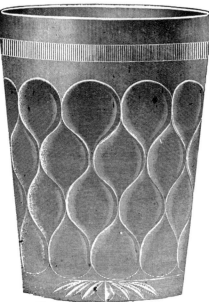

No. 298½ jelly tumbler.
shown without cap, capacity 8 ounces.
packed 24 dozen in barrel.

No. 308½ jelly tumbler and tin top.
capacity 8 ounces.
packed 20 dozen in barrel.

JADE SLAG

As Imperial's Caramel Slag and Purple Slag became popular, the firm sought to produce other versions of slag. A few pieces were made in 1966 as "Green Slag" (602 11" salad bowl and 602 6" salad bowl; No. 600 toothpick/cigarette holder; 1605 7½" bowl or ash tray; and 1608/1 square ash tray). This Green Slag, which appears in catalog 66A, was a combination of milk glass and green.

In 1975-1976, a line called "Jade Slag" was introduced. The catalog mentioned the "End O'Day" effect and went on to describe Jade Slag this way: "No two pieces are alike, and each reflects the individuality of the glassworker. Jade Slag, our newest color, brings an oriental feel in shades of turquoise-green with white milk glass; an exciting highlight of today's popular decorating colors."

Thirty-two Jade Slag items were illustrated in Imperial's 1975-1976 catalog, and all were available with glossy or satin finish. All of the articles are illustrated in this book (see Figs. 1797-1837), and some glossy and satin finished items are shown side by side. Several of the earlier "Green Slag" pieces are also illustrated.

JAMESTOWN FESTIVAL ITEMS

(see **Olde Jamestowne** in the next volume of this series)

JELLY TUMBLERS

Like many American glass plants, Imperial sought to fulfill the nation's almost insatiable need for common tumblers in which homemade jelly could be "put up" for later consumption. Many of these were illustrated in Imperial's May, 1911, catalogue. See also **packer's glassware** in the next volume of this series.

JEWELS, IMPERIAL

The misreading of Imperial advertising by some researchers has, unfortunately, led to the widespread notion that Imperial had a line of iridescent glassware originally called "Jewels." This is incorrect. The glassware in question, introduced in late 1916, was featured in ads in *Pottery, Glass and Brass Salesman* (December 16, 1916) and *Crockery and Glass Journal* (December 21, 1916). It was called simply "Art Glass" by the Imperial Glass Company (see the discussion of **Art Glass** in the previous volume of this series and the article "Imperial Jewels ... Not!" in *Glass Collector's Digest*, June/July, 1995).

Kallaglas

NEW!
Designed by Erwin Kalla
for

NEW ACCOUNTS:
We'll gladly tell you
how to become an Imperial Dealer.
Please, write us!

Order No. 990	List
12 oz. Footed Tumbler	$1.50
6 oz. Footed Sherbet	1.50
5½″ Nappy	1.00
18 oz. Tumbler	1.00
15 oz. Tumbler	.90
12 oz. Tumbler	.80
6 oz. Tumbler	.70
9½″ Plate	1.85
7½″ Plate (not shown)	1.50
Double Old Fashion (not shown)	.90

Never shown before . . . a completely new and different textured ware in four beautiful transparent pastel colors . . . Heather, Green, Brown and Turquoise. Gracefully shaped, yet so practical for every serving occasion.

As the name reveals, this highly textured ware was designed by Erwin Kalla. First marketed in 1961, Kallaglas is somewhat similar to the earlier Bambu line. There were ten items in the Kallaglas line: 6 oz. footed sherbet; 12 oz. footed tumbler; 18 oz. tumbler; 15 oz. tumbler; 12 oz. tumbler; 6 oz. tumbler; double old fashion; 5½″ nappy; 7½″ plate; and 9½″ plate. All were produced in Bead Green, Flask Brown, Heather, and Turquoise. In some Imperial advertising, Kallaglas plates were combined with Bambu items (see pp. 45-47 of the previous volume in this series).

KATY

This is Weatherman's name for Imperial's No. 749, which the factory called either"Lace Edge" or "Laced Edge" (see **Lace Edge** later in this book).

KEG TUMBLERS

As the name suggests, these resemble wooden kegs. Made in the mid-1960s, they come in three sizes—K1 (Cracker Barrel, intended for snacks such as chips and pretzels; see Fig. 967), K2 (Pony Keg; see Fig. 968), and K3 (Big Keg). All were made in crystal with bright gold decoration and in amber with bright gold decoration (these were called "two-tone crystal" and "two-tone amber," respectively, in Imperial's sales materials).

KENNEDY COIN PLATE

(see **Crystal Coins** earlier in this book)

do you WANT A MAN

—to be completely pleased with your personal thoughtfulness? Then give him EIGHT of these amberwood-hued, all-purpose hospitable "Cracker Barrel Tumblers," in the new, popular Squat Shape by Imperial. Pipe-Blown, Quality, stave-patterned Glass 13 oz. Keg Tumblers, hoops decorated by hand with 22 carat Gold, then kiln-fired. We'll insert your card. $12 per Set, Gift Boxed, Prepaid.

Old Hay Shed Gift Shop
P. O. Box 563
Bellaire, Ohio, U.S.A.

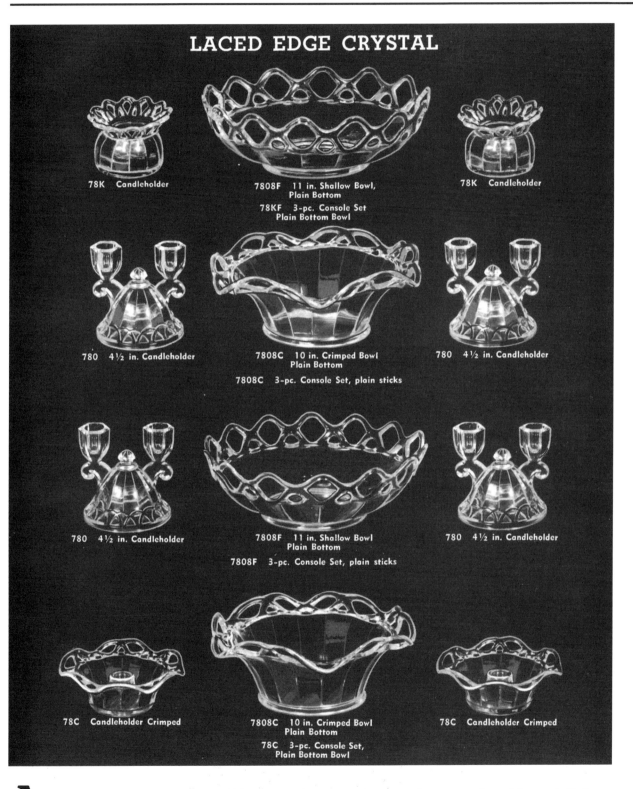

LACED EDGE CRYSTAL

78K   Candleholder

7808F   11 in. Shallow Bowl,
Plain Bottom
78KF   3-pc. Console Set
Plain Bottom Bowl

78K   Candleholder

780   4½ in. Candleholder

7808C   10 in. Crimped Bowl
Plain Bottom
7808C   3-pc. Console Set, plain sticks

780   4½ in. Candleholder

780   4½ in. Candleholder

7808F   11 in. Shallow Bowl
Plain Bottom
7808F   3-pc. Console Set, plain sticks

780   4½ in. Candleholder

78C   Candleholder Crimped

7808C   10 in. Crimped Bowl
Plain Bottom
78C   3-pc. Console Set,
Plain Bottom Bowl

78C   Candleholder Crimped

Although this line is not as well known as Cape Cod or Candlewick, Imperial's Lace Edge was an important Depression-era product which assured the factory's survival in difficult economic times. Imperial's records sometimes refer to the line as Laced Edge rather than Lace Edge, although collectors may call it "Katy" after Weath-erman's name. Some confound Imperial's Lace Edge with a similar line called Old Colony, which was marketed by the Hocking Glass Company of Lancaster, Ohio.

Imperial's Lace Edge was protected by two design patents, both filed by mould room foreman Charles W. Oldham in the spring of 1935. Patent
(text continued on p. 380)

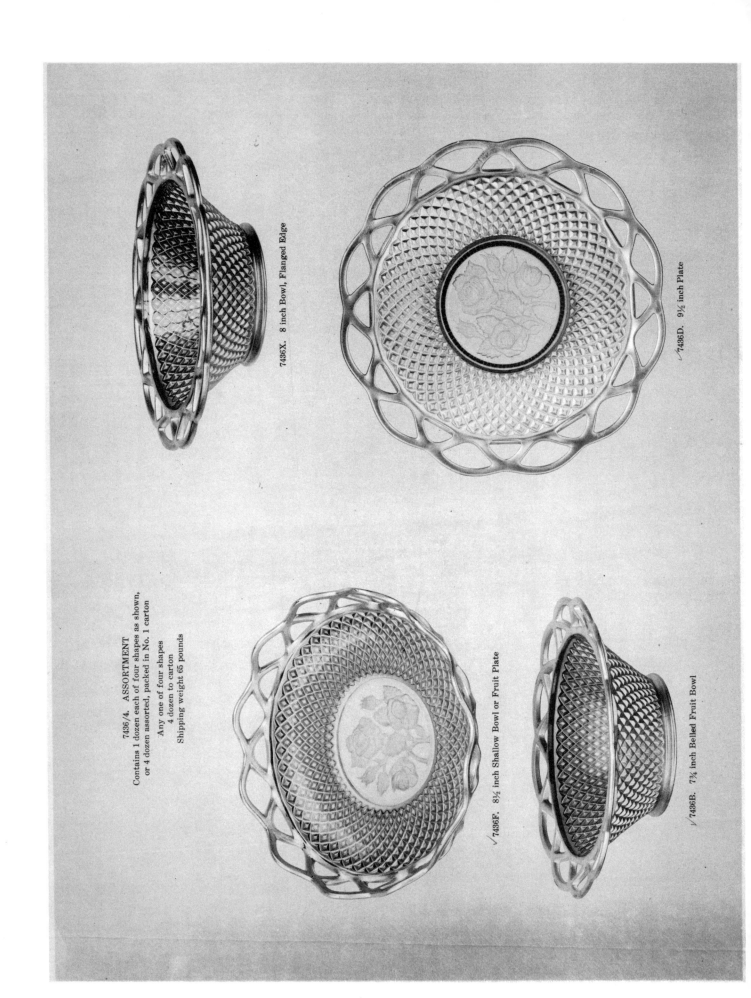

7436X.   8 inch Bowl, Flanged Edge

7436D.   9½ inch Plate

7436/4.   ASSORTMENT
Contains 1 dozen each of four shapes as shown,
or 4 dozen assorted, packed in No. 1 carton
Any one of four shapes
4 dozen to carton
Shipping weight 65 pounds

7436F.   8½ inch Shallow Bowl or Fruit Plate

7436B.   7¾ inch Belled Fruit Bowl

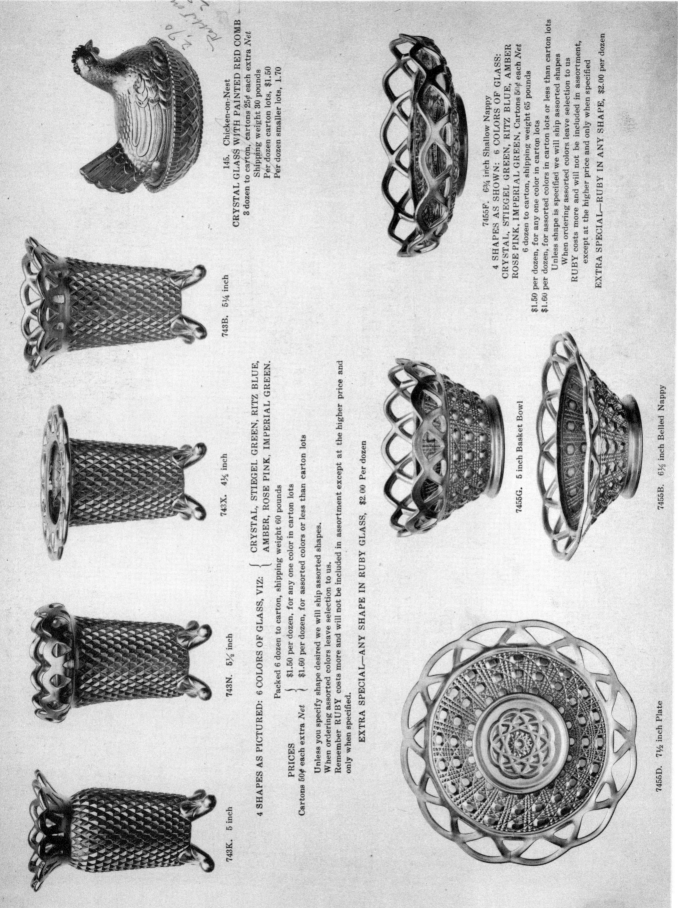

FOUR-TOED LACE EDGED VASES

743K. 5 inch

743N. 6½ inch

743X. 4½ inch

743B. 5¼ inch

145. Chicken-on-Nest
CRYSTAL GLASS WITH PAINTED RED COMB
3 dozen to carton, cartons 25¢ each extra Net
Shipping weight 30 pounds
Per dozen carton lots, $1.50
Per dozen smaller lots, 1.70

4 SHAPES AS PICTURED: 6 COLORS OF GLASS, VIZ: { CRYSTAL, STIEGEL GREEN, RITZ BLUE, AMBER, ROSE PINK, IMPERIAL GREEN.

Packed 6 dozen to carton, shipping weight 60 pounds

PRICES
Cartons 50¢ each extra Net
$1.50 per dozen, for any one color in carton lots
$1.60 per dozen, for assorted colors or less than carton lots

Unless you specify shape desired we will ship assorted shapes.
When ordering assorted colors leave selection to us.
Remember RUBY costs more and will not be included in assortment except at the higher price and only when specified.

EXTRA SPECIAL—ANY SHAPE IN RUBY GLASS, $2.00 Per dozen

7455F. 6¾ inch Shallow Nappy
4 SHAPES AS SHOWN: 6 COLORS OF GLASS:
CRYSTAL, STIEGEL GREEN, RITZ BLUE, AMBER
ROSE PINK, IMPERIAL GREEN, Cartons 51¢ each Net
6 dozen to carton, shipping weight 65 pounds
$1.50 per dozen, for any one color in carton lots
$1.60 per dozen, for assorted colors in carton lots or less than carton lots
Unless shape is specified we will ship assorted shapes
When ordering assorted colors leave selection to us
RUBY costs more and will not be included in assortment, except at the higher price and only when specified
EXTRA SPECIAL—RUBY IN ANY SHAPE, $2.00 per dozen

7455G. 5 inch Basket Bowl

7455B. 6½ inch Belled Nappy

7455D. 7½ inch Plate

L

#96,048, which depicted a two-handled sugar bowl, was granted in June, 1935, and patent #96,132, which depicted a plate, was granted a month later. Both patents show a design with oval-shaped openings and a three-pointed fan (or "crow's foot"). Imperial also made Lace Edge pieces with alternating small and large triangles forming the edge (these lack the fan element). In contrast, Hocking's Old Colony has openings which are generally circular in shape, and most of the pieces have a many-rayed star on the bottom or foot.

Most of Imperial's Lace Edge pieces bear No. 749 in the company's original catalogs, but some are designated No. 743, No. 745 or No. 780 (see the catalog page reproduced here as well as the Archers' book, pp. 156-157). Collectors have noted that individual items may exhibit different motifs on the exterior, but these differences do not seem to have been important during the 1930s. All variations were called Lace Edge by Imperial in original catalogs and other company records (see Figs. 1838-1905 for a wide variety of Lace Edge articles).

In April, 1935, the Butler Brothers wholesale house issued a brochure offering a number of pieces of Imperial's Lace Edge. Some of these were opalescent glass (dubbed Sea Green or Moonstone Blue) while others were in amber, crystal or green. Imperial's own catalogs mention these colors: crystal, Stiegel Green, Ritz Blue, amber, Rose Pink and green. The opalescent colors were called simply Sea Foam. Consumers who saved coupons from Friedman's Oak Grove or Cream of Nut oleomargarine in 1936 could redeem them at grocery stores for articles of Lace Edge in blue opalescent.

In the 1940s, Imperial made some Lace Edge articles on an exclusive basis for Sears, Roebuck and Co. These were advertised as "crocheted" glass, and the Imperial corporate name was not mentioned. One of salesman Ed Kleiner's notebooks notes that the Laced Edge handled baskets were first made for Sears.

Some Lace Edge articles were made with a grape motif or a rose motif in the bottom, which was then acid etched to accentuate the shadows and texture. A few of these were shown by the Butler Brothers in 1935 as well as in Imperial catalogs from the same era (see **Intaglio** earlier in this book).

Long after Imperial dropped the Lace Edge name, selected articles continued in the company's line. Several Lace Edge items are among the pieces in the 1958-59 Burgundy assortments (see pp. 69-70 of the previous volume in this series). Both the No. 780 6" covered bowl and its stemmed counterpart, the No. 78 footed jar and cover appear in various transparent colors or Caramel Slag in Imperial's catalogs or advertising throughout the

1960s. The No. 30 sugar and cream set in Caramel Slag is, in fact, the old No. 749 Lace Edge sugar and cream set shown on Imperial's illustrated sheets from the mid-1930s.

In 1968, Imperial marketed a number of Lace Edge pieces in its Belmont Crystal offerings for mass merchandisers. Despite the name, the articles were available in several colors, including Burgundy, Honey (amber), and Olive, which was much like Verde (see p. 54 of the previous volume in this series).

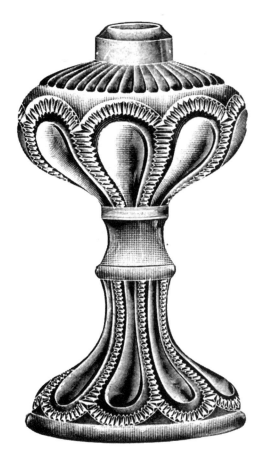

O stand lamp.

B hand lamp.

When Imperial first began production in 1904, the nation was in the midst of its gradual transition from gas and kerosene lighting to electricity. Like many early twentieth century glass factories, imperial made a wide range of lamps as well as shades and globes to serve the lighting industry (for information on these, see **electric shades, gas shades** and **illuminating goods** elsewhere in this book).

Imperial's earliest lamps ranged from plain kerosene lamps in crystal glass to lamps which were part of extensive pattern lines, such as No. 9. Several kerosene lamps were produced in iridescent Rubigold or Peacock, including No. 201 (the lamp now called Zipper Loop by Carnival glass collectors).

As a kind of illuminating glassware, lamps which used kerosene for fuel were key staple goods in the Imperial Glass Company's product lines. Typically, lamps were made in these types: hand lamps (always have a handle and may or may not be footed), stand lamps of various sizes and sewing lamps. There were also some "night lamps" (collectors call these miniature lamps today.

By the time of World War I, however, Imperial's production of kerosene lamps had been curtailed, although some shades and globes for lighting fixtures were being made. Decades later, kerosene lamps were made again, this time for reasons of nostalgia, when Imperial billed itself as the "House of Americana Glassware." Imperial's Supplement One to Our Catalog Number 62 shows several sizes of the No. 201 lamp. and these were available in milk glass, crystal and transparent colors (amber, Antique Blue and Mustard) as well as decorated versions ranging from gold or cranberry accents to all-over ruby stain.

In the mid-1960s, the Stamm House Dewdrop Opalescent line included several lamps. The No. 9 lamp reappeared as a "bundling lamp," and several of the No. 201 lamps were reissued in Rubigold and Peacock Carnival glass as well as popular transparent colors, such as amber and Antique Blue (see Figs. 1906-1921 for some of these lamps).

LEAD LUSTRE

This unique Imperial creation should be differentiated from the earlier Art Glass (see pp. 25-27 in the previous volume of this series) as well as its immediate predecessor, Free Hand (see pp. 328-330 in this book).

Unlike Free Hand, the short-lived Lead Lustre was made in paste moulds, not off hand. The Supplement to Imperial's Bargain Book (c. 1925) served to introduce Lead Lustre to the marketplace. The line was touted as "the highest type of Art Glass," and all of the articles were intended to be used as vases. A promotional circular prepared by Imperial said that the Lead Lustre vases were "made after our own recipes and by our own new method, a patent for which has been applied for, out of the best lead glass." An introductory sales offer consisted of thirty Lead Lustre vases for $50 plus $1.25 for the barrel in which they were packed; this was far less expensive than Free Hand.

More than 20 different effects were available in Lead Lustre; each was assigned a number, and three pages of color illustrations showed this interesting glassware. An undated color sales circular shows eight different colors and ten different shapes, and all the shapes could be ordered in any of the colors (see pp. 476-478).

Lead Lustre pieces are typically made of bone-white base glass blown in a paste mould so that there are no mould seams on the finished piece. While still hot, some pieces were sprayed with metallic salt solutions to create surface effects ranging from vivid iridescence to vibrant colors. Other pieces display a multi-colored marble effect or the "King Tut" (called "festoons" by Imperial) look reminiscent of Imperial's Free Hand glass. The "hanging hearts" motif (called "leaf and web" by Imperial) was also made on some Lead Lustre pieces. In one full-page ad (*China, Glass and Lamps*, January 12, 1925), Imperial repeated the "Why go to Europe?" line which had been used earlier in its Free Hand advertising.

Most Lead Lustre items were "stuck up" during production, so they will have ground, polished "pontil marks" on their bottoms (the ground, polished pontil mark readily reveals the bone-white glass). Original Imperial catalogs and sales brochures which illustrate Lead Lustre reflect at least seventeen different shapes and more than twenty exterior treatments. Each Lead Lustre vase was numbered (e. g., 418/10 or 418-10), so that the digits preceding the slash or hyphen are the "shape number," and the two digits following the slash or

SPECIAL LOT 2072 contains 2 each of the seven shapes shown, hand cut as shown, each in 2 colors, Gray Iridescent and Orange Iridescent, or 2⅓ dozen assorted Vases in one barrel.

619 Cut 93. 8 inch Bud Vase.

655 Cut 93. Vase. 6¾ inches High.

618 Cut 93. Rose Bowl. 6 inches High.

622 Cut 93. Vase. 8¾ inches High.

Why go to Europe,

to buy your fancy glassware, when a short trip to our factory will enable you to secure a better variety with a smaller investment?

at least this is what every buyer has told us, who visited our factory showroom during the last four months.

When in Pittsburgh, East Liverpool or Zanesville you can reach us by a few hours' ride.

Imperial glass company
Bellaire, Ohio.

L

hyphen are the "color & decoration" number.

The Lead Lustre shapes were numbered as follows: 319, 376, 412, 413, 415, 417, 418, 419, 618, 619, 622, 623, 643, 655, 3191, 3761, and 3762 (see p. 474). Presumably, each of these shapes was available in the different treatments as described in Imperial's Supplement to the Bargain Book and listed here:

5 dark green with bright orange interior
6 dark green with leaf and web ("hanging hearts")
10 dark blue with blue glaze, inside and outside
11 blue with opal swirled effect
12 blue with four opal festoons ("King Tut") and green interior
14 blue with opal swirled effect and green iridescence
20 bright orange inside and out
21 blue with opal swirled effect, bright orange interior
22 orange with blue festoons ("King Tut"), bright orange interior
25 green leaf and web ("hanging hearts"), bright orange interior
29 blue with opal leaf and web ("hanging hearts") and opal edge
30 blue with bright orange interior
31 gray iridescent with bright orange interior
32 blue with satin orange interior
35 canary yellow with bright orange interior
36 canary yellow with festoons ("King Tut")

37 bright orange with canary satin interior
38 canary yellow with satin orange interior
40 opal with green iridescence and bright orange interior
44 opal with green iridescence and gray interior
51 dark green with bright green interior
60 mulberry with bright orange interior
61 mulberry with satin orange interior

Several of the color and decorative effects (i. e., 6, 12, 22, 25, 29, and 36) are reminiscent of Free Hand, and these could be holdovers from Imperial's earlier, more expensive line which were combined with the paste mould Lead Lustre vases to create more attractive assortments.

One Lead Lustre assortment (Special Lot 2072) shown in Imperial's Supplement to the Bargain Book was decorated by wheel cutting. This process would remove the colored iridescent surface and allow the bone white opal glass to show. These Lead Lustre vases were apparently available in just two colors, gray iridescent and orange iridescent.

Lead Lustre is not mentioned in Imperial's catalog 200, but the firm's catalog 201 offers an assortment of eighteen Lead Lustre vases for about $1.00 each. Although the vases were "all different," this was obviously a close-out sale for, in the words of Imperial's price list, "the selection is left to us." Lead Lustre does not appear in any subsequent Imperial catalogs (see **lustre iridescent** later in this book).

This line of crystal and colored stemware and giftware began about 1979 and included candleholders and lamps. Featured on the front cover of the 1979 Catalog, Linear can also be found under "Giftables."

The Linear stemware included these items: 17 oz. iced beverage, 12 oz. wine/goblet and 12 oz. dessert. These were marketed in crystal, Nut Brown, Sunshine Yellow and Ultra Blue. Available in crystal only, the candleholders and lamps ranged from votive size to a hurricane lamp with chimney. The stemware was short-lived, but the lighting items were in the line for a few years.

LOGANBERRY

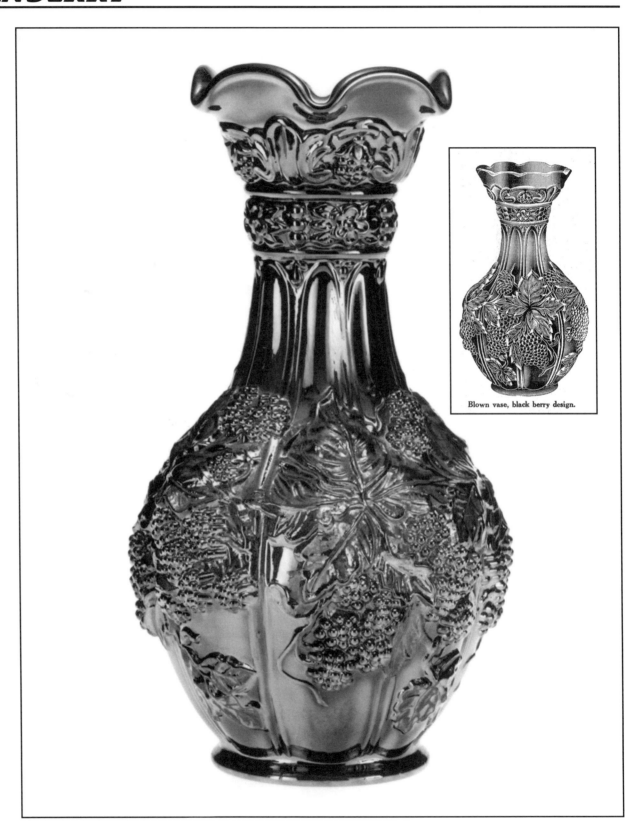

Blown vase, black berry design.

Although this vase has been called "Loganberry" for many, many years by Carnival glass collectors, it was originally Imperial's No. 477 and was, in fact, called "black berry"! When it reissued Carnival glass, Imperial adopted the popular Loganberry name.

LUCERNE CUT GLASS ASSORTMENT

Lucerne Cut Glass Assortment No. 2501 contains 1 dozen each of eight items shown, or 8 dozen assorted, packed in two cartons. Furnished in Topaz, Rose Pink, Green and Crystal Glass.

5991. 5 1/4"
Shallow Comport.

615 - 6 1/2 - 2 Hld.
Pickle Dish.

7275 W. 7"
Nappy

7255. W. 6"
2 Hld. Bowl

7255. H. 7 1/4"
2 Hld. Dish.

692/3
9" 10" Vase

7255. D. 6"
2 Hld. Plate

7605 W. 6 1/2"
Square Nappy

The No. 2501 Lucerne Cut Glass Assortment from the early 1930s brought individual articles together from several different lines—No. 599, No. 615, No. 725, No. 727, No. 760 and No. 692. The cut glass floral motif featured a stylized flower with six petals (the petals are pointed on most of these pieces, but the flower on the vase at lower left looks quite different). According to the original catalogue sheet, the Lucerne assortment was available "in Topaz, Rose Pink, Green and crystal glass."

LUNAR DOT CUTTING

L

Lunar Dot (C970) cutting on beverage items as shown in Imperial's 1953 catalogue.

The bottom two rows are shapes from Imperial's No. 785 "roly poly" line.

This cutting motif was popular through the 1950s. It is designated C970 in Imperial's 1953 catalogue, where it was shown on drinking glasses and pitchers. The large, randomly-placed "dots" are cut and polished.

SPECIAL LOT 2022

Contains 3 dozen assorted Vases, Hand Cut on
Iridescent, or ⅓ dozen each of 3 Vases shown,
each in above 3 colors.

768 Cut 12. Vase.
9 inch High.

771 Cut 12. Rose Bowl.
6 inch High.

223 Cut 12. Vase.
9½ inch High.

This line is closely related to Imperial's Lead Lustre, which was discussed earlier in this book. Unlike Lead Lustre which usually begins as opal glass blown in a paste mould, the lustre iridescent ware is a bright iridescent transparent glass. The Supplement to Imperial's Bargain Book mentions four lustre iridescent colors—Nuruby, Sapphire, Peacock and Purple Glaze—and all of these were used to make vases in nine different shapes (for several of the colors, see Figs. 1699 and 1702-1703). Some vases were also available with cut motifs.

L
MISCELLANEOUS

LA FRANCE STEMWARE

This was a short line bearing No. 2600 which consisted of just five stemware pieces , left to right: 12 oz. footed ice tea tumbler; 7 oz. footed water tumbler; 5 oz. footed juice tumbler; 3 oz. footed cocktail; and 6 oz. footed sherbet (the texture visible on the foot is on the underside). The La France items were shown in a 1943 Imperial folder along with Mardi Gras (No. 176), Twisted Crystal (No. 110), and Swedish Pinched Crystal (No. 220).

LALIQUE FINISH

Imperial used this phrase to denote crystal articles which had been satin-finished by the action of hydrofluoric acid. This treatment was popular during the 1940s and 1950s (see **Acid-etched glass** in the previous volume of this series).

LANTERN TUMBLER

(see **Marine Lights tumbler** in the next volume)

LAUREL CROWN CUTTING

This cutting, Imperial's C806, was shown on a goblet and plate in an original black-and-white photo from the factory archives.

Laurel Crown cutting

LA FRANCE STEMWARE

Leaf candy box

LEAF

This is the popular collectors' name for Imperial's No. 700, a short line of tableware which is well-known in milk glass and will be covered in the next volume of this series (in the meantime, see Myrna and Bob Garrison's *Imperial's Vintage Milk Glass*, pp. 77-80). The decorations on some pieces are worthy of note here; see Figs. 1892 and 1894, respectively for the Leaf 12 oz. footed ice tea with Aspen Green and Terra Cotta decoration (Denim Blue and Pewter Gray were also available).

LEAF CANDY BOX

Designated No. 312-A, this was a new item introduced in January, 1957. Both the base and lid are crystal, but the lid features an interesting applied colored handle in Bead Green, Flask Brown, Heather, or Stiegel Green. A memo to Imperial's sales representatives contained this note: "in case anyone wants to know, Carl Dorer, one of our mould makers and an authority on flowers, etc., says this is a Hibiscus leaf." These were also made without the handle as No. 312.

LEMON FROST

This pale, satin-finished hue is a "late" color in Imperial's history (see Fig. 1487), appearing in the 1982-83 catalogue not long after several other satin-finished colors (Blue Satin, Crystal Satin, Ivory Satin, Mint Green Satin and Pink Satin) had been in the line. Intended as.giftware, about 21 different articles were made in Lemon Frost, ranging from vases, covered boxes and dresser items to baskets, compotes and a 3-piece console set. One article, the 51792SYS candleholder, was also shown upside down by mistake and advertised as a "soap dish" to account for the error.

LICHEN GREEN

This opaque color was being developed by Imperial in 1954 for introduction in January, 1955, along with two other opaque colors, Forget-Me-Not Blue and Midwest Custard. There were considerable problems in obtaining the proper hue, as this memo (dated January 20, 1955) from Lucile Kennedy to Imperial's sales force indicates: "We just have not perfected the color we want and think it best to withdraw it before we get folks started on it. We will continue to experiment with this color and will offer it again when we are SURE we can produce and maintain a good green." The No. 132 urn was among the few items made in Lichen Green, and Imperial felt the color was too light. Further trials were not successful, and the color was not mentioned again.

LINDBURGH

This is Weatherman's name for Imperial's No. 719 line, which was described as polished crystal glass in the company's catalog 300 (see **No. 719** in the next volume of this series).

LONGHORN TUMBLER

This was Imperial's No. 779 tumbler. A stylized longhorn steer's head is shown on panels near the bottom. Made in crystal, the Longhorn tumbler is in Imperial's 1953 catalogue and was shown in sales notebooks in the early 1960s (see next page).

LOST SOUL TUMBLER

It's difficult to find the most apt adjective to describe this crystal tumbler which depicts human figures; terms such as "bizarre," "surrealistc" and "grotesque" are certainly applicable. Designated Imperial's No. 999, the Lost Soul tumbler was made in the early 1960s (see next page).

L
MISCELLANEOUS

Longhorn tumbler

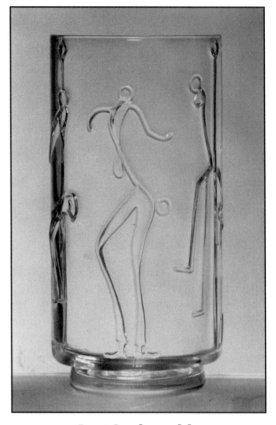

Lost Soul tumbler

LOVE BIRD ETCHING

This deep plate etching was Imperial's DE 432, and original publicity photos from Imperial's archives show only a goblet and a plate. The etching plates for this motif may have been acquired in Imperial's large purchase from the bankrupt Central Glass Company in 1940.

LUSTRE ROSE

This name is used by some Carnival glass collectors for Imperial's No. 489 line, which was originally called "American Beauty Rose" or "American Beauties" by the company. This motif was first made about 1911, and it was revived when Imperial re-issued Carnival glass in the 1960s (see **Carnival glass** and **Iridescent glass**; see also pp. 7-8 and 153 in the previous volume of this series).

Love Bird etching

COLOR PLATE DESCRIPTIONS

page 399
All of these are Imperial's Cape Cod. **891.** 160/163 ruby 30 oz. decanter and stopper. **892.** 160/163 Ritz Blue 30 oz. decanter and stopper. **893.** 160 Ritz Blue wine. **894.** 160/37 Ritz Blue saucer. **895.** 160/3D Ritz Blue 7" salad plate. **896.** 160 ruby wine. **897.** 160/5D ruby plate. **898.** 160 Ritz Blue juice tumbler. **899.** 160 Ritz Blue iced tea tumbler. **900.** 160 Ritz Blue sherbet. **901.** 160/37 Ritz Blue coffee cup. **902.** 160/1W Ritz Blue fruit bowl. **903.** 160 ruby sherbet. **904.** 160 ruby cocktail. **905.** 160/37 ruby coffee cup. **906.** 160 ruby juice tumbler. **907.** 160/37 ruby saucer. **908.** 160 ruby goblet. **909.** 160/34 ruby 4¹/₂" individual butter plate or coaster. **910.** 160 ruby whiskey. **911.** 160/53X ruby 6" baked apple. **912.** 160 4¹/₂" ruby finger bowl.

page 400
All of these are Imperial's Cape Cod. **913.** 160/3D amber 7" salad plate. **914.** 160/5D amber 8" salad plate. **915.** 160/5D Antique Blue 8" salad plate. **916.** 160/5D Azalea 8" salad plate. **917.** 160/5D 8" salad plate with yellow stain. **918.** 160/5D Verde 8" salad plate. **919.** 1602 amber wine. **920.** 1602 Verde footed juice tumbler. **921.** 1602 Azalea goblet. **922.** 1602 Antique Blue tall sherbet. **923.** 160 amber goblet. **924.** 1602 Antique Blue finger bowl. **925.** 160 old fashioned with light ruby stain. **926.** 160/119 Verde cruet.

page 401
All of these are Imperial's Cape Cod. **927.** 160/68D Sunshine Yellow pastry tray. **928.** 160/68D light yellow pastry tray. **929.** 160 Evergreen tumbler. **930.** 160/68D amber pastry tray. **931.** 1600 Evergreen goblet. **932.** 1602 amber goblet. **933.** 1600 Evergreen sherbet. **934.** Amber whimsey made from a vase. **935.** 160/119 Azalea cruet. **936.** 1602 sherbet with gold decoration. **937.** 160/105 Azalea 8" oval celery dish.

page 402
All of these are Imperial's Cape Cod. These pieces comprise the Cape Cod 160/20 fifteen-piece punch set. The cranberry rim treatment, Imperial's decoration #208, was introduced in 1943. **938.** 160/37 punch cup. **939.** 160/20V 16" cupped plate. **940.** 160/20B 12" six-quart punch bowl. **940A.** 160/91 ladle.

page 403
All of these are Imperial's Cape Cod which has been decorated with cranberry stain (this decoration, Imperial's #208, was introduced in 1943). **941.** 160/143 8¹/₂" flip vase. **942.** 160/163 30 oz. decanter and stopper. **943.** 1603 11" flip vase. **944.** 160/10D 10" dinner plate. **945.** 160/5D 8" salad plate. **946.** 160/1D 6¹/₂" bread and butter plate. **947.** 1600 goblet. **948.** 1600 wine. **949.** 1600 sherbet. **950.** 1600 footed ice tea. **951.** 160/37 punch cup. **952.** 160/35 tea cup and saucer.

page 404
953. Cape Cod 160/163 Ritz Blue 30 oz. decanter and stopper. **954.** Cape Cod 160 Ritz Blue 2¹/₂ oz. wine. **955.** Cape Cod 160 Ritz Blue 2¹/₂ oz. whiskey. **956.** Cape Cod 1602 Fern Green 11 oz. goblet. **957.** No. 104 Golden Shoji 10" vase (crystal glass painted black, then gold decorated and fired). **958.** Cape Cod 160 Evergreen 16 oz. tumbler. **959.** Cape Cod 160/116 Evergreen footed salt and pepper. **960.** Cape Cod 160 Evergreen 14 oz. goblet or ivy. **961.** Cape Cod 160/34 4¹/₂" individual butter plate (experimental color). **962.** Cape Cod Ritz Blue footed bowl. **963.** Heather Ranch Life tumbler. **964.** Heather No. 995 Concord tumbler. **965.** Heather No. 123 Chroma 12 oz. tumbler. **966.** Siamese Pink No. 221 Daisy and Button basket. **967.** Amber (satin-finished) Keg "Cracker Barrel" K1 snack bowl with gold decoration. **968.** Amber Keg "Pony Keg" On the Rocks K2 tumbler with gold decoration. **969.** Heather No. 1405 Ipswich (Heisey mould) covered jar. **970.** Nugreen No. 582 Fancy Colonial 8" salad bowl. **971.** Nugreen No. 582 Fancy Colonial 10³/₈" underplate.with gold band. **972.** Nugreen No. 582 Fancy Colonial 6¹/₄" footed bowl.

page 405
These four Caramel Slag place setting items were first made in 1964, and this color print was included in the Imperial salesmen's notebooks. **973.** No. 552 5¹/₂ oz. wine or juice. **974.** No. 552 11 oz. goblet. **975.** No. 552 5 oz. sherbet. **976.** No. 552 11 oz. iced drink tumbler.

page 406
Unless otherwise indicated, all of these Caramel Slag items have the glossy finish. Various mould numbers and names are given as well as the presence of ALIG marks on some items. **977.** No. 43154 (No. 6007) 36 oz. pitcher. **978.** Sample basket with milk glass handle. **979.** No. 43846 Dresden Girl bell, made from Cambridge mould No. 1123 (ALIG). **980.** No. 43771 (No. 965) 9¹/₂" footed vase. **981.** No. 48 7" "saddle" compote. **982.** No. 43759 (No. 613) 6" vase (ALIG). **983.** No. 1519/140 footed covered jar with seahorse handles (made from a Heisey Waverly line mould). **984.** Sample vase. **985.** No. 779 5" Dolphin candleholder. **986.** No. 297 7¹/₂" Shell tray. **987.** 43932 (No. 400) 8" Swan. **988.** 43636 (No. 104) miniature pitcher. **989.** Sample No. 463 10" oval bowl. **990.** 43863 5" Dog Collar ashtray (ALIG).

991-992. 43624 (No. 505) toothpick holders in satin (left) and glossy (right). **993.** 43528 (No. 123) 3" Cornucopia vase (ALIG). **994.** 43842 (No. 720) smooth bell (satin finish). **995.** 400/52B 6" two-handled bowl from Candlewick line. **996.** 400/62D 8¹/₂" two-handled plate from Candlewick line. **997.** Sample No. 736 Butterpat box and cover. **998.** Sample bowl. **999.** 43890 (1950/377) Pie Wagon box and cover (ALIG). **1000.** Sample No. 161 Rose butter and cover.

page 407

All of these glossy Caramel Slag items are shown in Imperial's last catalog, which was issued for 1982-83. Various mould numbers and names are given, and items should be marked ALIG. **1001.** 43771 (No. 965) 9¹/₂" footed vase. **1002.** 43401 (No. 514) 10³/₄" Windmill plate. **1003.** 43738 (No. 123) 6¹/₂" footed crimped compote. **1004.** 43735 (No. 123) 9¹/₂" footed compote and cover. **1005.** 43695 (No. 514C) 8¹/₂" crimped Windmill bowl with narrow panels on underside. **1006.** 43763 (No. 666) 6¹/₄" footed vase. **1007.** 43696 (No. 47C) 10" crimped Grape bowl. **1008.** 43641 (No. 514) 7" Windmill basket with milk glass handle. **1009.** 43794 (No. 671) 7" candleholder. **1010.** 43721 (No. 761) 5" footed compote with two-ball stem. **1011.** 43580 (No. 1950/199) 8" Shell tray. **1012.** 43199 (No. 822) Dog candy box and cover. **1013.** 43951 (Cambridge mould No. 1128) Scottie dog bookend. **1014.** 43933 (Heisey mould) small Elephant. **1015.** 43620 (No. 1) 2¹/₂" toothpick holder. **1016.** 43957 (Heisey mould) Tiger paperweight. **1017.** 43835 (Heisey mould) 4¹/₂" Minuet Girl. **1018-1019.** 43530 (No. 666) sugar and cream set.

page 408

Unless otherwise indicated, all of these Caramel Slag items have the glossy finish. Various mould numbers and names are given. **1020.** 43762 (No. 192) 8¹/₂" Tricorn vase. **1021.** No. 602 11" salad bowl. **1022.** 43698 (No. 737A) 8¹/₂" footed bowl. **1023.** 43770 (No. 529) 10" footed vase. **1024.** No. 611 covered jar. **1025.** No. 602 6" individual salad bowl. **1026.** 43693 (No. 74C) 8" three-toed Rose bowl (satin finish). **1027.** 43699 (No. 62C) 9" crimped rose bowl. **1028.** 43752 (No. 661) 5¹/₂" vase. **1029.** 43490 (No. 505) cruet and stopper. **1030.** No. 159 Lion box and cover (satin finish). **1031.** 43870 (No. 158) Rooster box and cover. **1032.** 43882 (No. 176) four-toed jar and cover (based on Northwood's Louis XV pattern). **1033-1034.** 43540 (No. 335) Owl sugar and cream set. **1035.** 43930 (No. 147) 4" Swan mint whimsey. **1036.** 43943 (No. 5/1) Bulldog Sitting (Parlour Pup). **1037.** No. 11 (Heisey mould) Scotty Champ. **1038.** No. 5/2 Scottie Dog standing (Parlour Pup). **1039.** No. 9/3 (Heisey mould) Mallard (wings down). **1040.** Loving Mice made in 1981 for PeeGee Glass of Fort Wayne, Indiana. **1041.** 43949 (No. 19) Woodchuck. **1042.** No. 14 (Heisey mould) Champ Terrier or Airdale. **1043.** 43639 (No. 459) Rooster holder.

page 409

Unless otherwise indicated, all of these Caramel Slag items have the glossy finish. Various mould numbers and names are given. **1044.** No. 52C 8" crimped Windmill bowl. **1045.** 43790 (No. 352) 7³/₈" candleholder. **1046.** 43858 (No. 1608/1) 6" square ash tray. **1047.** 43910 (No. 464) covered jar or pokal. **1048.** 43879 (No. 461) Eagle covered box. **1049.** 43574 (No. 478) 5¹/₂" Pansy handled nappy. **1050.** 43729 (No. 5930) 6" crimped compote (satin finish). **1051.** No. 156 5¹/₂" basket with milk glass handle. **1052.** Sample Flower Pot. **1053.** Sample No. 662 4¹/₂" vase. **1054.** 43723 (No. 727C) footed compote. **1055.** No. 6992 rectangular covered box with beaded edge. **1056.** 43865 (No. 1956) Hambone ash tray (Cambridge mould). **1057.** 43897 (No. 1560) box and cover. **1058.** 43325 (No. 210) Robin mug. **1059.** 43784 (No. 160) 3¹/₂" Rose candlestick (satin finish). **1060.** 43487 (No. 666) salt or pepper shaker (marked ALIG). **1061.** 43630 (No. 19) footed toothpick holder. **1062.** No. 600 toothpick holder. **1063.** 43320 (No. 1591) Storybook/Elephant mug (Heisey mould).

page 410

Imperial's Caramel Slag animals (made in glossy finish only) are among the more popular collectibles. The other two colors shown here—Ruby Slag and Purple Slag—will be covered in detail in the next volume of this series. **1064.** 43942 (No. 2) Eminent Elephant (Heisey mould). **1065.** 43941 (No. 1) Donkey/Wild Jack (Heisey mould). **1066.** 43931 (No. 10) Scolding Bird (marked ALIG). **1067.** 43900 (No. 800) Owl covered jar. **1068.** 43946 (No. 12/3) Standing Colt (Heisey mould). **1069.** 43939 (No. 9/1) Mallard, wings up (Heisey mould). **1070.** 43945 (No. 12/1) Pony Stallion (Heisey mould). **1071.** No. 12/4 Kicking Colt (Heisey mould). **1072.** 43938 (No. 8) Sittin' Duck (Heisey mould). **1073.** 43948 (No. 18) Hootless Owl. **1074.** 43920 (No. 146) Duck-on-Nest. **1075.** 43639 (No. 456) Rooster holder in Ruby Slag. **1076.** 43940 (No. 9/2) Mallard, wings halfway (Heisey mould). **1077.** No. 12/2 Balking Colt (Heisey mould). **1078.** No. 5/3 Terrier with tongue out (Parlour Pup). **1079.** 43935 Bunny, head down (Heisey mould; marked ALIG). **1080.** 43920 (No. 146) Duck-on-Nest in Purple Slag. **1081.** 43944 (No. 5/4) Terrier with tail up (Parlour Pup). **1082.** 43936 Cygnet (Heisey mould; marked ALIG).

page 411

This original ad for Rubigold glassware appeared in the April 2, 1923, issue of *The Pottery Gazette and Glass Trade Review*, a British publication. Johnsen & Jorgensen Flint Glass Ltd. imported glass from several American firms, including the Imperial Glass Company.

page 412

All of these are Imperial's "old" (pre-1930) iridescent ware, which is generally called "Carnival glass" today. Imperial's original numbers and other designations are noted, and names popularly used by collectors today are given. **1083.** Rubigold No. 496 (Hattie) bowl. **1084.** Rubigold No. 700 (Flute) crimped punch bowl and base. **1085.** Rubigold No. 492½ (Ripple) vase. **1086.** Rubigold No. 119 Crucifix candlestick. **1087.** No. 345½ Bellaire Good Will Tour (Bellaire Souvenir) bowl (Smooth Rib exterior). **1088.** Rubigold No. 473 Grape handled basket. **1089.** Rubigold No. 473 Grape tumbler. **1090.** Rubigold No. 473 Grape pitcher. **1091.** Rubigold No. 478 Pansy ruffled bowl (Arcs exterior). **1092.** Rubigold No. 405 (Morning Glory) jack-in-the-pulpit vase. **1093.** Rubigold No. 711 (Ranger) bowl **1094.** Rubigold No. 473 Grape plate. **1095.** Rubigold No. 629 (Star Spray or Strawflower) nappy in metal holder. **1096.** Rubigold No. 47½ (Ripple) sweet pea vase. **1097.** Not Imperial, this is Fenton's Peacock Tail. **1098.** Rubigold No. 582 Fancy Colonial (Optic and Buttons) bowl. **1099.** No. 452 Persian (Scroll Embossed) compote. **1100.** Rubigold No. 593 Colonial goblet. **1101.** Not Imperial, this is Fenton's Peacock Tail.

page 413

All of these are Imperial's "old" (pre-1930) iridescent ware, which is generally called "Carnival glass" today. Imperial's original numbers and other designations are noted, and names popularly used by collectors today are given. **1102.** Rubigold No. 489 American Beauty Rose (Lustre Rose) bowl. **1103.** Helios No. 452 Persian (Scroll Embossed) plate. **1104.** Old Gold No. 700 Grape (Heavy Grape) plate. **1105.** Helios No. 477 Black Berry (Loganberry) vase. **1106.** Rubigold No. 505 Bellaire (Octagon) goblet. **1107.** Rubigold No. 514 Windmill pitcher. **1108.** Rubigold No. 1 (Three in One) bowl. **1109.** Rubigold No. 74 (Poinsettia) pitcher. **1110.** Rubigold No. 473 Grape goblet. **1111.** Rubigold No. 246 (Columbia) salver. **1112.** Azur No. 473 Grape bowl. **1113.** Helios Shell and Sand ruffled bowl. **1114.** Rubigold No. 467½ (Parlor Panels) sweet pea vase. **1115.** Rubigold No. 473 Grape saucer. **1116.** Rubigold No. 473 Grape cup. **1117.** Rubigold No. 3 (Propeller) small compote.

page 414

All of these are Imperial's "old" (pre-1930) iridescent ware, which is generally called "Carnival glass" today. Imperial's original numbers and other designations are noted, and names popularly used by collectors are given. **1118.** Rubigold No. 409 (Crabclaw) pitcher. **1119.** Rubigold No. 409 (Crabclaw) tumbler. **1120.** Azur No. 434½ (Diamond Lace) pitcher. **1121.** Rubigold No. 484 Lily (Tiger Lily) tumbler. **1122.** Rubigold No. 484 Lily (Tiger Lily) pitcher. **1123.** No. 478 Pansy ruffled bowl (Arcs exterior). **1124.** Helios No. 489 American Beauty Rose (Lustre Rose or Open Rose) plate. **1125.** No. 465 (Acanthus) bowl. **1126.** Helios No. 514 Windmill ruffled sauce dish. **1127.** Peacock No. 514 Windmill sauce dish. **1128.** Rubigold No. 675 (Soda Gold) tumbler. **1129.** Peacock No. 675 (Soda Gold) tumbler. **1130.** Rubigold No. 670 Bird (Robin) mug. **1131.** Old Gold No. 478 Pansy oval bowl. **1132.** Rubigold No. 473 Grape blown wine bottle with stopper. **1133.** Not Imperial, this Scandinavian product is called Cathedral by Carnival glass collectors. **1134.** Helios No. 481½ (Ripple) sweet pea vase.

page 415

All of these are Imperial's "old" (pre-1930) iridescent ware, which is generally called "Carnival glass" today. Imperial's original numbers and other designations are noted, and the various names popularly used by collectors today are given. **1135.** Rubigold No. 700 candlesticks. **1136.** Rubigold No. 711 (Ranger) bowl. **1137.** "Amberina" No. 320 (Double Scroll or Packard) candlestick. **1138.** "Smoke" No. 320 (Double Scroll or Packard) candlestick. **1139.** Rubigold No. 320 (Double Scroll or Packard) candlestick. **1140.** Rubigold No. 313 (Double Scroll or Packard) candlestick; note the swirl optic. **1141.** Rubigold No. 635 (Premium) candlestick. **1142.** Rubigold No. 635 (Premium) candlestick; note the swirl optic. **1143.** Rubigold No. 419 candlestick. **1144.** Rubigold No. 470 (Beaded Bull's Eye) sweet pea vase. **1145.** Blue Ice Two-Handled candleholder. **1146.** Amber Ice No. 22/8 (Smooth Panels) vase.

page 416

These Azure Blue Carnival pieces were shown in Imperial's 1969 catalog. **1147.** No. 284 swung vase (made 11" to 14" tall). **1148.** No. 338 swung vase (made 9" to 12" tall). **1149.** No. 108 Rose vase. **1150.** No. 486 Masque (also known as Drama) vase. **1151.** No. 40 basket. **1152.** No. 619 Zodiac candy box and cover. **1153.** No. 505C crimped compote. **1154.** No. 473 crimped compote. **1155.** No. 975 jar and cover. **1156.** No. 11 jar and cover. **1157.** No. 163 decanter and stopper. **1158.** No. 473 wine. **1159.** No. 473 goblet. **1160.** No. 505 goblet. **1161.** No. 484 tumbler. **1162.** No. 484 pitcher. **1163.** No. 478 handled nappy. **1164.** No. 478C Pansy crimped oval bowl. **1165.** No. 454 Eagle trivet. **1166.** No. 102 urn. **1167.** No. 1 toothpick holder. **1168.** No 123 cornucopia. **1169.** No. 475 basket. **1170.** No. 100 boot. **1171.** No. 459 Rooster. **1172.** No. 10D Rose plate. **1173.** No. 5059 10" bowl. **1174.** No. 74C Rose 3-toed bowl. **1175.** No. 6122C crimped compote.

page 417

Except for item 1190, which is an "old" piece, all of these are Imperial's "new" Helios Carnival glass, which was made in the late 1960s. **1176.** No. 488 12" umbrella vase. **1177.** No. 505A tall compote. **1178.** No. 529 10" vase. **1179.** No. 473 Grape 10 oz. tumbler. **1180.** No. 473 Grape three-pint pitcher. **1181.** No. 62N Rose bowl. **1182.** No. 5059C 11" crimped bowl. **1183.** No. 47C Grape 9" bowl. **1184.** No. 474C 6" footed compote. **1185.** No. 40 9½" basket. **1186.** No. 478 Pansy 8" oval server. **1187.** No.

47A Grape 8" bowl. **1188.** No. 49 Grape 4¹/₂" bowl. **1189.** No. 282/1 jar and cover. **1190.** No. 52C Windmill 8" crimped bowl. **1191.** No. 473 Grape wine. **1192.** No. 478 Pansy handled nappy.

page 418
Pink Carnival glass was first made in 1978, and Meadow Green Carnival was added in 1980. **1193.** 42909PK (No. 146) Pink Carnival 4¹/₂" Duck-on-Nest. **1194.** 42920PK Pink Carnival 6¹/₂" box and cover (Cambridge mould 3800/165). **1195.** Pink Carnival No. 779 Dolphin candleholder. **1196.** 42904LG (No. 162) Meadow Green Carnival 5" Bunny-on-Nest. **1197.** 42920LG Meadow Green Carnival 6¹/₂" box and cover (Cambridge mould 3800/165). **1198.** 42904PK (No. 162) Pink Carnival Bunny-on-Nest. **1199.** 42933PK Pink Carnival 3¹/₂" small Elephant (Heisey mould). **1200.** 42909LG (No. 146) Meadow Green Carnival 4¹/₂" Duck-on-Nest. All of the following are Meadow Green Carnival glass: **1201.** 42772LG (No. 287C) Grape vase. **1202.** 42765LG (No. 662) 4¹/₂" vase. **1203.** 42774LG (No. 356) Loganberry 10" vase. **1204.** 42754LG (No. 109) Loganberry 6" vase. **1205.** 42686LG (No. 3897/3C) 7¹/₂" crimped bowl. **1206.** 42640LG (No. 73) 4¹/₂" basket. **1207.** 42932LG (No. 400) 8" Swan. **1208.** 42563LG (No. 555/52) 6¹/₂" nappy. **1209.** 42645LG (No. 404) 6¹/₂" bell. **1210.** 42620LG (No. 1) toothpick holder. **1211.** 42897LG (No. 156) 4¹/₂" box and cover.

page 419
All of these are Imperial's Rubigold Carnival glass. **1212.** No. 163 Grape decanter and stopper. **1213.** No. 787 Bambu tumbler. **1214.** No. 524 10¹/₂" Mum plate. **1215.** No. 514 Windmill 9 oz. tumbler. **1216.** No. 239 Windmill three pint pitcher. **1217.** No. 52C Windmill 8" crimped bowl. **1218.** No. 304 Spoonholder sugar and cover. **1219.** No. 301 cream pitcher. **1220.** No. 400 8" Swan bowl. **1221.** No. 473 Grape 10 oz. goblet. **1222-1223.** No. 478 Pansy sugar and creamer. **1224.** No. 438 8" bowl. **1225.** No. 473 Grape 10 oz. tumbler. **1226.** No. 212 4¹/₂" compote. **1227.** No. 276 Grape 1/4 pound butter and cover. **1228.** No. 149 5¹/₂" Turkey-on-nest. **1229.** No. 241 Grape cruet and stopper. **1230.** No. 478 Pansy 5¹/₂" handled nappy.

page 420
Carnival glass from Imperial's sales materials. **1231-1232.** Rubigold No. 2526 Rose sugar and cream set. **1233-1234.** Peacock No. 2526 Rose sugar and cream set. **1235.** Peacock No. 161 Rose butter and cover. **1236.** Rubigold No. 161 Rose butter and cover. **1237.** Peacock No. 474 10 oz. tankard mug. **1238.** Rubigold No. 474 10 oz. tankard mug. **1239.** Rubigold No. 241C Grape bud vase. **1240.** Peacock No. 241C Grape bud vase.

page 421
Carnival glass from Imperial's sales materials. **1241.** Rubigold No. 176 4-toed jar and cover. **1242.** Peacock No. 282 covered jar. **1243.** Rubigold No. 425 footed jar and cover. **1244.** Rubigold No. 975 box and cover. **1245.** Rubigold No. 159 Lion box and cover. **1246.** Rubigold No. 158 Cockerel (Rooster) box and cover. **1247.** Peacock No. 40 Daisy basket. **1248.** Rubigold No. 972 (Dewey) box and cover. **1249.** Rubigold No. 304 spoonholder sugar and cover. **1250.** Rubigold No. 40 Daisy basket.

page 422
Carnival glass from Imperial's sales materials. **1251.** Rubigold No. 492 swung vase, 8-12." **1252.** Rubigold No. 481 swung vase, 10-14." **1253.** Peacock No. 481 swung vase, 10-14." **1254.** Peacock No. 492 swung vase, 8-12." **1255.** Rubigold No. 286B 5" 4-toed vase, open edge (Lace Edge). **1256.** Rubigold No. 181 Rose vase. **1257.** Rubigold No. 192 Tricorn vase. **1258.** Rubigold No. 529 Nucut 10" vase. **1259.** Rubigold No. 536 Nucut 6" vase. **1260.** Rubigold No. 287 Grape 10" vase. **1261.** Rubigold No. 356 Loganberry vase. **1262.** Rubigold No. 480 Floral vase. **1263.** Rubigold No. 486 Drama/Masque vase.

page 423
Carnival glass from Imperial's sales materials. **1264.** Rubigold No. 612 Nucut 3 oz. footed wine. **1265.** Rubigold No. 612 Nucut decanter and stopper. **1266.** Rubigold No. 163 Grape decanter and stopper. **1267.** Rubigold No. 473 Grape 3 oz, wine. **1268.** Rubigold No. 225 Grape egg cup/juice/wine. **1269.** Rubigold No. 307 6 oz. footed juice/wine (the three wines—No. 473, No. 225 and No. 307—were also available with the No. 163 decanter as wine sets). **1270.** Rubigold Salz and **1271.** Peacock Pfeffer (these were sold as the No. 267 Salz and Pfeffer set). **1272.** Rubigold No. 304 spoonholder sugar and cover. **1273.** Rubigold No. 304/1 open edge bowl. **1274.** Rubigold No. 301 cream pitcher. **1275.** Rubigold No. 749B 6¹/₂" compote. **1276-1277.** Rubigold and Peacock No. 239 Windmill pitchers. **1278.** Rubigold No. 678 pitcher. **1279.** Peacock No. 489 Rose pitcher. **1280-1281.** Rubigold and Peacock No. 514 Windmill tumblers. **1282.** No. 678 Rubigold Cosmos tumbler. **1283.** No. 489 Peacock Rose tumbler (pitchers and tumblers were available as 7-pc. water sets).

page 424
Carnival glass from Imperial's sales materials. **1284.** Rubigold No. 473 Grape 10 oz, goblet. **1285.** Rubigold No. 473 Grape 6 oz. sherbet. **1286.** Rubigold No. 473 Grape 3 oz. wine. **1287.** Rubigold No. 473 Grape 10 oz. tumbler. **1288.** Rubigold No. 307 Grape 6 oz. footed juice/wine. **1289.** Rubigold No. 225 Grape egg cup/juice/wine. **1290.** Rubigold No. 96 Grape salt/pepper shakers. **1291.** Rubigold No. 276 Grape 1/4 pound butter and cover. **1292-1293.** Rubigold No. 831 Grape footed sugar and cream

set. **1294.** Rubigold No. 899C Grape 4³/₄" crimped bowl. **1295.** Rubigold No. 241 Grape cruet and stopper. **1296.** Rubigold No. 473 Grape 1 pint pitcher. **1297.** Rubigold No. 49 Grape 4¹/₂" bowl. **1298.** Rubigold No. 3D Grape 7¹/₂" plate. **1299.** Rubigold No. 858 Grape 6" handled oval pickle. **1300.** Peacock No. 473 Grape three pint pitcher. **1301.** Peacock No. 473 Grape 10 oz. goblet. **1302.** Rubigold No. 473 Grape 12 oz. tumbler. **1303.** Rubigold No. 473 Grape three pint pitcher.

page 425

Carnival glass from Imperial's sales materials. **1304.** Rubigold No. 500 15 pc. punch set (base/vase, 12 cups, punch bowl, and ladle). **1305.** Peacock No. 500 15 pc. punch set.

page 426

Carnival glass tumblers from Imperial's sales materials. **1306.** Rubigold No. 106 13 oz. Colonial Cabin tumbler. **1307.** Peacock No. 106 13 oz. Colonial Cabin tumbler. **1308.** Peacock No. 787 14 oz. Bambu tumbler. **1309.** Rubigold No. 787 14 oz. Bambu tumbler. **1310.** Rubigold No. 7243 14 oz. Hobnail tumbler. **1311.** Peacock No. 7243 14 oz. Hobnail tumbler. **1312.** Rubigold No. 113 Aloha tumbler. **1313.** Peacock No. 113 Aloha tumbler.

page 427

All of these are Imperial's Sunset Ruby Carnival glass. **1314.** No. 404 9" footed vase. **1315.** No. 474 6¹/₂" vase. **1316.** No. 22C 6" blown vase (Cambridge mould). **1317.** No. 505 8" footed vase. **1318.** No. 976 jar and cover. **1319.** No. 3800/165 covered box (Cambridge mould). **1320.** No. 3800/165C 7" three-toed compote (Cambridge mould). **1321.** No. 474C 7¹/₂" compote. **1322.** No. 3800/42C 5" compote (Cambridge mould). **1323.** No. 3800/27 sugar and cream set (Cambridge moulds). **1324.** No. 210 Robin mug. **1325.** No. 402 toothpick holder. **1326.** No. 494 9 oz. tumbler. **1327.** No. 494 9" pitcher/vase. **1328.** No. 434N 7" bowl. **1329.** No. 5057 8" bowl. **1330.** No. 489C 8" bowl. **1331.** No. 329 9" three-toed bowl. **1332.** No. 3800/72 3" candleholders (Cambridge mould). **1333.** No. 3800/49B 7" four-toed bowl (Cambridge mould). **1334.** No. 3800/57B 8" four-toed bowl (Cambridge mould). **1335.** No. 3800/57A 8" four-toed bowl (Cambridge mould).

page 428

Imperial's White Carnival glass. **1336.** 42400 (No. 525) Homestead 10¹/₂" plate. **1337.** 42062 (No. 670) Robin tumbler. **1338.** 42162 (No. 670) Robin three pint pitcher. **1339.** 42150 (No. 473) Grape one pint pitcher. **1340.** 42774 (No. 356) Loganberry 10" vase. **1341.** 42894 (No. 619) Zodiac box and cover (Heisey mould). **1342.** 42786 (No. 1155) 3" candleholder (Cambridge mould). **1343.** 42784 (No. 160) Rose candleholder. **1344.** 42615 (No. 161) Rose butter and cover. **1345.** 42622 (No. 7) toothpick holder. **1346.** 42844 (No. 809) Suzanne bell. **1347.** 42891 (No. 975) box and cover. **1348.** 42754 (No. 109) Loganberry 6¹/₂" vase. **1349.** 42756 (No. 536) 6" vase. **1350.** 42725 (No. 3800/520) 5" compote (Cambridge mould). **1351.** 42728 (No. 505A) 4³/₄" compote. **1352.** 42551 (No. 1155N) three-toed nappy (Cambridge mould). **1353.** 42701 (No. 1152) 10" three-toed bowl (Cambridge mould). **1354.** 42699 (No. 62C) Rose 9" crimped bowl. **1355.** 42685 (No. 489) Rose 7¹/₂" three-toed bowl. **1356.** 42574 (No. 478) Pansy 5¹/₂" handled nappy. **1357.** 42695 (No. 478C) Pansy 8¹/₂" oval bowl. **1358.** 42930 (No. 147) 4" Swan.

page 429

These large plates are E. Ward Russell's America the Beautiful Series in new Carnival glass. In addition to the initials EWR, the plates may have others, as follows: CJU for Carl J. Uhrmann (Imperial's president); LJK for Lucile Jean Kennedy (Imperial's sales manager); BMH for B. Marvin Hardy (Imperial's hot metal superintendent); JW for Joseph Weishar (proprietor of Island Mould & Machine Co.); RR for Robert Rupp (Westmoreland Glass Co.); RW for Robert Wheeler (Imperial/Lenox executive); and JC for John "Jack" Choko (designer for all plates except 1972). **1359.** Ruby iridescent (48 satin-finished, others iridized) "U. S. Capitol Washington, D. C." (1969). **1360.** Green iridescent with frosted center "Mount Rushmore South Dakota" (1970). **1361.** Amber iridescent "Statue of Liberty, Liberty Island, New York" (1971). **1362.** Rubigold "Monument Valley Arizona" (1972; designed by Elizabeth Cox). **1363.** Crystal iridescent "Declaration of Independence 200 Years Ago 1776-1876 Philadelphia, PA" (1973). **1364.** Dark plum iridescent "Golden Gate Bridge San Francisco, Calif." (1974; made at Westmoreland because Imperial was on strike and has "WG" mark). **1365.** Sunshine Yellow "Mount Vernon Virginia" (1975). **1366.** This blue tumbler was made as a souvenir for the first Holmes County, Ohio, Fall Antique Festival. **1367.** Rubigold insulator, marked "HUMAN SERVOT." **1368.** Iridescent blue mug, marked "Presznick's Carnival Glass Museum." **1369.** Iridescent blue mug with sueded panels: "Los Angeles, California, American Carnival Glass Association, July Fourth, 1969." **1370.** Iridescent red oval bowl "ACGA July 7, 1973 Staunton, Virginia" (depicts natural bridge). **1371-1372.** Sample Kittens basket for Dorothy Taylor and Kittens "bowl" before being made into basket [according to Taylor's Carnival Glass Encore, October, 1982, this mould was at Imperial to make samples, but it later went to Fenton where production was done]. The Storybook mugs were made in limited quantities by Imperial for E. Ward Russell, who called it the Nursery Rhyme mug. **1373.** Iridescent blue Storybook/Nursery Rhyme mug, marked: IG (ground bottom, only 20 made). **1374.** Helios Carnival Storybook/Nursery Rhyme mug, marked: IG EWR (ground bottom, 351 made). **1375.** Amber Carnival Storybook/Nursery Rhyme mug, marked: EWR (484 made). **1376.** Sunset Ruby Carnival Storybook/Nursery Rhyme mug, marked: IG

EWR (ground bottom, 390 made). **1377.** Amber Carnival Storybook/Nursery Rhyme mug, marked: IG EWR Nixon-Agnew (467 made). **1378.** Ultra Blue Storybook/Nursery Rhyme mug, marked: IG H-in-diamond EWR 1895 HEISEY 1975 (338 made). **1379.** Fern Green Storybook/Nursery Rhyme mug, marked: IG H-in-diamond EWR 1901 IMPERIAL 1976.

page 430
These colored pieces had their origins in Imperial's Cathay line. **1380.** Jade 51886 Scolding Bird. **1381.** Black Empress book-stop. **1382.** Dynasty Jade Bamboo urn. **1383.** Crystal Wedding lamp with ruby base. **1384.** Frosted Verde Bamboo urn. **1385.** Jade 51638 Mandarin book holder. **1386.** Dynasty Jade Phoenix bowl. **1387.** Black Fan sweetmeat box. **1388.** Jade 51888 Pillow box and cover. **1389.** Cranberry Fu wedding vase. **1390.** Midwest Custard satin Phoenix bowl. **1391.** Cranberry Wu Ling ash tray. **1392.** Frosted Verde Junk flower bowl. **1393.** Blue Shen candle base. **1394.** Dynasty Jade Shen flower box-bowl. **1395.** Moonstone white Shang candy jar. **1396.** Black Ming jar. **1397.** Ruby Yang and Yin ash tray. **1398.** Frosted Wu Ling ash tray.

page 431
These satin-finished Cathay items were shown in the January, 1964, Imperial salesmen's notebooks. **1399.** No. 5017 Verde Egrette. **1400.** No. 5016 Verde Fu wedding vase. **1401.** No. 5020/1 Cranberry Shen bowl. **1402.** 5017 Cranberry Egrette. **1403.** No 5010 Verde Junk center bowl. **1404.** No. 5011 Cranberry Wu Ling ashtray. **1405.** 5016 Cranberry Fu wedding vase. **1406.** 5020/2 Verde Shen candle-holders. **1407.** 5020/1 Verde Shen bowl. **1408.** 5010 Cranberry Junk center bowl. **1409.** 5011 Verde Wu Ling ashtray. **1410.** 5020/2 Cranberry Shen candleholders.

page 432
These satin-finished Cathay items were shown in the July, 1964, Imperial salesmen's notebooks. **1411.** 5002 Verde Shang jar and cover. **1412.** 5014 Cranberry Bamboo jar and cover. **1413.** 5026 Cranberry Phoenix bowl. **1414.** 5026 Verde Phoenix bowl. **1415.** 5014 Verde Bamboo jar and cover. **1416.** 5002 Cranberry Shang jar and cover.

page 433
These Twelve Days of Christmas plates were also made in satin-finished clear glass, but the iridescent Carnival glass versions are the most popular. **1417.** Partridge in a Pear Tree (blue, 1970). **1418.** Two Turtle Doves (dark green, 1971). **1419.** Three French Hens (amber, 1972). **1420.** Four Colly Birds (white, 1973). **1421.** Five Golden Rings (Verde, 1974). **1422.** Six Geese-a-Laying (yellow, 1975); some of these were also made in Ultra Blue with iridescent finish in 1976 (these have "Plate No. 7" on the back). **1423.** Seven Swans-a-Swimming (Ultra Blue, 1976). **1424.** Eight Maids-a-Milking (Nut Brown, 1977). **1425.** Nine Drummers Drumming (pink, 1978). **1426.** Ten Pipers Piping (Horizon Blue, 1979). **1427.** Eleven Ladies Dancing (light green, 1980). **1428.** Twelve Lords-a-Leaping (ruby amberina, 1981).

page 434
Most of these items are from Imperial's No. 123, which was named Coronet in 1938-40, but changed to Victorian in 1941 and then to Chroma in the early 1950s. All of the Chroma stemware has texture on the stem; the earlier Coronet or Victorian pieces lack the texture on the lower ball on the stem. **1429.** Evergreen 8" salad plate. **1430.** Madeira 12 oz. ice tea. **1431.** Burgundy 8" salad plate. **1432.** Evergreen 12 oz. tumbler. **1433.** Madeira 8" salad plate. **1434.** 43735 Caramel Slag compote (lacks cover; compare the color to the covered compote at the end of the row). **1435.** Pale yellow "cakestand" whimsey made from 43735 compote. **1436.** Sample 43735 Purple Slag covered compote. **1437.** Ruby Victorian 8 oz. goblet (note the smooth lower ball on the stem). **1438.** Indigo 8 oz. goblet. **1439.** Burgundy 8 oz. goblet. **1440.** Crystal Victorian 8 oz. goblet (note the smooth lower ball on the stem). **1441.** Madeira 8 oz. goblet. **1442.** Midwest Custard 8 oz. goblet. **1443.** Evergreen 8 oz. goblet. **1444.** Burgundy 5½ oz. juice. **1445.** Evergreen 5½ oz. juice. **1446.** Indigo 5½ oz. juice. **1447.** Evergreen 6 oz. sherbet. **1448.** Ruby Victorian 6 oz. sherbet (note the smooth lower ball on the stem). **1449.** Burgundy 6 oz. sherbet.

page 435
This original color advertisement shows articles from Imperial's Hoffman House, Provincial (made by Imperial from Heisey moulds) and Concord lines.

page 436
Imperial's No. 153 twin candlesticks were combined with either round or oval bowls to form three-piece console sets in many different colors. **1450.** Green No. 153B round bowl. **1451.** Rose Marie/Rose Pink No. 153B round bowl. **1452.** Amber No. 153B round bowl. **1453.** Amber No. 153 oval bowl. **1454.** Ritz Blue No. 153 twin candlesticks. **1455.** Ritz Blue No. 153B round bowl. **1456.** Stiegel Green No. 153 oval bowl. **1457.** Stiegel Green No. 153B round bowl. **1458.** Milk glass No. 153B round bowl. **1459.** Ruby No. 153B round bowl. **1460.** Stiegel Green No. 153 twin candlestick. **1461.** Green No. 153 twin candlestick. **1462.** Black No. 153 twin candlestick. **1463.** Ruby No. 153 twin candlestick. **1464.** Ritz Blue No. 153 twin candlestick. **1465.** Milk glass No. 153 twin candlestick. **1466.** Amber No. 153 twin candlestick. **1467.** Viennese Blue No. 153 twin candlestick.

891

892

893

894

895

896

897

898

899

900

901

902

903

904

905

906

907

908

909

910

911

912

CAPE COD

913

914

915

916

917

918

919

920

921

922

923

924

925

926

927

928

929

930

931

932

933

934

935

936

937

938

940

940A

939

940

941

942

943

944

945

946

947

948

949

950

951

952

CAPE COD, ETC.

953

954

955

956

957

958

959

959

960

961

962

963

964

965

966

967

968

969

970

971

972

973

974

975

Olden
End O' Day
Glass
(Caramel Slag)
Place Setting
Items
by
Imperial

976

CARAMEL SLAG

977

978

979

980

981

982

983

984

985

986

987

988

989

990

991

992

993

994

995

996

997

998

999

1000

1001

1002

1003

1004

1005

1006

1007

1008

1009

1010

1011

1012

1013

1014

1015

1016

1017

1018

1019

Caramel Slag

1020

1021

1022

1023

1024

1025

1026

1027

1028

1029

1030

1031

1032

1033

1034

1035

1036

1037

1038

1039

1040

1041

1042

1043

1044

1045

1046

1047

1048

1049

1050

1051

1052

1053

1054

1055

1056

1057

1058

1059

1060

1061

1062

1063

Caramel Slag

1064

1065

1066

1067

1068

1069

1070

1071

1072

1073

1074

1075

1076

1077

1078

1079

1080

1081

1082

RUBIGOLD GLASSWARE

A Golden Opportunity to Secure
"A Splendid Seller"

JOHNSEN & JORGENSEN FLINT GLASS L^TD

26-27, Farringdon Street.
LONDON · E · C · 4 ·

Telephone: City 8882.
Telegrams: "Fish. London"

CARNIVAL GLASS (OLD)

1083

1084

1085

1086

1087

1088

1089

1090

1091

1092

1093

1094

1095

1096

1097

1098

1099

1100

1101

1102

1103

1104

1105

1106

1107

1108

1109

1110

1111

1112

1113

1114

1115

1116

1117

CARNIVAL GLASS (OLD)

1118   1119   1120   1121   1122

1123   1124   1125

1126   1127   1128   1129   1130

414   1131   1132   1133   1134

1135

1135

1136

1137

1138

1139

1140

1141

1142

1143

1144

1145

1146

CARNIVAL GLASS (NEW)

1147   1148   1149   1150   1151   1152

1153   1154   1155   1156

1157   1158   1159   1160   1161   1162

1163   1164   1165   1166   1167   1168   1169   1170   1171

416   1172   1173   1174   1175

1176 **1177** **1178** **1179** **1180**

1181 **1182** **1183**

1184 **1185** **1186** **1187**

1188 **1189** **1190** **1191** **1192**

CARNIVAL GLASS (NEW)

1193 1194 1195 1196 1197 1198 1199 1200

1201 1202 1203 1204 1205 1206 1207 1208 1209 1210 1211

1212

1213

1214

1215

1216

1217

1218

1219

1220

1221

1222

1223

1224

1225

1226

1227

1228

1229

1230

CARNIVAL GLASS (NEW)

1231

1232

1233

1234

1235

1236

1237

1238

1239

1240

1241   1242   1243   1244

1245   1246

1247

1248   1249   1250

CARNIVAL GLASS (NEW)

1251

1252

1253

1254

1255

1256

1257

1258

1259

1260

1261

1262

1263

1264

1265

1266

1267

1268

1269

1270

1271

1272

1273

1274

1275

1276

1277

1278

1279

1280

1281

1282

1283

CARNIVAL GLASS (NEW)

1284   1285   1286   1287   1288   1289

1290   1291   1292   1293

1294   1295   1296   1297   1298   1299

1300   1301   1302   1303

1304

1305

CARNIVAL GLASS (NEW)

COMMON
ICED TEA
BECOMES
UNCOMMON
WHEN SERVED
IN
DISTINCTIVE
TUMBLERS

1306

1307

1308

1309

1310

1311

1312

1313

1314   **1315**   **1316**   **1317**

1318   **1319**   **1320**   **1321**   **1322**

1323   **1324**   **1325**   **1326**   **1327**

1328   **1329**   **1330**   **1331**

1332   **1333**   **1332**   **1334**   **1335**

Carnival Glass (new)

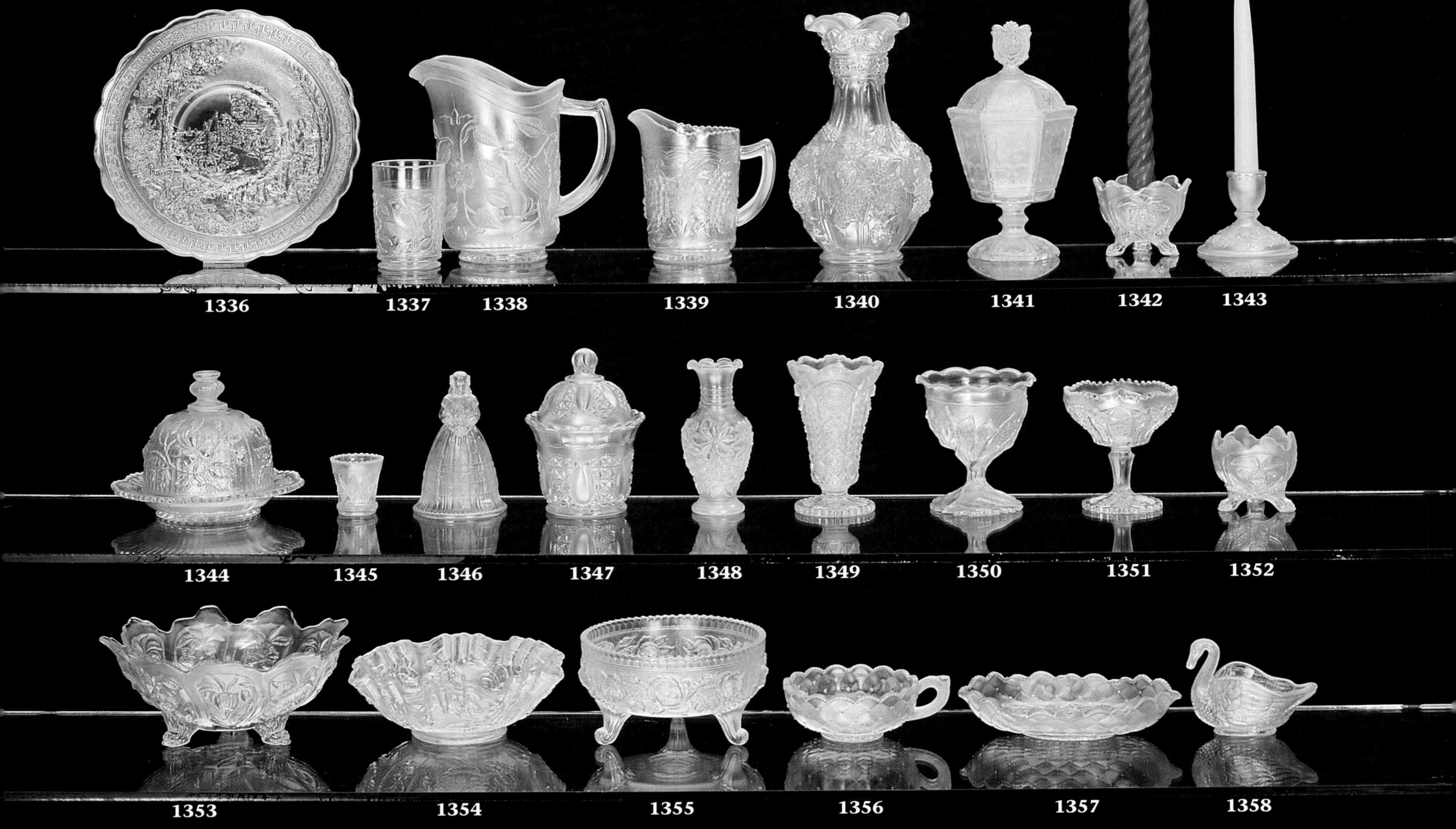
1336
1337
1338
1339
1340
1341
1342
1343
1344
1345
1346
1347
1348
1349
1350
1351
1352
1353
1354
1355
1356
1357
1358

CARNIVAL GLASS (NEW)

1359

1360

1361

1362

1363

1364

1365

1366

1367

1368

1369

1370

1371

1372

1373

1374

1375

1376

1377

1378

1379

429

CATHAY

1380 **1381** **1382** **1383** **1384** **1385**

1386 **1387** **1388** **1389**

1390 **1391** **1392**

1393 **1394**

1395 **1396** **1397** **1398**

1399   1400   1401   1402

1403   1404   1405

1406   1407   1406

1408

1409

1410

1412

1411

1413

1414

1415

HAND
CRAFTED
CATHAY
GLASS
by
IMPERIAL
U.S.A.

1416

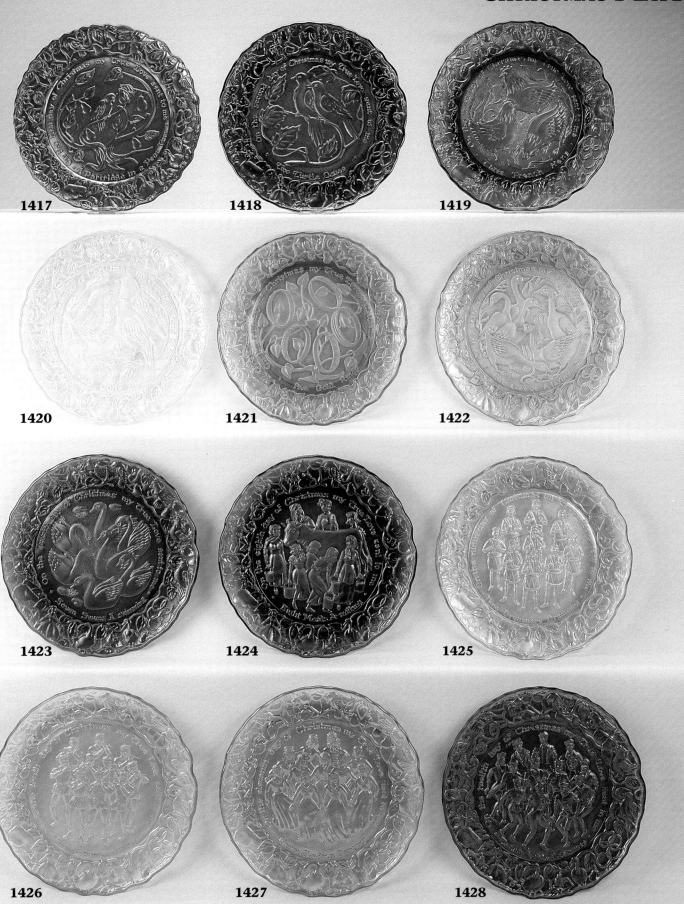

1417

1418

1419

1420

1421

1422

1423

1424

1425

1426

1427

1428

CHROMA

1429   1430   1431   1432   1433

1434   1435   1436

1437   1438   1439   1440   1441   1442   1443

1444   1445   1446   1447   1448   1449

COLORFUL, CASUAL ELEGANCE!

Variety in lovely,
hand-fashioned glassware.
Variety in decorator-accepted
colors: Heather, Verde,
Amber and Crystal.
Variety in styling, shapes,
sizes. Match or contrast
with accessories — create
a hospitable mood.
Better stores everywhere
should have these colorful,
American-made
Imperial Glass patterns.

Hoffmann House

Provincial

Concord

AMERICANA
Is Here to Stay!

. . . and will continue to grow year
after year. Imperial is proud to be
recognized as the TOP SOURCE for
the finest in this type of American
Handmade Glassware. Ask your
Imperial representative about these
and other wanted, fast-moving lines
from the "House of Americana."

CONSOLE SETS

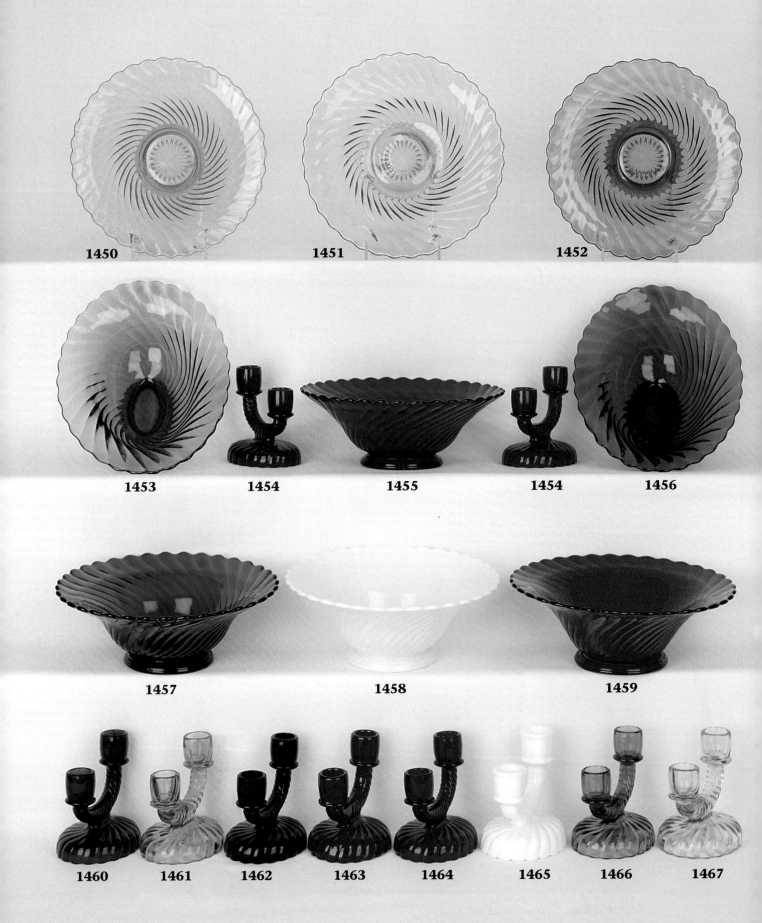

1450   **1451**   **1452**

1453   **1454**   **1455**   **1454**   **1456**

1457   **1458**   **1459**

1460   **1461**   **1462**   **1463**   **1464**   **1465**   **1466**   **1467**

| 1468 | 1469 | 1468 | 1470 | 1471 | 1470 |

| 1472 | 1473 | 1472 | 1474 | 1475 | 1474 |

| 1476 | 1477 | 1476 |

| 1478 | 1479 |

1480

1481

1482

1483

1484

1485

1486

1487

1488

1489

1490

1491

1492

1493

1494

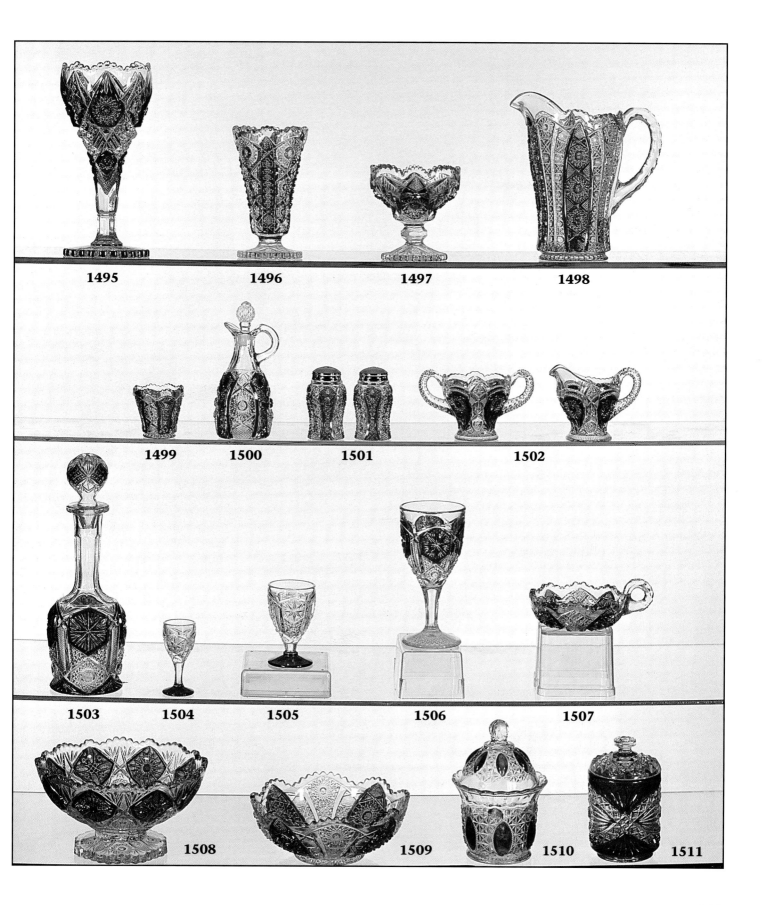

1495   1496   1497   1498

1499   1500   1501   1502

1503   1504   1505   1506   1507

1508   1509   1510   1511

DEW DROP

1512 1513 1514 1515 1516 1517 1518

1519 1520 1521 1522 1523

1524 1525 1526 1527

1528 1529 1530 1531

Genuine
OPALESCENT
Victorian Era
DEWDROP GLASS

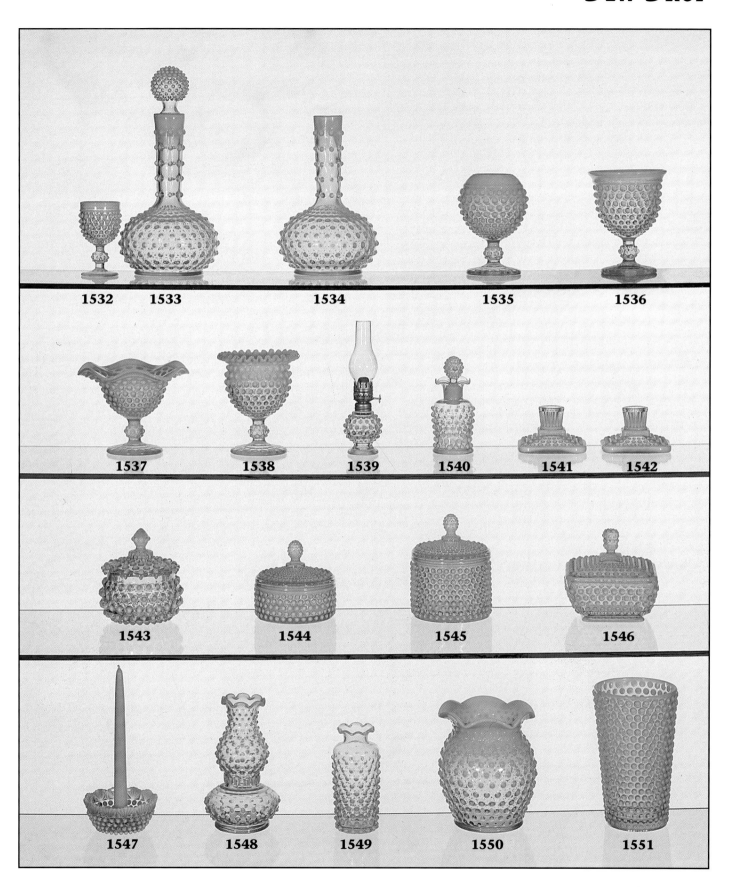

1532 **1533** **1534** **1535** **1536**

1537 **1538** **1539** **1540** **1541** **1542**

1543 **1544** **1545** **1546**

1547 **1548** **1549** **1550** **1551**

FANCY COLONIAL

1552   1553   1554   1555

1556   1557   1558   1559

1560   1561   1562   1563   1564

1566   1568   1570   1571   1573   1575

1567   1569   1572   1574

1576

1577

1578

1579

1580

1581

1582

1583

1584

1585

1586

1587

1588

1589

1590

1591

1592

1593

1594

1595

1596

1597   1598   1599   1600   1601   1602

1603   1604   1605   1606

1607   1608   1609   1610   1611   1612   1613

1614   1615   1616   1617   1618

1619   1620   1621   1620   1622

1623 1624 1625 1626 1627

1628 1629 1630 1631 1632 1633 1634 1635

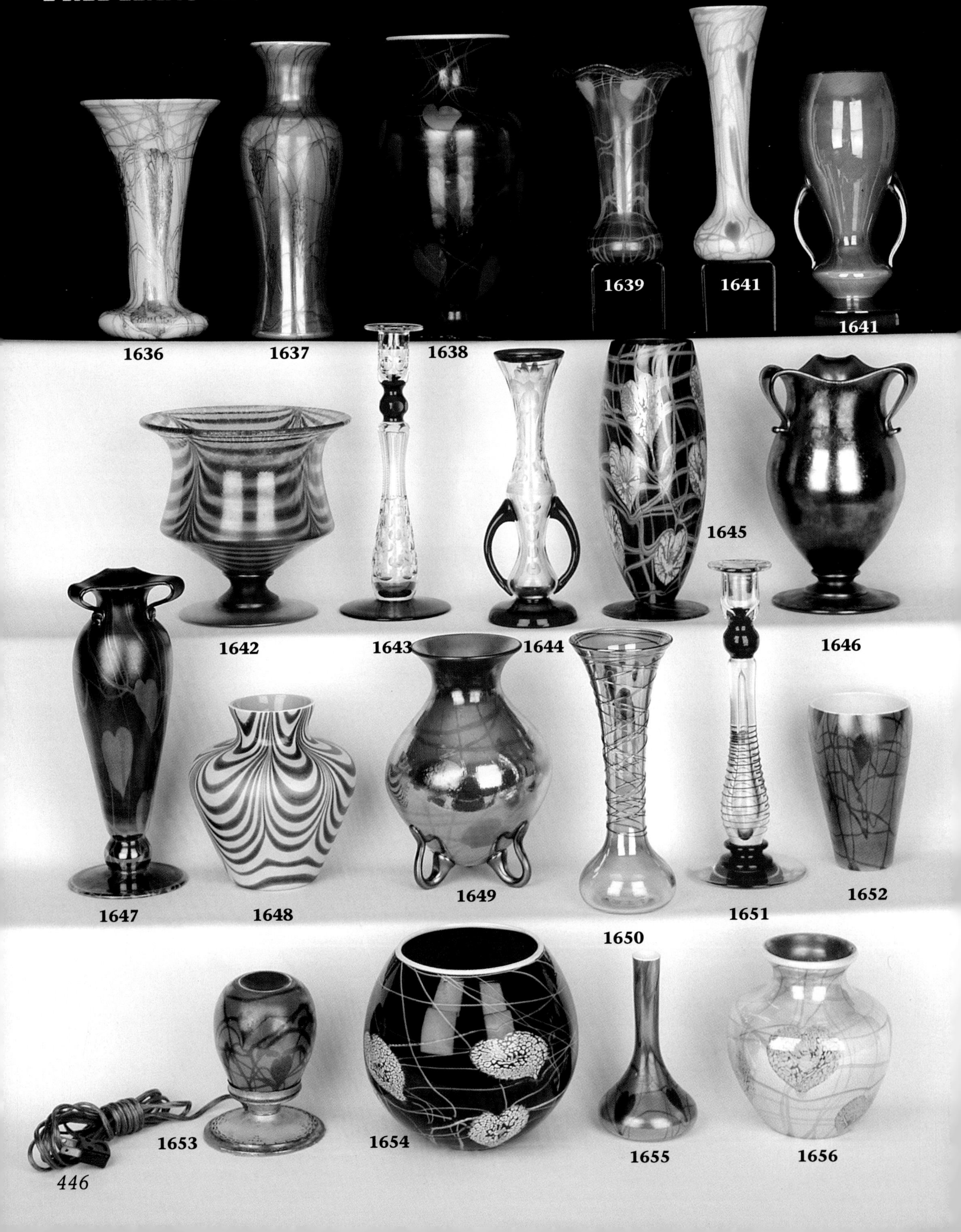

1636

1637

1638

1639

1641

1641

1642

1643 1644

1645

1646

1647

1648

1649

1650

1651

1652

1653

1654

1655

1656

446

1657
1658
1659
1660
1661
1662
1663

1664
1665
1666
1667
1668
1669

1670
1671
1672
1673

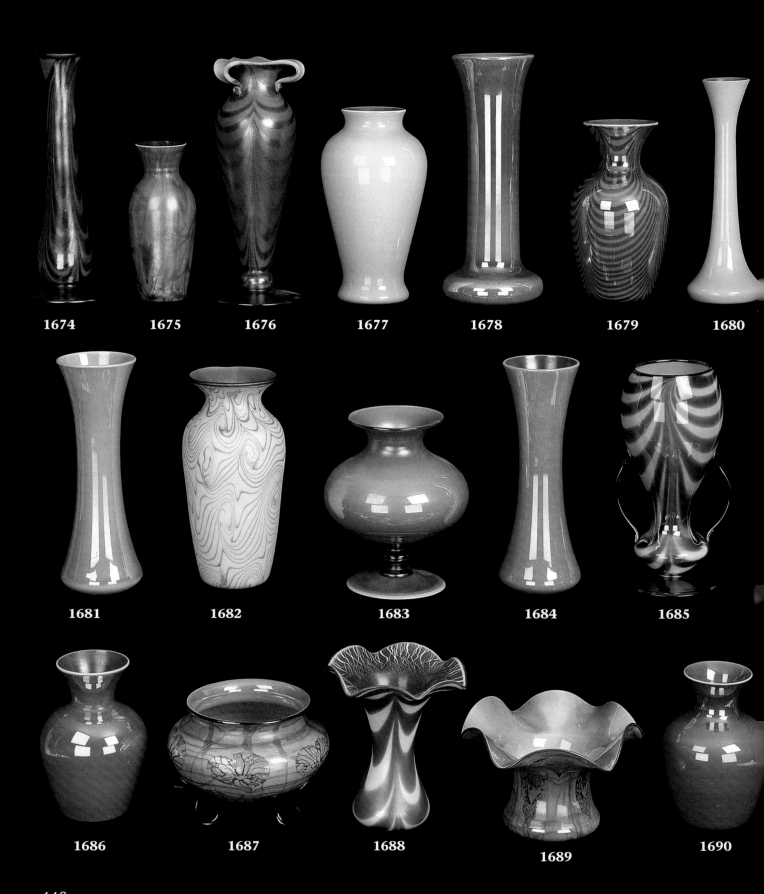

1674 1675 1676 1677 1678 1679 1680

1681 1682 1683 1684 1685

1686 1687 1688 1689 1690

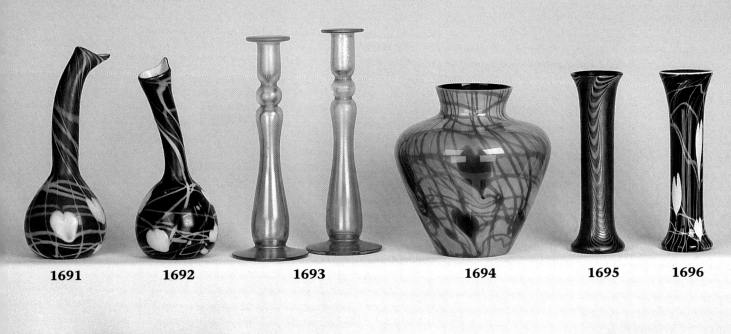

1691   1692   1693   1694   1695   1696

1697   1698   1699   1700   1701

1702   1703   1704

Free Hand and Lead Lustre

1705   1706   1707   1708   1709   1710

1711   1712   1713   1714   1715   1716   1717

1718   1719   1720

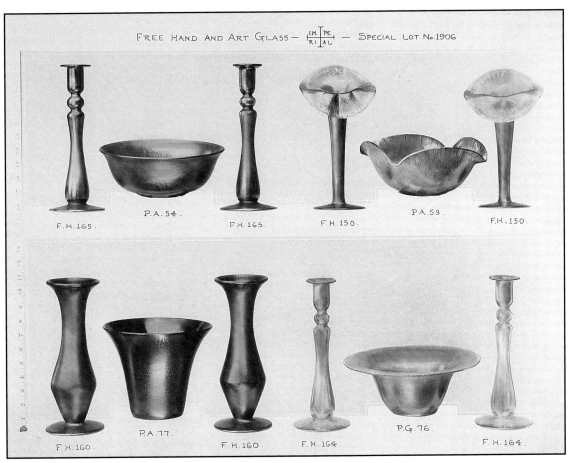

FREE HAND AND ART GLASS — IM PE RI AL — SPECIAL LOT No. 1906

F.H. 165.   P.A. 54.   F.H. 165.   F.H. 150.   P.A. 59.   F.H. 150.

F.H. 160.   P.A. 77.   F.H. 160.   F.H. 164.   P.G. 76.   F.H. 164.

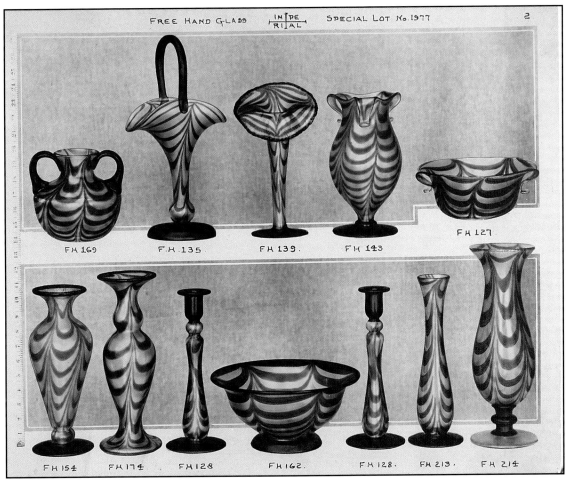

FREE HAND GLASS   IM PE RI AL   SPECIAL LOT No. 1977   2

FH 169   F.H. 135.   FH 139.   FH 143   FH 127

FH 154   FH 174   FH 128   FH 162.   FH 128.   FH 213.   FH 214

FREE HAND CATALOG

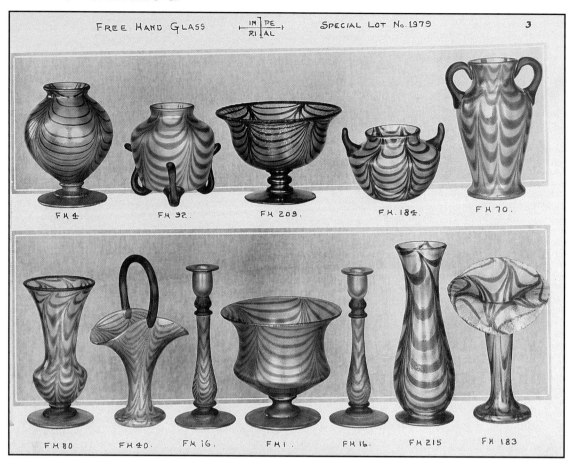

FREE HAND GLASS — IMPERIAL — SPECIAL LOT No. 1979 — 3

FH 4.   FH 92.   FH 209.   F.H.184.   FH 70.

FH 80   FH 40.   FH 16.   FH 1.   FH 16.   FH 215   FH 183

FREE HAND GLASS. — IMPERIAL — SPECIAL LOT No. 1976. — 4.

FH 181.   F.H.180.   FH 193.   FH.185.   FH 199.

FH 186.   FH 192.   FM 195   FH 179.   FH 195.   FH 175   FH 205

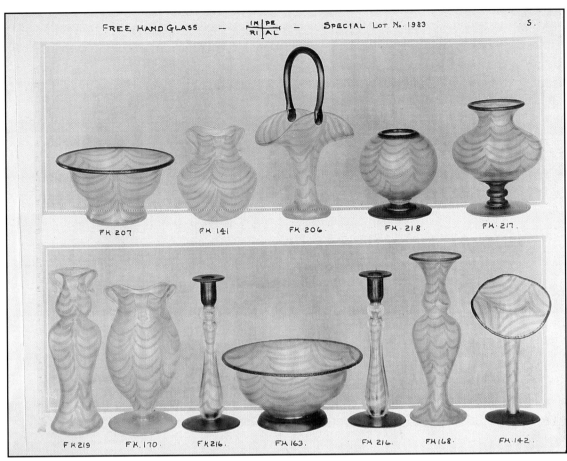

FREE HAND GLASS — IMPERIAL — SPECIAL LOT No. 1983   5.

FH 207   FH 141   FH 206   FH 218   FH 217.

FH 219   FH 170.   FH 216.   FH 163.   FH 216.   FH 168.   FH 142.

FREE HAND GLASS.   IMPERIAL   SPECIAL LOT No. 1978   6

FH 10   FH 21.   FH 57.   FH 210   FH 17.   FH 189.

FH 109   FH 13   FH 165   FH 208   FH 165   FH 190.

FREE HAND CATALOG

FREE HAND GLASS [IM PE / RI AL] SPECIAL LOT No. 1973   7.

FH 201.   FH 196.   FH 197.   FH 202   FH 203

FH 157   FH 200   FH 194.   FH 204.   FH 194.   FH 191   FH 198

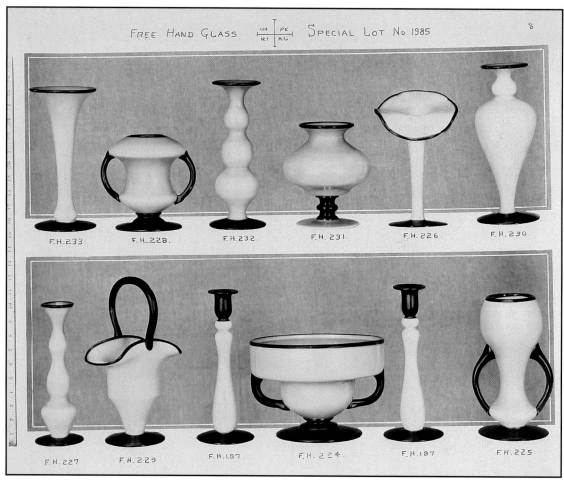

FREE HAND GLASS [IM PE / RI AL] SPECIAL LOT No. 1985   8

F.H. 233.   F.H. 228.   F.H. 232.   F.H. 231.   F.H. 226   F.H. 230.

F.H. 227   F.H. 229.   F.H. 187.   F.H. 224.   F.H. 187.   F.H. 225.

FREE HAND GLASS · IMPERIAL · SPECIAL LOT No. 1986. 9.

F. H. 240. F. H. 237. F. H. 242. F. H. 241. F. H. 236.

F. H. 235. F. H. 238. F. H. 234. F. H. 223. F. H. 234. F. H. 239. F. H. 243.

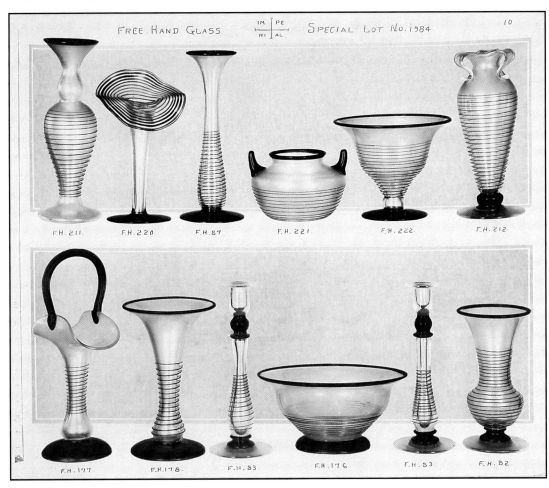

FREE HAND GLASS · IMPERIAL · SPECIAL LOT No. 1984 10

F. H. 211. F. H. 220. F. H. 87. F. H. 221. F. H. 222. F. H. 212.

F. H. 177. F. H. 178. F. H. 83. F. H. 176. F. H. 83. F. H. 82.

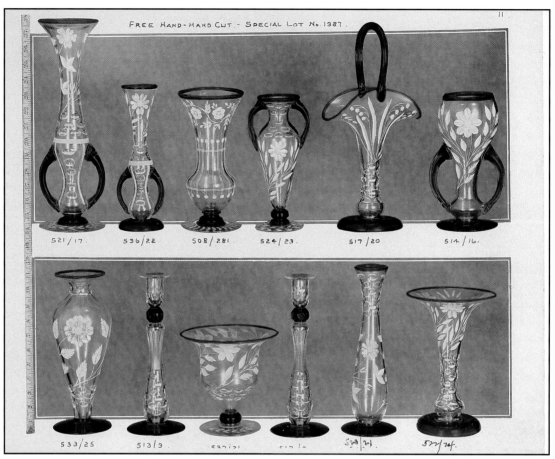

FREE HAND - HAND CUT - SPECIAL LOT No. 1987.

521/17.   536/22.   508/2.81.   524/23.   517/20.   514/16.

533/25.   513/9.   522/21.   512/0.   522/21.   522/24.

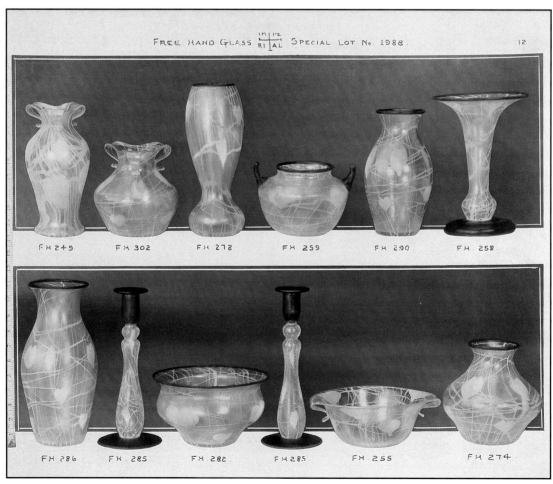

FREE HAND GLASS IMPERITAL SPECIAL LOT No. 1988.

FH 249.   FH 302.   FH 272.   FH 259.   FH 290.   FH 258.

FH 286.   FH 285.   FH 282.   FH 285.   FH 255.   FH 274.

FREE HAND GLASS [IMPERIAL] SPECIAL LOT No. 1989.   13.

F.H. 310.   F.H. 301.   F.H. 316.   F.H. 292.   F.H. 298.   F.H. 292.

F.H. 318   F.H. 312.   F.H. 306.   F.H. 313.   F.H. 314   F.H. 315.

FREE HAND GLASS [IMPERIAL] SPECIAL LOT No. 1990.   14.

F.H. 271   F.H. 293.   F.H. 303.   F.H. 247   F.H. 266.   F.H. 265.

F.H. 288   F.H. 317.   F.H. 279.   F.H. 276   F.H. 248.   F.H. 273.

FREE HAND CATALOG

FREE HAND GLASS ⊞ SPECIAL LOT 1991.   15

F.H. 309   F.H. 281   F.H. 244   F.H. 262   F.H. 294   F.H. 264

F.H. 322   F.H. 326   F.H. 272   F.H. 275   F.H. 260   F.H. 257

FREE HAND GLASS ⊞ SPECIAL LOT No. 2000.   17.

F.H. 338   F.H. 358   F.H. 324   F.H. 343   F.H. 339   F.H. 323

F.H. 342   F.H. 344   F.H. 325   F.H. 341   F.H. 345   F.H. 340

FREE HAND GLASS [IM|PE / RI|AL] SPECIAL LOT No. 2003.   18.

F.H. 357.   F.H. 307.   F.H. 356   F.H. 355   F.H. 361.   F.H. 354.

F.H. 353.   F.H. 362.   F.H. 352.   F.H. 360.   F.H. 352   F.H. 295.

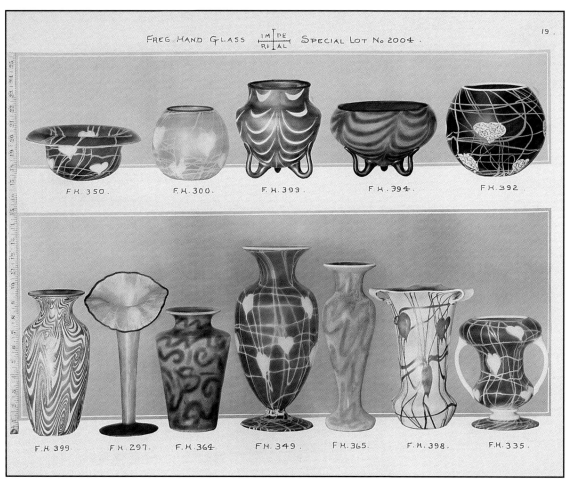

FREE HAND GLASS [IM|PE / RI|AL] SPECIAL LOT No. 2004.   19.

F.H. 350.   F.H. 300.   F.H. 393.   F.H. 394.   F.H. 392.

F.H. 399   F.H. 297.   F.H. 364   F.H. 349.   F.H. 365.   F.H. 398.   F.H. 335.

FREE HAND CATALOG

FREE HAND GLASS ⊞ IM|PE / RI|AL SPECIAL LOT No. 2001.   '20

F.H. 336.   F.H. 331   F.H. 329   F.H. 332.   F.H. 359.

F.H. 337.   F.H. 327.   F.H. 330.   F.H. 333.   F.H. 330.   F.H. 334.   F.H. 328.

FREE HAND — HAND CUT — IM|PE / RI|AL — SPECIAL LOT No. 2005.   21.

F.H. 700/51.   F.H. 703/48   F.H. 709/46.   F.H. 701/48   F.H. 704/48.

F.H. 706/47.   F.H. 707/52.   F.H. 711/9.   F.H. 714/50.   F.H. 711/9.   F.H. 708/49.   710/47.

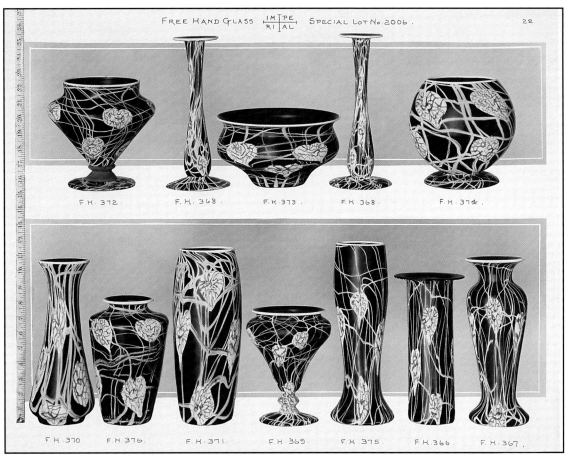

Free Hand Glass IMPERIAL Special Lot No. 2006. 22

F.H. 372. F.H. 368. F.H. 373. F.H. 368. F.H. 374.

F.H. 370 F.H. 376. F.H. 371. F.H. 369. F.H. 375. F.H. 366. F.H. 367.

Free Hand Glass IMPERIAL Special Lot No. 2007. 23.

F.H. 386. F.H. 381. F.H. 384. F.H. 383. F.H. 388. F.H. 380.

F.H. 378. F.H. 387. F.H. 379. F.H. 382. F.H. 379. F.H. 385.

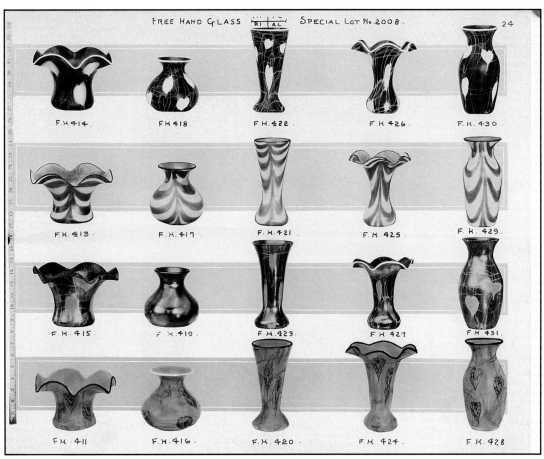

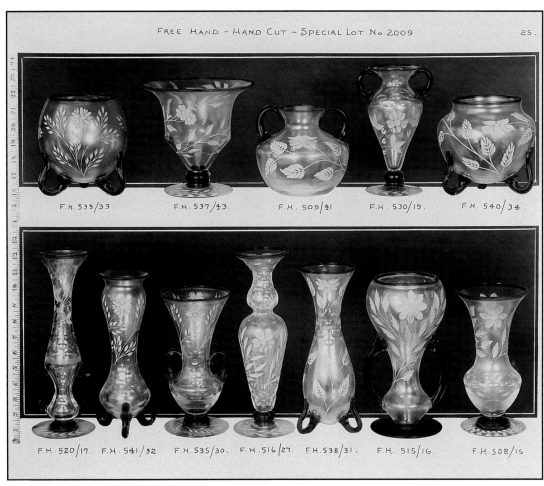

1721 1722 1723 1724 1725 1726

1727 1728 1729 1730 1731

1732 1733 1734 1735 1736

1737 1738 1739 1740 1741

HOFFMAN HOUSE

1742   1743   1744   1745   1746   1747

1748   1749   1750   1751

1752   1753   1754   1755   1756

1757

1758

1759

1760

1761

1762

1763

1764

1765

1766

1767

1768

1769

1770

1771

1772

1774

1775

1776

1777

1778

1779

1780

1781

1782

1783

1784

1785

1786

1787

1788

1789

1790

1791

1792

1793

1794

1793

1795

1796

1795

1797   1798   1799   1800   1801

1802   1803   1804   1805

1806   1807   1808   1809   1810   1811   1812

1813   1814   1815   1816   1817

JADE SLAG

1818

1819

1820

1821

1822

1823

1824

1825

1826

1827

1828

1829

1830

1831

1832

1833

1834

1835

1836

1837

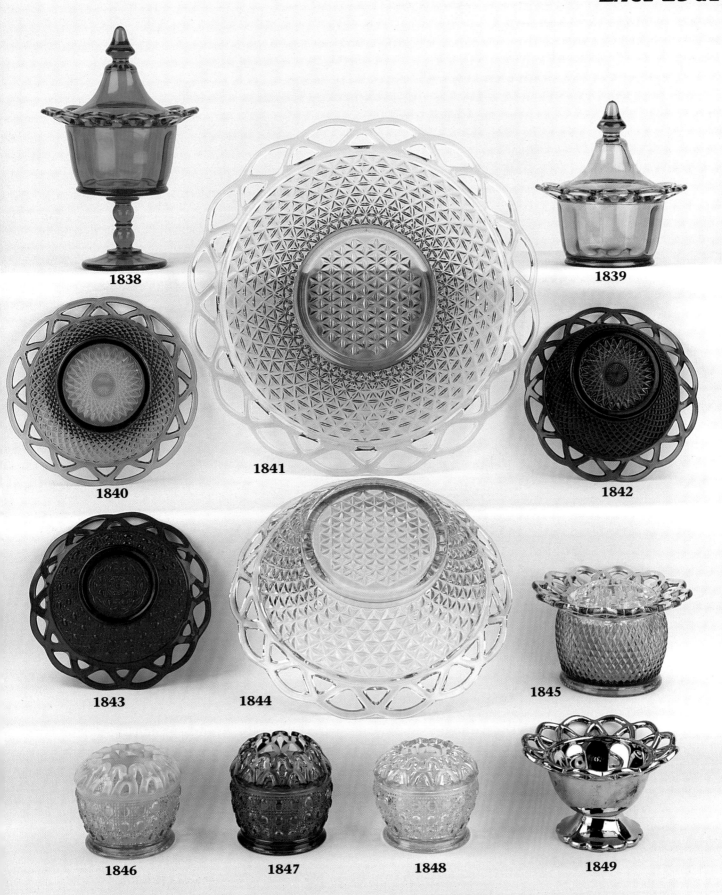

1838

1839

1840

1841

1842

1843

1844

1845

1846

1847

1848

1849

1850 1851 1852 1853 1854

1855 1856 1857

1858 1859 1860 1861

1862 1863 1864 1865

1866   1867   1868   1869   1870   1871   1872

1873   1874   1875   1876   1877   1878

1879   1880   1881   1882

1883   1884

LACE EDGE

1885

1886

1887

1889

1888

1890

1891

1892

1893

1894

1895

1896

1897

1898

1899

1900 1901 1902 1903 1904 1905

1906   **1907**   **1908**   **1909**   **1910**

1911   **1912**   **1913**   **1914**   **1915**

1916   **1917**   **1918**   **1919**

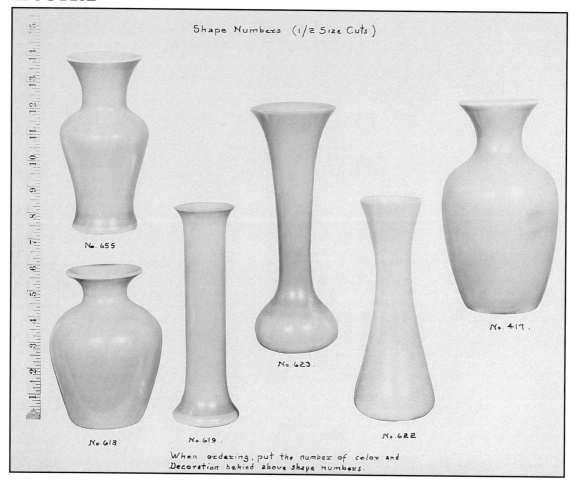

Shape Numbers (1/2 Size Cuts.)

No. 655.

No. 623.

No. 417.

No. 618.

No. 619.

No. 622

When ordering, put the number of color and Decoration behind above shape numbers.

Shape Numbers. (1/2 Size Cuts)

No. 418.

No. 419

No. 412.

No. 415.

When ordering, put the number of color & decoration behind above shape number.

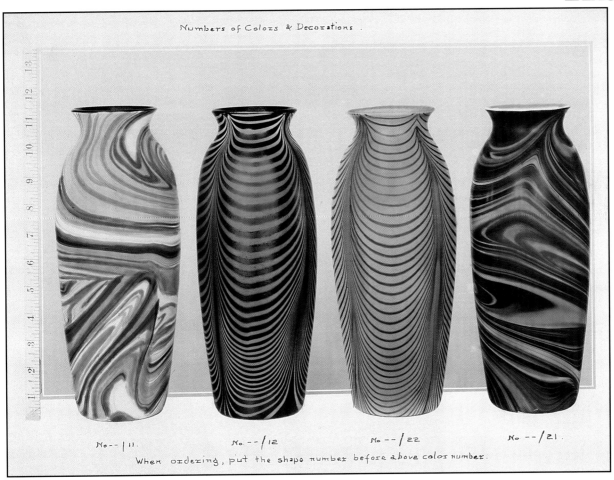

Numbers of Colors & Decorations.

No--/11.   No--/12   No--/22   No--/21.

When ordering, put the shape number before above color number.

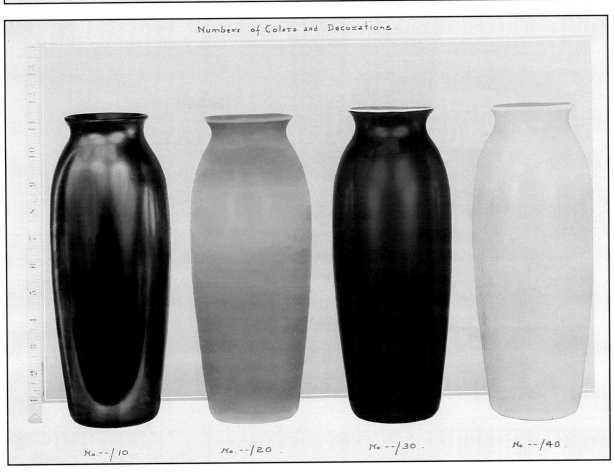

Numbers of Colors and Decorations.

No.--/10.   No.--/20.   No.--/30.   No.--/40.

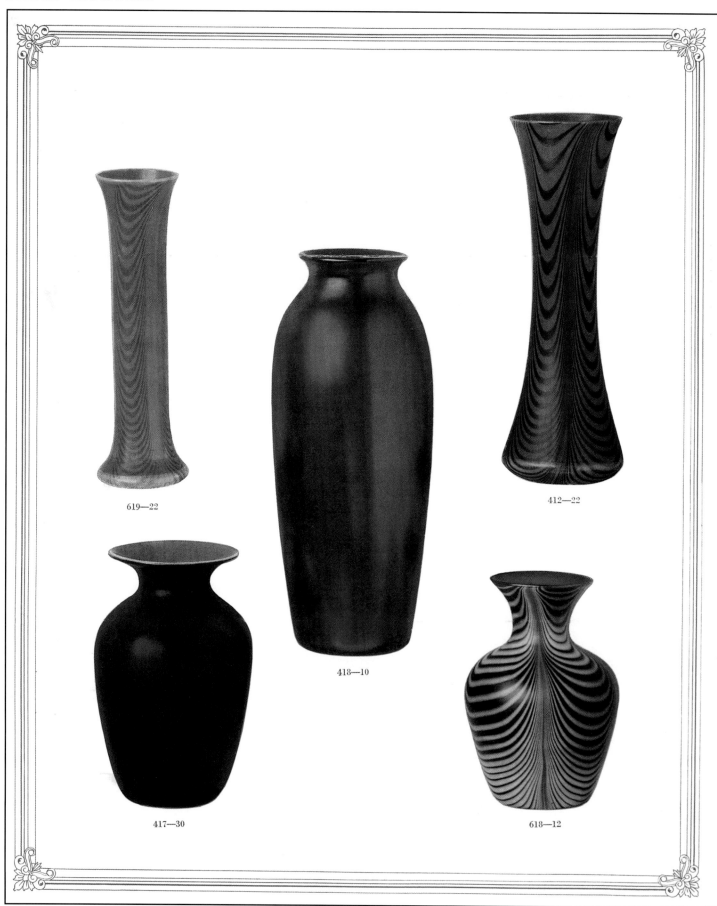

619—22

412—22

418—10

417—30

618—12

623—21

418—12

622—11

413—14

419—44

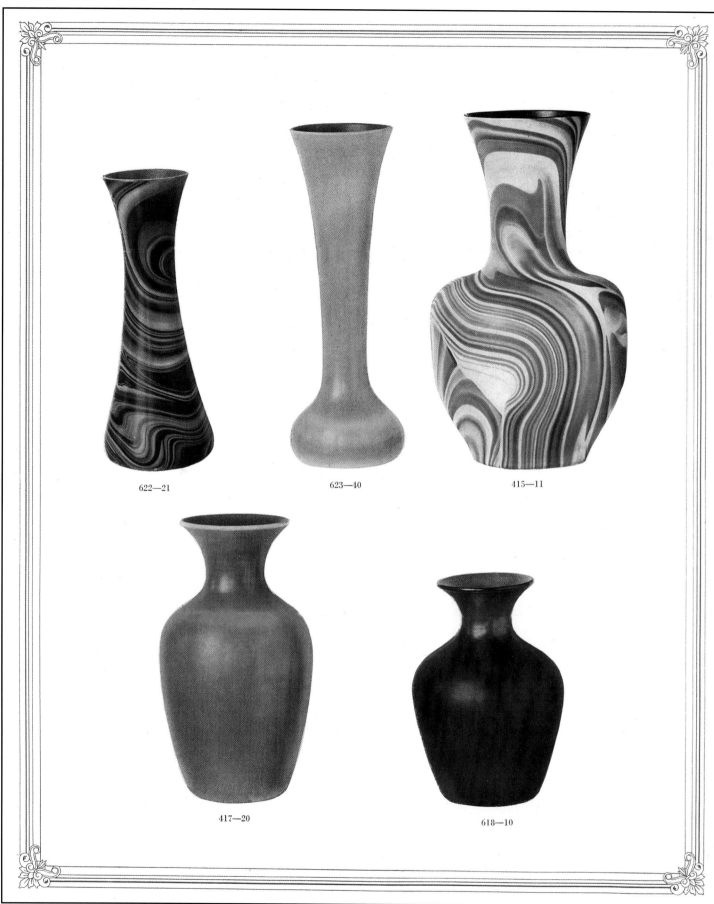

622—21

623—40

415—11

417—20

618—10

page 437

Items from Imperial's No. 320 line were combined to make console sets, as shown here. When made with a swirl optic effect, these were re-numbered as No. 313 (Weatherman, who called all of these Packard, did not differentiate between the plain and optic versions). Carnival collectors refer to Imperial's No. 320 as Double Scroll. **1468.** Blue No. 320 oval 8¹/₄" candlesticks. **1469.** Blue No. 320 10¹/₂" oval bowl. **1470.** Golden Green No. 320 oval 8¹/₄" candlesticks. **1471.** Golden Green No. 320 10¹/₂" oval bowl. **1472.** Green No. 313 oval candlestick (note swirl optic). **1473.** Green No. 313 10¹/₂" oval bowl (note swirl optic). **1474.** Rubigold No. 320 oval candlestick. **1475.** Rubigold No. 320 10¹/₂" oval bowl. **1476.** Amber No. 320/cut 200 oval candleholder. **1477.** Amber No. 320/cut 200 10¹/₂" oval bowl (Weatherman calls this cutting "Roma"). **1478.** Black No. 320 10¹/₂" oval bowl with gold trim and Maytime floral decoration. **1479.** Black footed compote with Maytime floral decoration.

page 438

1480. Midwest Custard Atterbury Scroll covered compote. **1481.** Ivory No. 109 Rose 6" bud vase. **1482.** Midwest Custard 10" Loganberry vase. **1483.** Midwest Custard No. 123 Chroma 12 oz. ice tea. **1484.** Midwest Custard No. 123 Chroma 8" salad plate. **1485.** Midwest Custard No. 123 Chroma 6 oz. sherbet. **1486.** Midwest Custard No. 123 Chroma 8 oz. goblet. **1487.** Lemon Frost 51844 Colonial Bell. **1488.** Ivory 4¹/₂" basket. **1489.** Midwest Custard Phoenix bowl. **1490.** Midwest Custard (satin-finished) 5002 Sheng jar and cover. **1491.** "Gaffer Gaines" No. 83 vase (blue opal cased with opal). **1492.** Milk glass Leaf No. 700 12 oz. footed ice tea with Aspen Green decoration (Denim Blue, Pewter Gray and Terra Cotta were also available). **1493.** Hobnail No. 615 footed bowl with cover (amber bowl and milk glass cover and foot; these were also made with bowls in Antique Blue, Heather and Mustard). **1494.** Milk glass Leaf No. 700 12 oz. footed ice tea with Terra Cotta decoration (Aspen Green, Denim Blue and Pewter Gray were also available).

page 439

These decorated cranberry items from Imperial's Catalog 69 were also made in Collectors Crystal. **1495.** No. 404/Dec 9" footed vase. **1496.** No. 536/Dec 6" vase. **1497.** No. 537/Dec 4¹/₂" compote. **1498.** No. 505/Dec pitcher/vase. **1499.** No. 505/Dec toothpick holder. **1500.** No. 506/Dec cruet and stopper. **1501.** No. 505/Dec salt and pepper set. **1502.** No. 402/Dec individual sugar and cream set. **1503.** No. 612/Dec decanter and stopper. **1504.** No. 612/Dec cordial. **1505.** No. 612/Dec wine. **1506.** No. 612/Dec goblet. **1507.** No. 568/Dec 5" handled nappy. **1508.** No. 737A/Dec 8¹/₂" footed bowl. **1509.** No. 5057/Dec 8" bowl. **1510.** No. 975/Dec covered jar. **1511.** No. 282/1/Dec covered jar.

page 440

Stamm House Dewdrop Opalescent items from the initial offering in January, 1965. **1512.** No. 1886 goblet. **1513.** No. 1886 sherbet. **1514.** No. 1886 juice. **1515.** No. 1886 wine. **1516.** No. 1886 water tumbler. **1517.** No. 1886 ice tea. **1518.** No. 624 pitcher/vase (56 oz.). **1519.** No. 635 5¹/₂" square box and cover. **1520.** No. 631 footed sugar and cream set. **1521.** No. 285 square candleholders. **1522.** No. 742 5" round box and cover. **1523.** No. 188 footed ivy ball. **1524.** No. 188A footed goblet/vase. **1525.** No. 188C crimped compote (5" tall). **1526.** No. 641 8" bowl. **1527.** No. 188P footed posie bowl (6" tall). **1528.** No. 742 10" flip vase. **1529.** No. 635 5¹/₂" square bowl. **1530.** No. 642 10" bowl. **1531.** No. 7423 6¹/₂" blown vase.

page 441

Most of these Stamm House Dewdrop Opalescent items appeared in Imperial's catalog 66A, which was published in 1967. By this time, the 1886 prefix was added to many of the item numbers, and some item descriptions were changed slightly. **1532.** No. 1886 wine. **1533.** No. 1886/163 38 oz. bottle and stopper. **1534.** No. 1886/163/1 bottle. **1535.** No. 1886/188 6" tall ivy. **1536.** No. 1886/188A 6" tall footed vase. **1537.** No. 1886/188C 5" tall crimped compote. **1538.** No. 1886/188P 6" tall posie bowl. **1539.** No. 1886/216 boutique lamp. **1540.** No. 1886/741 cologne and stopper. **1541-1542.** No. 1886/285 square candleholders. **1543.** No. 1886/270 jar and cover. **1544.** No. 1886/742 box and cover. **1545.** No. 1886/886 jar and cover. **1546.** No. 1886/635 box and cover. **1547.** No. 1886/643 4" candleholder. **1548.** No. 1886/114 7¹/₄" lamp/vase. **1549.** No. 1886/724 6" bud vase. **1550.** No. 1886/7423 6¹/₂" blown vase. **1551.** No. 1886/742/1 8" flip vase.

page 442

Although Imperial's No. 582 Fancy Colonial line had been introduced in 1914, it was still selling well when the Rose Marie color debuted in late 1926. **1552.** 10 oz, goblet. **1553.** 12" celery. **1554.** 5¹/₄" footed bowl. **1555.** Water bottle. **1556.** 8" nut bowl. **1557.** 7" nut bowl. **1558.** 8" berry bowl. **1559.** Three-piece mayonnaise set. **1560.** 5" two-handled footed bowl. **1561.** Hotel sugar. **1562.** Hotel cream. **1563.** 10 oz. tumbler. **1564.** 5¹/₂" handled bon-bon. **1566.** Egg cup. **1567.** Salt or pepper shaker. **1568.** Custard. **1569.** 1 oz. cordial. **1570.** Oil bottle. **1571.** Sherbet. **1572.** 4¹/₂" nappy. **1573.** 4¹/₂ oz. cocktail. **1574.** 5" berry. **1575.** 3 oz. cocktail.

page 443

All of these are from Imperial's No. 582 Fancy Colonial line. **1576.** Rubigold 7¹/₂" salad plate. **1577.** Rubigold 10¹/₂" cake plate. **1578.** Nugreen 8" salad bowl and underplate with platinum decoration. **1579.** Green 10¹/₂" cake plate **1580.** Nugreen 6 oz. saucer champagne. **1581.** Rubigold 6" nappy. **1582.**

Iris Ice 10½" cake plate (narrow bottom). **1583.** Rubigold three-pint jug. **1584.** Nugreen 5¼" footed bowl. **1585.** Rubigold crimped nappy. **1586.** Rubigold 6 oz. champagne. **1587.** Rubigold two-handled berry. **1588.** Nugreen 7" nappy. **1589.** Green 1 oz. cordial. **1590.** Rainbow or Rubigold (very light) footed creamer. **1591.** Rubigold 9" ice cream. **1592.** Nugreen 9" ice cream. **1593.** Nugreen 5½" handled bon-bon. **1594.** Rubigold 8" deep salad. **1595.** Green 6" nut or lily bowl. **1596.** Nugreen 8" oval spoon tray.

page 444

These Fired Gold on Crystal items appeared in Imperial's 1972 catalog, where the prefix "G" indicated the gold decoration. Quite a few of these pieces were also in the Collectors Crystal line, and some were also available in Decorated Cranberry (see p. 307). **1597.** G194 9½" celery vase. **1598.** G404 9" footed vase. **1599.** G505 8" footed vase. **1600.** G536 6" vase. **1601.** G555 4½" footed compote. **1602.** G537 4½" footed compote. **1603.** G506 cruet and stopper. **1604.** G505 salt and pepper set. **1605.** G402 individual sugar and cream set. **1606.** G505 toothpick holder. **1607.** G52 bottle and stopper (Cambridge mould). **1608.** G52 4 oz. wine (Cambridge mould). **1609.** G612 decanter and stopper. **1610.** G612 cordial. **1611.** G736 Butterpat box and cover. **1612.** G973 covered compote. **1613.** G505 pitcher/vase. **1614.** G503 6½" oval nappy. **1615.** G568 5" handled nappy. **1616.** G466/1 11½" tray. **1617.** G1467 3½" coaster (Heisey mould). **1618.** G1468 4" coaster (Heisey mould). **1619.** G737A 8½" footed bowl. **1620.** G352 7⅜" candleholder. **1621.** G5059 10" bowl. **1622.** G5057 8" bowl.

page 445

These Flask Brown pieces appeared in Imperial's catalog 66A, which was published in 1967. **1623.** No. 466 5¼" flower arranger. **1624.** No. 207K 5" flower arranger (note crystal flower frog). **1625.** No. 618 Springerle covered sweetsbowl. **1626.** No. 159/1 7¼" bowl. **1627.** No. 159 Atterbury Lion box and cover. These Flower Fair stemware items are from the Imperial/Lenox 1976-1977 catalog. All were available in Fern Green, Nut Brown, Sunshine Yellow and Ultra Blue. **1628.** Ultra Blue 24200 12 oz. goblet. **1629.** Nut Brown 24200 12 oz. goblet. **1630.** Fern Green 24200 12 oz. goblet. **1631.** Sunshine Yellow 24200 12 oz. goblet. **1632.** Fern Green 24220 10 oz. dessert. **1633.** Fern Green 24240 9 oz. wine. **1634.** Fern Green 24200 12 oz. goblet. **1635.** Fern Green 24260 13 oz. iced beverage.

page 446

1636. This interesting vase with hanging hearts motif might be Imperial's Free Hand or a Durand product. **1637.** Free Hand vase with hanging hearts motif. **1638.** Free Hand vase (F. H. 353). **1639.** Free Hand vase with hanging hearts motif. **1640.** Lead Lustre 623/25 vase with hanging hearts motif. **1641.** Free Hand vase. **1642.** Free Hand footed bowl (F. H. 1). **1643.** Free Hand candlestick (F. H. 513/9) with cut motif. **1644.** Free Hand vase (F. H. 520/17) with cut motif. **1645.** Free Hand vase with hanging hearts motif. **1646.** Free Hand vase (similar to F. H. 21). **1647.** Free Hand vase (F. H. 362). **1648.** Possibly a Free Hand vase, but the shape seems to match Imperial's 771, which may have been used for Lead Lustre. **1649.** Free Hand vase. **1650.** Possibly Free Hand, but this threaded piece seems to match Lead Lustre shape 623. **1651.** Free Hand candlestick (F. H. 83). **1652.** Free Hand vase with hanging hearts motif (this piece may have been ground down considerably). **1653.** Free Hand perfume lamp with hanging hearts motif. **1654.** Free Hand bowl (F. H. 392). **1655.** Free Hand vase. **1656.** Free Hand vase.

page 447

1657. Probably a Free Hand vase with hanging hearts motif (possibly a ground down piece from Lead Lustre shape 768). **1658.** Free Hand vase made into a lamp. **1659.** Lead Lustre 412/22 vase. **1660.** Free Hand vase (F. H. 243). **1661.** Lead Lustre 655/25 vase. **1662.** Free Hand atomizer with hanging hearts motif. **1663.** Possibly Free Hand, but this threaded piece seems to match Lead Lustre shape 623. **1664.** Free Hand vase. **1665.** Lead Lustre 417/35 vase. **1666.** Lead Lustre 619 vase. **1667.** Free Hand vase (F. H. 238). **1668.** Lead Lustre 622/20 vase. **1669.** Lead Lustre 619/11 vase. **1670.** Free Hand vase. **1671.** Free Hand footed vase (F. H. 4). **1672.** Free Hand bowl. **1673.** Free Hand vase.

page 448

1674. Free Hand footed vase (F. H. 235). **1675.** Free Hand vase with hanging hearts motif. **1676.** Free Hand vase (similar to F. H. 236). **1677.** Lead Lustre 643/35 vase. **1678.** Lead Lustre 419/20 vase. **1679.** Lead Lustre 417/22 vase. **1680.** Lead Lustre 3191/35 vase. **1681.** Lead Lustre 412/44 vase. **1682.** Free Hand vase (F. H. 399). **1683.** Free Hand footed vase. **1684.** Lead Lustre 412/31 vase. **1685.** Free Hand vase (similar to F. H. 241). **1686.** Lead Lustre 618/40 vase. **1687.** Free Hand bowl (F. H. 387). **1688.** Free Hand vase (similar to F. H. 425). **1689.** Free Hand vase (F. H. 411). **1690.** Lead Lustre 618/20 vase.

page 449

The un-numbered piece on this page is Imperial's Murrhina c. 1959, which will be discussed in the next volume of this series. **1691.** Unusual Free Hand vase with hanging hearts motif. **1692.** Unusual Free Hand vase with hanging hearts motif. **1693.** Free Hand candlesticks (similar to F. H. 164 and F. H. 165). **1694.** Lead Lustre 771 vase, decoration number not known. **1695.** Lead Lustre 619/12 vase. **1696.** Lead Lustre 619/29 vase. **1697.** Lead Lustre 619/20 vase. **1698.** Lead Lustre 619/5 vase. **1699.** Nuruby lustre iridescent No. 771 blown vase. **1700.** Lead Lustre 655/20 vase. **1701.** Lead Lustre 417/20 vase. **1702.** Purple Glaze lustre iridescent No. 771 blown vase. **1703.** Purple Glaze lustre iridescent bowl. **1704.** Free Hand vase (F. H. 359).

page 450
1705. Lead Lustre 415/11 vase. **1706.** Free Hand candlesticks. **1707.** Lead Lustre 418/12 vase. **1708.** Free Hand candlestick (F. H. 285). **1709.** Free Hand vase (F. H. 328). **1710.** Lead Lustre 415/6 vase. **1711.** Lead Lustre 417/30 vase. **1712.** Lead Lustre 3191/61 vase. **1713.** Free Hand vase (F. H. 240). **1714.** This vivid iridescent Free Hand vase is similar in shape to F. H. 306 and F. H. 307. **1715.** Probably a Free Hand vase with hanging hearts motif. **1716.** Lead Lustre 319/30 candlestick. **1717.** Free Hand atomizer with hanging hearts motif. **1718.** Free Hand bowl with hanging hearts motif. **1719.** Free Hand vase (F. H. 180). **1720.** Free Hand bowl (similar to F. H. 255).

page 451
These two pages are from an original Imperial catalog. **Top::** Free Hand and Art Glass Special Lot No. 1906. These console sets contain two pieces (vases or candlesticks) of Free Hand as well as a bowl from the earlier Art Glass line ("P. A." stands for Pearl Amethyst and "P. G." denotes Pearl Green); no other Art Glass is shown in this catalog. The Free Hand pieces have a green iridescent finish. **Bottom:** Free Hand Glass Special Lot No. 1977. These Free Hand pieces have a silvery iridescent body with cobalt blue stripes and/or handles and/or joint and/or foot.

page 452
These two pages are from an original Imperial catalog. **Top:** Free Hand Glass Special Lot No. 1979. These pieces have a silvery iridescent body with red-colored stripes and/or handles and/or joints. **Bottom:** Free Hand Glass Special Lot No. 1976. These pieces have a light greenish-silver iridescent body with cobalt blue stripes and/or handles and/or foot.

page 453
These two pages are from an original Imperial catalog. **Top:** Free Hand Glass Special Lot No. 1983. These pieces have a very light silvery iridescent body with green stripes and/or edges and/or handles and/or foot. **Bottom:** Free Hand Glass Special Lot No. 1978. These pieces are all-over iridescent, and the dominant color is green, Several pieces (F. H. 17 and F. H. 208) have some of the stretch effect typically associated with Imperial's Art Glass.

page 454
These two pages are from an original Imperial catalog. **Top:** Free Hand Glass Special Lot No. 1973. These Free Hand pieces feature a strong, all-over iridescent finish. Note the vivid iridescence on some of the footed pieces. **Bottom:** Free Hand Glass Special Lot No. 1985. These Free Hand pieces have an opaque ivory body with some pale iridescence on the outside; the insides of some pieces—F. H. 224, F. H. 227 and F. H. 233—may be pale orange. The applied handles and/or edge and/or feet are cobalt blue.

page 455
These pages are from an original Imperial catalog. **Top:** Free Hand Glass Special Lot No. 1986. These Free Hand pieces have a light orange iridescence on ivory glass; the handles and/or edges and/or feet are cobalt blue. **Bottom:** Free Hand Glass Special Lot No. 1984. These Free Hand pieces have a transparent crystal body. Pieces in the top row have cobalt blue threading and/or joint and/or handles and/or feet, while those in the bottom have ruby threading and/or joint and/or handles and/or feet.

page 456
These two pages are from an original Imperial catalog. **Top:** Free Hand Cut Special Lot No. 1987. These Free Hand pieces are crystal with elaborate wheel-cut motifs ranging from florals to polished circles and ovals. The applied handles and/or edges and/or feet and/or joints are cobalt blue. The Free Hand shape number is followed by a number for the cutting. Most of the cuttings have numbers below 30, so 281 could be a mistake. **Bottom:** Free Hand Glass Special Lot No. 1988. These Free Hand pieces have a nearly transparent silvery body with a slight iridescence. They display the "hanging hearts" motif. The applied handles and/or edges and/or feet are cobalt blue.

page 457
These two pages are from an original Imperial catalog. **Top:** Free Hand Glass Special Lot No. 1989. Most of these Free Hand pieces display the "hanging hearts" motif, but several different colors are shown. The Free Hand pieces in the upper left are iridescent orange with a cobalt blue edge; these should not be confused with Lead Lustre pieces. **Bottom:** Free Hand Glass Special Lot No. 1990. These Free Hand pieces all display the "hanging hearts" motif, but two different colors are shown, dark blue body and orange iridescent body.

page 458
These two pages are from an original Imperial catalog. **Top:** Free Hand Glass Special Lot No. 1991. Most of these Free Hand pieces display the "hanging hearts" motif. **Bottom:** Free Hand Glass Special Lot No. 2000. This Free Hand assortment reflects a wide variety of colors and motifs, ranging from "hanging hearts" to applied threading. Several of these shapes (F. H. 358 and F. H. 342) are similar to the later Lead Lustre pieces.

page 459

These two pages are from an original Imperial catalog. **Top:** Free Hand Glass Special Lot No. 2003. These Free Hand "hanging hearts" pieces have dark bodies with strong orange/green iridescence. **Bottom:** Free Hand Glass Special Lot No. 2004. This Free Hand assortment reflects a wide variety of colors and motifs. Note the mottled hearts (F. H. 392). The treatments shown on F. H. 399 and F. H. 364 are the only ones like this depicted in this original catalog.

page 460

These two pages are from an original Imperial catalog. **Top:** Free Hand Glass Special Lot No. 2001. These Free Hand pieces with hanging hearts motif have a dark cobalt blue body with opal edges and/or feet and/or joint. **Bottom:** Free Hand Hand Cut Special Lot No. 2005. These Free Hand pieces are a silvery iridescent crystal with elaborate wheel-cut motifs. The applied handles and/or edges and/or feet and/or stems/joints are yellow-green. The Free Hand shape number is followed by a number for the particular cutting; several pieces have the same cutting (47 or 48), and the candleholders have the same cutting (9) as those shown earlier in this original catalog.

page 461

These two pages are from an original Imperial catalog. **Top:** Free Hand Glass Special Lot No. 2006. These Free Hand pieces display the hanging hearts motif on a dark blue body, usually with opal edge. The applied glass for the hanging hearts is opal and light blue threads are applied to create a mottled effect. **Bottom:** Free Hand Glass Special Lot No. 2007. These Free Hand pieces display the hanging hearts motif on an opal body with vivid orange iridescence.

page 462

These two pages are from an original Imperial catalog. **Top:** Free Hand Glass Special Lot No. 2008. This assortment of Free Hand vases in four different colors shows that Imperial was trying to make vases in the the same shape (vertical columns) in a variety of treatments, perhaps reflecting the company's desire to standardize the line. **Bottom:** Free Hand Hand Cut Special Lot No. 2009. These Free Hand pieces are crystal with wheel-cut motifs, including florals and polished circles and ovals. The Free Hand shape number is followed by a number for the cutting. The applied handles and/or edges and/or feet and/or stems/joints are cobalt blue.

page 463

Imperial often used gold decoration on its glassware, and this page shows a wide variety of products. **1721.** No. 701 Reeded 7" covered jar. **1722.** No. 701 Reeded 8" covered jar. **1723.** No. 701 Reeded 5" covered jar. **1724.** No. 701 Reeded 8" vase (all of these gold-decorated No. 701 pieces were also called Midas). **1725.** No. 777 Cow Brand 16 oz. tumbler. **1726.** Zodiac tumbler. All of these gold-decorated Candlewick pieces have the Rose of Sharon deep plate etching. **1727.** Candlewick 400/45 DE 5$\frac{1}{2}$" tall compote. **1728.** Candlewick 400/37 DE cup and saucer. **1729.** Candlewick 400/124 DE 12$\frac{1}{2}$" oval plate. **1730.** Candlewick 400/107 DE 5$\frac{3}{4}$" footed vase. **1731.** Candlewick 400/188 DE 7" ivy or brandy vase. **1732.** Santa bell. **1733.** No. 702 DE covered jar (Rose of Sharon etching). **1734.** Candlewick 400/100/2-2 twin Eagle candleholder. **1735.** Sample shaker with gold panels and Rose of Sharon etching. **1736.** Candlewick 400/40/o DE 6$\frac{1}{2}$" handled basket. **1737.** Goboons medium vase. **1738.** Goboons large vase. **1739.** Goboons small vase (all of these gold-decorated Goboons pieces were also called Midas). **1740.** Cape Cod 160/180 4$\frac{1}{2}$" spider. **1741.** Sample 5001 Pagoda (from Cathay line), no base.

page 464

These Hoffman House items were shown in Imperial's catalog 69. **1742.** Ruby No. 46 12 oz. goblet. **1743.** Ruby No. 46 10 oz. goblet. **1744.** Ruby No. 46 5$\frac{1}{2}$ oz. sherbet. **1745.** Ruby No. 46 6 oz. wine. **1746.** Ruby No. 46 4$\frac{3}{4}$" nappy. **1747.** Ruby No. 46 7$\frac{1}{2}$" plate. **1748.** Amber No. 46 12 oz. goblet. **1749.** Verde No. 46 12 oz. goblet. **1750.** Nut Brown No. 46 12 oz. goblet. **1751.** Antique Blue No. 46 12 oz. goblet. These Hoffman House items from 1974-75 are all Verde: **1752.** 22240 6 oz. wine. **1753.** 22260 16 oz. iced beverage. **1754.** 12 oz. goblet. **1755.** 22200 10 oz. goblet. **1756.** 22220 6 oz. dessert.

page 465

1757. Amethyst Ice 8" plate. **1758.** Probably Rose Ice 12" bowl. **1759.** Iris Ice 12" Colonial No. 600 bowl. **1760.** Blue Ice sandwich tray (with cut decoration). **1761.** Blue Ice 8" plate. **1762.** Blue Ice comport. **1763.** Amber Ice 8" plate. **1764.** Probably Rose Ice octagonal plate. **1765.** Green Ice plate. **1766.** Iris Ice comport. **1767.** Iris Ice plate. **1768.** Green Ice sugar. **1769.** Green Ice mayonnaise bowl. **1770.** Iris Ice large comport. **1771.** Green Ice plate. **1772.** Green Ice sherbet.

page 466

Items in Imperial ruby from catalog 69. **1774.** No. 356 10" vase. **1775.** 572. 6$\frac{1}{4}$" vase (Cambridge mould). **1776.** No. 573C 6" crimped vase (Cambridge mould). **1777.** No. 461C 5" crimped compote. **1778.** 165/45 5$\frac{1}{2}$" compote (Cambridge mould). **1779.** No. 109 6" bud vase. **1780.** No. 76 5$\frac{1}{2}$" vase. **1781.** No. 123 3" cornucopia (Cambridge mould). **1782.** No. 5006 3$\frac{1}{2}$" ash tray (Cathay Butterfly). **1783.** No. 5004 4$\frac{1}{2}$" ash tray (Cathay Yang and Yin). **1784.** No. 282 4$\frac{1}{2}$" candleholder. **1785.** No. 1956

8" ash tray (Cambridge mould). **1786.** No. 280/84 bowl. **1787.** No. 280/85 box and cover. **1788.** No. 165/85 three-toed box and cover (Cambridge mould). **1789.** No. 170 box and cover. **1790.** No. 464 pokal. **1791.** No. 1575B 9¹/₂" bowl (Heisey mould). **1792.** No. 1575 F 10¹/₂" float bowl (Heisey mould). **1793.** No. 341/2 7¹/₂" candleholder (Heisey mould). **1794.** No. 574B 9" crimped bowl (Cambridge mould. **1795.** No. 1503/80 candleblock (Heisey mould). **1796.** No. 1575N 6¹/₂" bowl (Heisey mould).

page 467
Except for Fig. 1805, all of these Jade Slag items were made in both glossy and satin finishes during 1975-1976. **1797.** 43770 (No. 529) 10" footed vase (satin finish). **1798.** 43900 (No. 800) Owl covered jar. **1799.** 43150 (No. 240) one-pint Windmill pitcher. **1800.** 43699 (No. 62C) 9" crimped Rose bowl. **1801.** 43762 (No. 192) 8¹/₂" tricorn vase (satin finish). **1802.** 43870 (No. 158) Rooster covered box. **1803.** 43574 (No. 478) Pansy 5¹/₂" handled nappy. **1804.** 43910 (No. 464) covered jar or pokal (satin finish). **1805.** 43858 (1608/1) 6" square ash tray, c. 1962-66. **1806.** 43842 (No. 720) bell. **1807.** 43906 (No. 60) Beehive covered honey jar (satin finish). **1808.** 43920 (No. 146) Duck-on-Nest (satin finish). **1809.** 43642 (No. 156) basket with milk glass handle. **1810.** 43636 (No. 104) miniature pitcher (satin finish). **1811.** 43528 (No. 123) cornucopia toothpick holder (satin finish; Cambridge mould). **1812.** 43639 (No. 459) Rooster holder. **1813.** 43540 (No. 335) Owl sugar. **1814.** 43630 (No. 19) footed toothpick holder (satin finish). **1815.** 43865 (No. 1956) Hambone ash tray (satin finish; Cambridge mould). **1816.** 43624 (No. 505) toothpick holder. **1817.** 43540 (No. 335) Owl creamer.

page 468
Except for a few items as indicated, all of these Jade Slag items were made in both glossy and satin finishes during 1975-1976. **1818.** 43681 (No. 1605) 7¹/₂" bowl or ash tray possibly c. 1962-66). **1819.** 43490 (No. 505) cruet and stopper. **1820.** 43752 (No. 661) 5" vase. **1821.** 43752 (No. 661) 5" vase (satin finish). **1822.** 43699 (No. 62C) 9" crimped Rose bowl. **1823.** 43723 (No. 727C) 4" crimped hexagon Grape footed compote (satin finish). **1824.** 43723 (No. 727C) 4" crimped hexagon Grape footed compote. **1825.** 43729 (No. 5930) crimped compote (satin finish). **1826.** 43932 (No. 400) 8" open Swan. **1827.** 43882 (No. 176) four-toed covered jar. **1828.** 43897 (No. 1560) 5¹/₂" covered box. **1829.** 43897 (No. 1560) 5¹/₂" covered box (satin finish). **1830.** 43784 (No. 160) pair of 3¹/₂" Rose candlesticks. **1831.** Sample No. 46 Hoffman House 6 oz. wine. **1832.** No. 602 6" salad bowl, c. 1966. **1833.** 43930 (No. 147) 4" open Swan mint whimsey (satin finish). **1834.** 43930 (No. 147) 4" open Swan mint whimsey. **1835.** 43784 (No. 160) pair of 3¹/₂" Rose candlesticks (satin finish). **1836.** No. 600 two-handled toothpick holder, c. 1966. **1837.** 43320 Storybook/Elephant mug (No. 1591; Heisey mould).

page 469
All of these are Imperial's Lace Edge. **1838.** Antique Blue No. 78 footed jar and cover. **1839.** Amber No. 780 jar and cover. **1840.** Amber No. 749 7¹/₄" bowl. **1841.** Amber No. 749 14" plate. **1842.** Burgundy No. 207F bowl. **1843.** Ritz Blue No. 743 7¹/₄" bowl. **1844.** Viennese Blue No. 749 10" bowl. **1845.** Amberglo No. 207 flower arranger. **1846.** Sea Foam Blue [opalescent] No. 745 ivy ball. **1847.** Amber No. 745 ivy ball. **1848.** Rose Pink No. 745 ivy ball. **1849.** Silver decorated No. 780 footed compote.

page 470
All of these are Imperial's Lace Edge. **1850.** Rubigold No. 743 5¹/₂" vase. **1851.** Ruby No. 745 7¹/₂" plate. **1852.** Antique Blue No. 780 14" shallow bowl. **1853.** Ultra Blue No. 745 7¹/₂" plate. **1854.** Ruby No. 743 5¹/₂" vase. **1855.** Stiegel Green No. 743 bowl. **1856.** Verde tidbit set from Imperial's Belmont Crystal line (similar to No. 7432/86 2-tier tidbit set). **1857.** Burgundy No. 207F bowl. **1858.** Ritz Blue No. 745 nappy. **1859.** Turquoise Opaque No. 745 nappy. **1860.** Rose Pink No. 745 nappy. **1861.** Ruby No. 745 nappy. **1862.** Ruby No. 745 nappy. **1863.** Verde No. 207 flower arranger. **1864.** Sunset Ruby Carnival No. 274C 7" four-toed compote. **1865.** Stiegel Green No. 745 nappy.

page 471
All of these are Imperial's Lace Edge. **1866.** Stiegel Green No. 743 vase. **1867.** Ritz Blue No. 743 vase. **1868.** Ruby No. 743 vase. **1869.** Amber No. 743 vase. **1870.** Teal No. 743 vase. **1871.** Sea Foam Blue [opalescent] No. 743 vase. **1872.** Amber No. 743 vase. **1873.** Heather No. 749 flower arranger. **1874.** Amber No. 780 vase. **1875.** Teal No. 780 vase. **1876.** Ritz Blue No. 780 vase. **1877.** Amber No. 780 vase. **1878.** Ritz Blue No. 780 rose bowl. **1879.** Amber No. 780 vase. **1880.** Viennese Blue No. 780 four-toed footed bowl. **1881.** Amber No. 780 bowl. **1882.** Amber No. 780 comport. **1883.** Amber No. 780 6" shallow bowl. **1884.** Verde No. 780 large shallow bowl.

page 472
All of these are Imperial's Lace Edge. **1885.** Sea Foam Green [opalescent] No. 749 11" plate. **1886.** Ultra Blue 9" mint tray with center handle. **1887.** Verde No. 749 11" plate (note black/gold Belmont Crystal label). **1888.** Ritz Blue No. 745 nappy. **1889.** Amber No. 745 nappy. **1890.** Azalea No. 780 jar and cover. **1891.** Base of Azalea No. 780 jar to show bottom detail. **1892.** Stiegel Green No. 745 nappy. **1893.** Ruby No. 745 "basket bowl" [shape name from 1930s]. **1894.** Sea Foam Blue [opalescent] No. 745 plate. **1895.** Amber four-toed covered jar. **1896.** Amber covered bowl. **1897.** Amber No. 745 ivy ball. **1898.** Amber flower arranger. **1899.** Amber No. 274C four-toed footed bowl. **1900.** Sea Foam

Blue [opalescent] No. 743 vase. **1901.** Sea Foam Green [opalescent] No. 743 vase. **1902.** Stiegel Green No. 745 nappy. **1903.** Sea Foam Blue [opalescent] No. 743 vase. **1904.** Sea Foam Green [opalescent] No. 743 vase. **1905.** Ruby No. 743 vase.

page 473
1906. Honey Amber No. 201 Peacock Feather lamp. **1907.** Amber No. 201 Peacock Feather 12" hand lamp. **1908.** Mustard No. 201 Peacock Feather hand lamp. **1909.** Antique Blue 1886/350 Hobnail lamp. **1910.** Verde 1886/350 Hobnail lamp. **1911.** Heather No. 9 Bundling Lamp with sueded crystal shade. **1912.** Green No. 9 Bundling Lamp with ruby shade. **1913.** Crystal No. 9 Bundling Lamp with amber shade. **1914.** Green No. 9 Bundling Lamp with sueded crystal shade. **1915.** Antique Blue No. 9 Bundling Lamp. **1916.** Antique Blue No. 216 Boutique Lamp. **1917.** Honey Amber No. 216 Boutique Lamp. **1918.** Amber No. 216 Boutique Lamp. **1919.** 1886/216 boutique lamp from the Stamm House Dewdrop Opalescent line.

page 474
These two pages from an Imperial sales brochure show the original numbers for many of the shapes available in the Lead Lustre line (417, 618, 619, 622, 623 and 655; 412, 415, 418 and 419).

page 475
These two pages from an Imperial sales brochure show the original numbers for some of the colors and decorative treatments available in the Lead Lustre line (11, 12, 21 and 22; and 10, 20, 30 and 40) .

page 476
This color page from an Imperial sales brochure shows five items from the Lead Lustre line (the three-digit shape number precedes the two-digit number designating the color and/or decorative treatment).

page 477
This color page from an Imperial sales brochure shows five items from the Lead Lustre line (the three-digit shape number precedes the two-digit number designating the color and/or decorative treatment).

page 478
This color page from an Imperial sales brochure shows five items from the Lead Lustre line (the three-digit shape number precedes the two-digit number designating the color and/or decorative treatment).

BIBLIOGRAPHY

Archer, Douglas and Margaret. *Imperial Glass* (1978). Paducah, KY: Collector Books.

Burns, Carl O. *Imperial Carnival Glass* (1995). Paducah, KY: Collector Books.

Edwards, Bill. *The Standard Encyclopedia of Carnival Glass*, 4th ed. (1994). Paducah, KY: Collector Books.

Garrison, Myrna and Bob. *Imperial's Boudoir, Etcetera ... A Comprehensive Look at Dresser Accessories for Irice and Others* (1996). Order ($26.95 plus $3.00 shipping and $2.09 tax for Texas residents) from Collector's Loot, 3816 Hastings Drive, Arlington, TX 76013.

Garrison, Myrna and Bob. *Imperial Cape Cod: Tradition to Treasure* (1982; revised 1991). Order ($14.95 plus $2.00 shipping and $1.16 tax for Texas residents) from Collector's Loot, 3816 Hastings Drive, Arlington, TX 76013.

Garrison, Myrna and Bob. *Imperial's Vintage Milk Glass* (1992). Order ($16.95 plus $2.00 shipping and $1.32 tax for Texas residents) from Collector's Loot, 3816 Hastings Drive, Arlington, TX 76013.

Ross, Richard and Wilma. *Imperial Glass: Imperial Jewels, Free Hand and Pressed Glass* (1971). Des Moines, IA: Wallace-Homestead.

Pages 1-226 are in Volume 1 and pages 227-494 are in this book.

IMPERIAL GLASS ENCYCLOPEDIA
Volume II, "Cape Cod - L"
National Imperial Glass Collectors' Society, Inc. — Edited by James Measell
Value Guide 1997 - 1998

This value guide embraces more than 1,000 articles pictured in the color pages of this book, as well as two pages of Cathay shown in black and white. The price ranges given reflect items in "mint" condition. For some items, no price (NP) is indicated because the item is seldom seen and/or has not changed hands for some time.

Neither the author nor the publishers can be liable for any losses incurred when using this guide as the basis for any transaction.

FRONT COVER:	BACK COVER:
A- 700-800	G- 200-250
B- 12-15	H- 120-130
C- 750-800	I- 100-125
D- 300-325	J- 600-700
E- 45-50	K- 500-600
F- NP	L- 25-30

CATHAY P. 260:	
A- NP	891- 225-250
B- 750-800	892- 300-325
C- 175-200	893- 45-50
D- 300-350	894- 30-35
E- 650-750	895- 35-40
F- 200-250	896- 35-40
G- 350-400	897- 25-30
H- 650-725	898- 30-35
I- 35-40	899- 25-30
J- 35-40	900- 25-30
K- 35-40	901- 35-40
L- 250-300	902- 25-30
M- 125-150	903- 25-30
N- 75-100	904- 25-30
O- 200-250	905- 30-35
P- 150-175	906- 25-30
	907- 15-20
	908- 20-25
CATHAY P. 261:	909- 20-25
A- 325-350	910- 40-45
B- 225-250	911- 20-25
C- 275-300	912- 20-25
D- 500-575	913- 25-30
E- 275-300	914- 15-20
F- 200-225	915- 20-25
G- 175-200	916- 20-25
H- 325-350	917- 25-30
I- 250-275	918- 15-20
J- 200-225	919- 15-20
K- NP	920- 15-20
L- 225-250	921- 25-30
M- 250-275	922- 25-30
N- 200-225	923- 25-30
O- 125-140	924- 30-35
P- 125-150	925- 30-35
Q- 75-100	926- 30-35

927- 125-135	971- 60-65	1016- 125-140	
928- 125-135	972- 40-45	1017- 50-60	
929- 60-65	973- 80-90	1018- 35-40	
930- 115-120	974- 80-90	1019- 35-40	
931- 50-55	975- 80-90	1020- 145-160	
932- 15-20	976- 70-80	1021- 360-380	
933- 50-55	977- 95-100	1022- 90-100	
934- NP	978- NP	1023- 150-165	
935- 50-55	979- 75-80	1024- 250-275	
936- 45-50	980- 115-125	1025- 110-120	
937- 70-80	981- 95-110	1026- 50-55	
938- 30-35	982- 50-55	1027- 45-50	
939- 200-225	983- 110-120	1028- 45-50	
940- 400-450	984- NP	1029- 50-55	
940A- 30-35	985- 40-45	1030- 150-170	
941- 165-175	986- 45-50	1031- 145-155	
942- 165-175	987- 85-95	1032- 60-65	
943- 175-200	988- 20-25	1033- 20-25	
944- 45-50	989- NP	1034- 20-25	
945- 35-40	990- 45-50	1035- 30-35	
946- 30-35	991- 20-25	1036- 40-45	
947- 30-35	992- 20-25	1037- 165-175	
948- 35-40	993- 25-30	1038- 65-75	
949- 30-35	994- 50-55	1039- 200-225	
950- 40-45	995- 150-175	1040- 25-30	
951- 30-35	996- 175-200	1041- 40-45	
952- 50-60	997- NP	1042- 95-105	
953- 300-325	998- NP	1043- 75-80	
954- 45-50	999- 165-175	1044- 45-50	
955- 50-55	1000- NP	1045- 35-45	
956- NP	1001- 115-125	1046- 20-25	
957- NP	1002- 135-150	1047- 120-130	
958- 60-65	1003- 75-85	1048- 110-120	
959- 65-75	1004- 125-135	1049- 35-40	
960- 50-55	1005- 50-55	1050- 35-40	
961- NP	1006- 85-95	1051- 45-50	
962- NP	1007- 100-115	1052- NP	
963- 30-35	1008- 100-115	1053- NP	
964- 20-25	1009- 45-50 each	1054- 40-45	
965- 25-30	1010- 40-45	1055- 250-275	
966- 75-85	1011- 45-50	1056- 35-40	
967- 40-45	1012- 125-135	1057- 40-45	
968- 20-25	1013- 135-150	1058- 35-40	
969- 55-60	1014- 75-85	1059- 25-30	
970- 55-60	1015- 20-25	1060- 25-30	

1061- 20-25	1119- 35-40	1177- 30-35	1235- 35-40	1293- 18-20
1062- 35-40	1120- 365-375	1178- 65-75	1236- 35-40	1294- 20-25
1063- 40-45	1121- 30-35	1179- 25-30	1237- 25-30	1295- 55-60
1064- 50-55	1122- 155-165	1180- 50-55	1238- 25-30	1296- 35-40
1065- 45-50	1123- 130-140	1181- 45-50	1239- 55-65	1297- 15-20
1066- 100-110	1124- 175-185	1182- 65-75	1240- 55-65	1298- 45-50
1067- 80-90	1125- 100-110	1183- 60-70	1241- 30-35	1299- 20-25
1068- 40-45	1126- 30-35	1184- 30-35	1242- 45-50	1300- 65-75
1069- 40-45	1127- 35-40	1185- 60-70	1243- 35-40	1301- 12-15
1070- 45-50	1128- 40-45	1186- 35-40	1244- 35-40	1302- 25-30
1071- 145-170	1129- 55-65	1187- 45-50	1245- 110-130	1303- 65-75
1072- 45-50	1130- 55-60	1188- 20-25	1246- 110-130	1304- 250-270
1073- 35-40	1131- 65-75	1189- 30-35	1247- 45-50	1305- 250-270
1074- 40-45	1132- 102-112	1190- 35-40	1248- 60-70	1306- 60-70
1075- 50-55	1133- NP	1191- 20-25	1249- 40-45	1307- 65-75
1076- 40-45	1134- 50-55	1192- 25-30	1250- 45-50	1308- 55-65
1077- 145-170	1135- 45-55 pr.	1193- 30-35	1251- 25-30	1309- 55-65
1078- 75-80	1136- 40-45	1194- 40-45	1252- 30-35	1310- 45-50
1079- 45-50	1137- 45-50	1195- 75-85	1253- 30-35	1311- 45-50
1080- 45-50	1138- 50-55	1196- 30-35	1254- 25-30	1312- 130-145
1081- 45-50	1139- 35-40	1197- 45-50	1255- 30-35	1313- 130-145
1082- 45-50	1140- 40-45	1198- 30-35	1256- 35-40	1314- 65-75
1083- 45-50	1141- 30-35	1199- 40-45	1257- 45-50	1315- 35-40
1084- 250-300	1142- 35-40	1200- 35-40	1258- 45-50	1316- 55-60
1085- 50-60	1143- 175-195	1201- 45-50	1259- 20-22	1317- 25-30
1086- 775-800	1144- 45-55	1202- 30-35	1260- 40-45	1318- 45-50
1087- 55-65	1145- NP	1203- 60-70	1261- 50-55	1319- 30-35
1088- 85-100	1146- 55-65	1204- 25-30	1262- 65-70	1320- 25-30
1089- 25-30	1147- 45-50	1205- 30-35	1263- 40-45	1321- 30-35
1090- 75-80	1148- 50-55	1206- 35-40	1264- 22-25	1322- 30-35
1091- 45-55	1149- 30-35	1207- 50-55	1265- 70-80	1323- 45-50
1092- 45-55	1150- 65-70	1208- 30-35	1266- 70-80	1324- 25-30
1093- 45-55	1151- 60-70	1209- 40-45	1267- 15-20	1325- 20-25
1094- 50-55	1152- 75-80	1210- 25-30	1268- 30-35	1326- 20-25
1095- 80-90	1153- 35-40	1211- 40-45	1269- 30-35	1327- 75-85
1096- 45-50	1154- 35-40	1212- 70-80	1270- 25-30	1328- 35-40
1097- NP	1155- 50-55	1213- 55-65	1271- 25-30	1329- 35-40
1098- 25-30	1156- 85-95	1214- 45-50	1272- 40-45	1330- 35-40
1099- 120-140	1157- 90-100	1215- 18-20	1273- 35-40	1331- 45-50
1100- 25-30	1158- 25-30	1216- 85-95	1274- 30-35	1332- 35-40 pr.
1101- NP	1159- 30-35	1217- 35-40	1275- 25-30	1333- 35-40
1102- 50-60	1160- 35-40	1218- 40-45	1276- 85-95	1334- 45-50
1103- 130-140	1161- 25-30	1219- 30-35	1277- 90-100	1335- 40-45
1104- 100-115	1162- 120-130	1220- 45-55	1278- 85-95	1336- 40-45
1105- 195-215	1163- 25-30	1221- 12-15	1279- 80-90	1337- 10-15
1106- 45-50	1164- 30-35	1222- 22-25	1280- 18-20	1338- 70-80
1107- 65-75	1165- 35-40	1223- 22-25	1281- 20-22	1339- 30-35
1108- 35-40	1166- 25-30	1224- 35-40	1282- 18-20	1340- 45-50
1109- 60-65	1167- 20-25	1225- 15-20	1283- 16-18	1341- 50-60
1110- 35-45	1168- 25-30	1226- 25-30	1284- 12-15	1342- 15-20
1111- 85-95	1169- 70-80	1227- 25-30	1285- 30-35	1343- 15-20
1112- 120-130	1170- 35-40	1228- 35-40	1286- 15-20	1344- 30-35
1113- 75-80	1171- 50-55	1229- 55-60	1287- 15-20	1345- 15-20
1114- 85-95	1172- 80-85	1230- 20-25	1288- 30-35	1346- 35-40
1115- 35-40	1173- 50-55	1231- 18-20	1289- 30-35	1347- 25-30
1116- 35-40	1174- 45-50	1232- 18-20	1290- 35-40	1348- 15-20
1117- 30-35	1175- 45-50	1233- 18-20	1291- 25-30	1349- 25-30
1118- 175-185	1176- 150-170	1234- 18-20	1292- 18-20	1350- 25-30

1351- 20-25	1409- 35-40	1467- 20-25	1525- 40-45	1583- 165-175
1352- 20-25	1410- 45-50 pr.	1468- 25-30	1526- 35-40	1584- 45-50
1353- 35-40	1411- 65-70	1469- 45-50	1527- 45-50	1585- 25-30
1354- 30-35	1412- 75-80	1470- 45-50	1528- 45-50	1586- 55-60
1355- 30-35	1413- 65-75	1471- 80-85	1529- 25-30	1587- 65-70
1356- 20-25	1414- 50-55	1472- 25-30	1530- 45-50	1588- 40-45
1357- 25-30	1415- 60-70	1473- 45-50	1531- 55-65	1589- 40-45
1358- 30-35	1416- 70-75	1474- 30-35	1532- 20-25	1590- 35-40
1359- 50-55	1417- 30-35	1475- 65-70	1533- 75-85	1591- 35-40
1360- 25-30	1418- 25-30	1476- 25-30	1534- 65-70	1592- 60-65
1361- 20-25	1419- 25-30	1477- 60-65	1535- 50-55	1593- 45-50
1362- 25-30	1420- 25-30	1478- 75-80	1536- 40-45	1594- 30-35
1363- 65-70	1421- 25-30	1479- 35-40	1537- 40-45	1595- 40-45
1364- 45-50	1422- 25-30	1480- 50-55	1538- 45-50	1596- 50-55
1365- 50-55	1423- 25-30	1481- 15-20	1539- 50-55	1597- 30-35
1366- 65-75	1424- 25-30	1482- 55-60	1540- 45-50	1598- 35-40
1367- 35-40	1425- 40-45	1483- 35-40	1541- 25-30	1599- 30-35
1368- 30-35	1426- 60-70	1484- 35-40	1542- 25-30	1600- 30-35
1369- 35-40	1427- 40-45	1485- 30-35	1543- 40-45	1601- 25-30
1370- 35-40	1428- 45-50	1486- 30-35	1544- 40-45	1602- 25-30
1371- NP	1429- 18-20	1487- 40-45	1545- 45-50	1603- 40-45
1372- NP	1430- 35-40	1488- 30-35	1546- 45-50	1604- 20-25
1373- 50-55	1431- 18-20	1489- 75-80	1547- 15-20	1605- 30-35
1374- 50-55	1432- 35-40	1490- 85-95	1548- 45-50	1606- 15-20
1375- 40-45	1433- 18-20	1491- NP	1549- 20-25	1607- 75-80
1376- 50-55	1434- 60-65	1492- 85-95	1550- 55-65	1608- 20-25
1377- 50-55	1435- 80-90	1493- 55-60	1551- 40-45	1609- 65-70
1378- 45-50	1436- NP	1494- 85-95	1552- 30-40	1610- 15-20
1379- 45-50	1437- 25-30	1495- 50-55	1553- 50-60	1611- 35-40
1380- 75-80	1438- 25-30	1496- 30-35	1554- 25-30	1612- 45-50
1381- 65-75	1439- 25-30	1497- 30-35	1555- 80-90	1613- 45-50
1382- 75-90	1440- 10-12	1498- 60-65	1556- 50-55	1614- 20-25
1383- 75-90	1441- 25-30	1499- 18-22	1557- 50-55	1615- 20-25
1384- 60-70	1442- 30-35	1500- 45-50	1558- 30-35	1616- 35-40
1385- 70-75	1443- 25-30	1501- 25-30	1559- 60-65	1617- 8-10
1386- 75-80	1444- 20-25	1502- 40-45	1560- 35-40	1618- 10-12
1387- 100-125	1445- 20-25	1503- 75-85	1561- 30-35	1619- 35-40
1388- 50-60	1446- 20-25	1504- 18-22	1562- 30-35	1620- 25-30
1389- 60-65	1447- 18-20	1505- 15-20	1563- 30-35	1621- 35-40
1390- 70-75	1448- 25-30	1506- 18-22	1564- 25-30	1622- 30-35
1391- 40-45	1449- 18-20	1507- 20-25	1565- NP	1623- 20-25
1392- 65-70	1450- 40-45	1508- 40-45	1566- 35-40	1624- 20-25
1393- NP	1451- 45-50	1509- 35-40	1567- 40-45	1625- 30-35
1394- 70-75	1452- 40-45	1510- 35-40	1568- 15-20	1626- 20-25
1395- 100-125	1453- 40-45	1511- 35-40	1569- 40-50	1627- 60-65
1396- 65-75	1454- 35-40	1512- 20-25	1570- 75-85	1628- 14-16
1397- 40-45	1455- 80-90	1513- 15-20	1571- 30-35	1629- 12-14
1398- 40-45	1456- 50-55	1514- 12-15	1572- 15-20	1630- 10-12
1399- 80-90	1457- 50-55	1515- 20-25	1573- 25-30	1631- 12-14
1400- 55-60	1458- 35-40	1516- 15-20	1574- 15-20	1632- 8-10
1401- 65-70	1459- 80-85	1517- 15-20	1575- 25-30	1633- 6-8
1402- 85-100	1460- 20-25	1518- 60-65	1576- 30-35	1634- 10-12
1403- 65-70	1461- 15-20	1519- 45-50	1577- 55-60	1635- 8-10
1404- 40-45	1462- 18-22	1520- 35-40	1578- 130-140	1636- 500-550
1405- 60-65	1463- 35-40	1521- 50-60	1579- 45-50	1637- 550-650
1406- 40-45 pr.	1464- 40-45	1522- 40-45	1580- 40-45	1638- 850-950
1407- 60-65	1465- 12-15	1523- 50-55	1581- 20-25	1639- 500-600
1408- 75-85	1466- 15-20	1524- 40-45	1582- 60-65	1640- 400-500

1641- 700-800	1699- 200-250	1757- 35-40	1815- 50-55	1873- 20-25
1642- 800-900	1700- 150-175	1758- 45-50	1816- 25-30	1874- 20-25
1643- 500-600	1701- 175-200	1759- 45-50	1817- 35-40	1875- 25-30
1644- 600-700	1702- 250-300	1760- 65-70	1818- 40-45	1876- 25-30
1645- 700-800	1703- 250-275	1761- 35-40	1819- 75-85	1877- 20-25
1646- 750-850	1704- 425-500	1762- 35-40	1820- 65-70	1878- 35-40
1647- 700-800	1705- 400-475	1763- 25-30	1821- 70-75	1879- 20-25
1648- 550-650	1706- 800-850	1764- 30-35	1822- 70-80	1880- 30-35
1649- 700-800	1707- 400-450	1765- 50-55	1823- 65-70	1881- 15-20
1650- 425-475	1708- 425-475	1766- 25-30	1824- 60-65	1882- 25-30
1651- 600-700	1709- 600-700	1767- 25-30	1825- 50-55	1883- 15-20
1652- 325-275	1710- 450-500	1768- 55-60	1826- 135-145	1884- 25-30
1653- 500-600	1711- 250-275	1769- 35-40	1827- 80-90	1885- 60-65
1654- 650-760	1712- 250-275	1770- 25-30	1828- 55-60	1886- 35-40
1655- 300-375	1713- 1150-1250	1771- 45-50	1829- 60-65	1887- 20-25
1656- 500-575	1714- 575-625	1772- 40-45	1830- 60-65 pr.	1888- 20-25
1657- 275-325	1715- 475-525	1773- NP	1831- NP	1890- 35-40
1658- NP	1716- 250-275	1774- 65-75	1832- 145-165	1891- NP
1659- 250-300	1717- 800-900	1775- 30-35	1833- 55-60	1892- 25-30
1660- 750-850	1718- 750-850	1776- 35-40	1834- 50-55	1893- 30-35
1661- 350-450	1719- 700-800	1777- 20-25	1835- 65-70 pr.	1894- 25-30
1662- 800-900	1720- 750-800	1778- 45-50	1836- 40-45	1895- 30-35
1663- 250-350	1721- 65-70	1779- 15-20	1837- 60-65	1896- 30-35
1664- 675-725	1722- 75-85	1780- 15-20	1838- 25-30	1897- 20-25
1665- 250-275	1723- 55-60	1781- 15-18	1839- 25-30	1898- 20-25
1666- 300-350	1724- 75-85	1782- 20-25	1840- 20-25	1899- 20-25
1667- 650-750	1725- NP	1783- 25-30	1841- 25-30	1900- 30-35
1668- 125-150	1726- NP	1784- 20-25	1842- 35-40	1901- 30-35
1669- 250-275	1727- NP	1785- 15-20	1843- 35-40	1902- 25-30
1670- 650-750	1728- 100-125	1786- 15-18	1844- 40-45	1903- 30-35
1671- 800-900	1729- NP	1787- 25-30	1845- 20-25	1904- 30-35
1672- 725-800	1730- NP	1788- 45-50	1846- 25-30	1905- 30-35
1673- 475-575	1731- NP	1789- 30-35	1847- 20-25	1906- 100-125
1674- 575-625	1732- NP	1790- 30-35	1848- 20-25	1907- 85-95
1675- 575-625	1733- 65-70	1791- 25-30	1849- 35-40	1908- 95-100
1676- 700-800	1734- NP	1792- 25-30	1850- 20-25	1909- 85-95
1677- 275-300	1735- NP	1793- 40-50 pr.	1851- 20-25	1910- 85-95
1678- 225-250	1736- NP	1794- 40-45	1852- 30-35	1911- 80-90
1679- 250-300	1737- 65-70	1795- 18-20	1853- 20-25	1912- 75-80
1680- 250-275	1738- 75-85	1796- 30-35	1854- 25-30	1913- 75-80
1681- 200-250	1739- 55-60	1797- 170-190	1855- 25-30	1914- 75-80
1682- 500-600	1740- NP	1798- 90-100	1856- NP	1915- 75-80
1683- 750-850	1741- NP	1799- 90-100	1857- 30-35	1916- 75-80
1684- 200-250	1742- 14-16	1800- 70-80	1858- 20-25	1917- 45-50
1685- 900-1000	1743- 14-16	1801- 160-175	1859- 25-30	1918- 40-45
1686- 175-200	1744- 10-12	1802- 175-200	1860- 20-25	1919- 50-55
1687- 700-800	1745- 12-14	1803- 50-55	1861- 25-30	
1688- 525-575	1746- 8-10	1804- 155-175	1862- 25-30	
1689- 525-625	1747- 8-10	1805- 25-30	1863- 20-25	
1690- 175-200	1748- 12-14	1806- 65-75	1864- 35-40	
1691- NP	1749- 12-14	1807- 65-70	1865- 25-30	
1692- NP	1750- 12-14	1808- 70-75	1866- 25-30	
1693- 650-750	1751- 14-16	1809- 55-60	1867- 30-35	
1694- 500-600	1752- 8-10	1810- 45-50	1868- 30-35	
1695- 200-250	1753- 8-10	1811- 30-35	1869- 20-25	
1696- 225-275	1754- 12-14	1812- 75-80	1870- 25-30	
1697- 200-250	1755- 12-14	1813- 35-40	1871- 30-35	
1698- 275-300	1756- 6-8	1814- 30-35	1872- 20-25	